Essentials of Logic Programming

Essentials of
Logic Programming

CHRISTOPHER JOHN HOGGER

*Senior Lecturer in Computing, Imperial
College of Science and Technology, London*

CLARENDON PRESS · OXFORD
1990

Oxford University Press, Walton Street, Oxford OX2 6DP
Oxford New York Toronto
Delhi Bombay Calcutta Madras Karachi
Petaling Jaya Singapore Hong Kong Tokyo
Nairobi Dar es Salaam Cape Town
Melbourne Auckland
and associated companies in
Berlin Ibadan

Oxford is a trade mark of Oxford University Press

Published in the United States
by Oxford University Press, New York

British Library Cataloguing in Publication Data
Hogger, Christopher John
Logic programming.
1. Computer systems. Programming
I. Title II. Series
005.1
ISBN 0–19–853820–0
ISBN 0–19–853832–4 pbk

Library of Congress Cataloging in Publication Data
Hogger, Christopher John.
Logic programming / Christopher John Hogger.
p. cm.—(Graduate texts in computer science; 1)
Includes bibliographical references and index.
1. Logic programming. I. Title. II. Series.
QA76.63.H64 1990 005.1—dc20 90–7847
ISBN 0–19–853820–0
ISBN 0–19–853832–4 (Paperback)

Printed in Great Britain by
Bookcraft Ltd.
Midsomer Norton, Bath

Preface

I began writing my first book *Introduction to Logic Programming* ten years ago and it took me three years to complete it. Although it was well received, I vowed afterwards that I would never again write a book dealing with the general features of the logic programming formalism. There surely has to be a limit on how many times one can bear to explain what is meant by clausal form, computation rules, unifiers and all the other paraphernalia. Nonetheless, time mellows one's attitudes and the field moves on. Moreover, the present book began with an advantage which the first one did not—the availability of a sufficient body of lecture notes and exercises evolved from the courses which I teach to my students, thus making the enterprise altogether less arduous.

In the text this book therefore often refers to itself as a "course", although it is my hope and intention that various courses might be culled from it by other persons responsible for teaching logic programming. To this end the text consists not of a few large and monolithic chapters but sixty short 'Themes' from which various subsets may be selected and permuted as appropriate. The Themes fall into various natural groupings, as depicted in the *Contents* pages. The group entitled *Background* gives a brief indication of the aims of logic programming together with recommended sources of further reading material; by this device I have been able to avoid peppering the text as a whole with references and other such distractions. The *Overview* group says more about what logic programming is and how it arose, and offers some comments upon what are commonly seen as its main strengths and weaknesses.

For readers having little or no acquaintance with logic I have included two further groups on *First-order logic* and *Clausal-form logic*, followed by another one on *Problem solving* describing how logic may be adapted towards computational ends. For many students of computing science this will be the staple material of courses unconcerned with logic programming.

I decided to introduce as early as possible the notion of the Herbrand domain, which can be regarded as containing the basic data over which logic programs operate. This notion is also fundamental to the procedures by which problems formulated in clausal-form logic had to be tackled in ancient times. These matters are briefly discussed in another group entitled *The Herbrand domain.*

Logic programs are conventionally executed by theorem provers implementing the inference system known as resolution. It is not essential to view their execution in theorem-proving terms, but the strong results already available about the soundness and completeness of resolution afford important guarantees about the correctness of program execution, and so are worth understanding. The group on *Resolution* introduces these topics from a general viewpoint and is followed by a rather longer one on *SLD-resolution*, which is the core execution system for standard logic programming.

At this stage we are about half-way through the book, having established the structure and computational properties of so-called definite programs. The principal remaining obligation is to consider what such programs mean. Here we have to return once more to the Herbrand domain and consider how programs may be interpreted in terms of the relations they define upon it. This leads naturally to the idea of the minimal Herbrand model as the meaning of a logic program. All this is dealt with in the group entitled *Semantics of definite programs*. I have included here a short Theme on partial orders and lattices, whilst recognizing that this material will be familiar to many students through their more general courses on discrete mathematics.

Within the quite large body of knowledge that now exists about how to modify programs in logically defensible ways, the techniques known as unfolding and folding predominate. Their justification in logical terms requires reference not only to the explicit content of the programs but also to their implicit content under the so-called closed-world assumption, which may in turn be formalized through the operation known as program completion. The group on *Transforming and completing programs* deals with these issues.

The only significant extension to definite-clause programming discussed in this book is the finite failure extension, which yields the capability for default reasoning. The group *Programming with finite failure* examines the operational and semantical aspects of the extension, its implementation in the SLDNF inference system and some of its applications. For the semantics, more use has to made here of the earlier Themes on program completion.

Lastly, under the title *Verifying programs*, I have given two Themes which briefly consider ways of demonstrating the termination of definite programs relative to classes of queries and their correctness relative to logical specifications.

Having summarized what the book is about, I ought also to indicate what it is not about. It is *not* about Prolog programming, although the relationship of Prolog to pure logic programming receives attention in many of the Themes. Already there are a great many—possibly too many—books describing Prolog and its applications. One concession which I *have* made in deference to Prolog is to abide—more or less—by its conventions for naming constants and variables. In my first book I steadfastly employed the opposite conventions, which I personally prefer, but suffered quite a few complaints as a result. Neither is this a book about the *theory* of logic programming, although a certain amount of formality is needed here and there for the sake of precision and justification. John W. Lloyd's unique and well-known book on the *Foundations of Logic Programming* will, I am sure, long remain the best source for those interested chiefly in theoretical issues. Neither is this a book about the research frontier in logic programming. Unlike the position ten years ago, so much is now happening in the field, and at such a pace, that it is no longer possible to describe that frontier comprehensively in one book. Serious researchers wanting to keep abreast of what is currently going on should read the proceedings of the principal conferences, which are cited in Theme 3. This book is intended only to provide a start towards understanding the core features of the formalism.

There are all sorts of topics which I have had to omit, despite their interest and importance. They include constraint logic programming, concurrency, meta-order and higher-order features, the relationship to functional and object-oriented programming, deductive databases and much else besides. It is my longer-term intention to write further texts dealing with these more specialized issues, since no proper treatment of them could be accommodated within the present text.

My first book was also criticized for having no exercises (and hence no answers) and very few pictures. By contrast, half of this one consists of nothing else. In particular, the worked answers will, I hope, prove to be almost as informative as the main text.

The Themes vary in length depending upon how complicated are the issues they address. In my courses I typically present two to four Themes in each lecture. The set of exercises attending each Theme might occupy the average student for one tutorial period; this depends, of course, upon their pre-existing competence in matters such as Prolog programming and mathematical logic. Such competence is not a prerequisite for following this book, but it certainly helps.

As a final note, I hope that the fine granularity of the Themes together with the index—which I assure you is *not* machine-generated—will enable readers to find their way about the text without difficulty. In the index, the principal page reference to an item is shown in italic; on the page referred to, the principal occurrence of that item appears in bold face.

Acknowledgements

The writing of this book owes much to the encouragement given by various of my colleagues in the Department of Computing at Imperial College, and was undertaken at the initial suggestion of Chris Hankin as Series Editor, for whose supportiveness I am most grateful. It also owes a great deal to what I have learnt over the years from working with Bob Kowalski, Dov Gabbay and many others in the Computational Logic Group.

The book covers most of what I teach to my students in various courses on logic programming. Their responses both to the material presented and to the exercises required of them have contributed substantially to the improvement of the text and the correction of errors. However, since I suspect that every technical book, though finite, nevertheless contains an infinite number of errors whose emergence continues for an infinite period of time, I shall not be greatly surprised if mistakes begin to turn up after publication. If you should find any then please don't rush to tell me—editing the present edition of the manuscript has already consumed quite enough time and energy.

Which reminds me to acknowledge my debt to Apple Computer, Inc., makers of the Macintosh II—surely one of the most noble of all computing engines. At any rate, it was the only kind of computer available to me for the preparation of the manuscript, besides being the only kind I actually know how to use. I would not have known even this were it not for the assistance of my good friend and colleague Frank Kriwaczek, who on many occasions rescued me from deep mysteries concerning fonts, bit-maps and other such imponderables which lie at the remotest frontiers of human knowledge.

Many other friends and associates contributed advice on both matters of exposition, typesetting and specific technical points, or helped in the rectification of mistakes. Included amongst these are Krysia Broda, Jane Spurr, Graem Ringwood, Marek Sergot, Yonni Cosmadopoulos, Ian Hodkinson, Barry Richards, John Shepherdson and Hirohisa Seki. My thanks to you all and to any others whom I may have omitted to mention.

Finally, I acknowledge the forbearance of my wife Elizabeth and my two young children Brendon and Emlyn for tolerating my long leave of absence from domestic matters as I worked away in solitude at the aforesaid noble computing engine. By way of a lasting testament I have incorporated their names as constant symbols in some of the examples used in the text. I hope this will be sufficient compensation.

CONTENTS

The Herbrand domain

Resolution

Programming with SLD-resolution

Semantics of definite programs

Transforming and completing programs

Programming with finite failure

Verifying programs

Theme 1

Introduction

The first priority of this course must be to explain the *logical basis* of "logic programming". To omit this would be to omit the reason why logic programming has any significance at all. We shall need this basis in many of the Themes which lie ahead, not only to understand the formalism in its unadulterated form but also to assess certain features of its less virtuous, but eminently more popular, relation—the Prolog programming language. Our logical foundation will equip us to say, for instance, what logic programs can or cannot express or compute—in short, what they *mean*. Besides looking at semantical and other theoretical matters, however, we shall also comment when appropriate upon the *practical* significance of the topics under discussion.

It is important from the start to resist taking on a narrow conception of logic as just another language available for solving routine computational problems. The point of chief significance is that logic can be used to represent knowledge pertinent to many different contexts and can be animated, or mechanized, in many different ways. For example, we shall see later on how the basic paradigm can be applied directly—that is, without first having to compose special-purpose software—to such tasks as comparing programs and testing the integrity of databases. Thus we have the makings of a broad perspective: logic programming potentially serves any computing context offering scope for *mechanized reasoning*.

Throughout the course we shall restrict attention to logic programming based upon classical logic. This is partly because classical logic is understood better than other species of logic, partly because those other species are best appreciated only when the classical one has been adequately explored, but mostly because up to now only the classical one has been turned to computational purposes with any real degree of success.

There are two main avenues of approach to uncovering the mathematical content of logic—**model theory** and **proof theory**. Model theory examines the relationships between sentences of logic once they have been interpreted, by association with external domains, such as to give them truth-values. The vocabulary of elementary model theory employs such terms as *true, false, interpretation, satisfaction, model, implication* and *semantic consequence*. Proof theory examines the relationships between sentences in terms of their derivability from other sentences using rules which operate only upon the structural content of sentences. The vocabulary of elementary proof theory uses words such as *axiom, inference rule, theorem, proof, consistency* and *syntactic consequence*.

Both approaches are of value in understanding logic programming, and we shall see that for classical logic there are simple but important connections between them. The most important connection is that the things we desire to be true should coincide with the things we are capable of proving; equivalently, that the answers implied by a program should coincide with the answers computable from it.

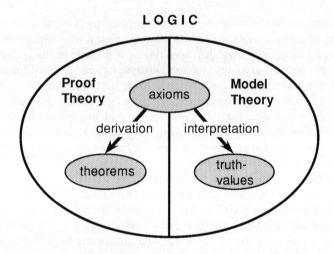

Figure 1.1. The two views of logic.

Exercises 1

1. Since we have not yet presented anything of a technical nature, the best exercise for the moment is probably to take a nice long walk in the country, and prepare yourself spiritually for what lies ahead.

Theme 2

Supplementary texts

Many books have been published on the subjects of logic programming, Prolog and sundry topics relating to them. Most of them are tutorial guides to Prolog programming in the context of artificial intelligence applications such as expert systems. They vary widely both in their degree of sophistication and in the extent to which they acknowledge and exploit underlying logical principles.

Itemized below are a few books selected according to their appropriateness as supplementary material for this course. None of them is strictly necessary to the course, but each of them can contribute usefully to the assimilation of the material presented.

"Logic for Problem Solving"
Author: Robert A. Kowalski
Publisher: Elsevier North Holland, New York (1979)
ISBN: 0-444-00365-7

This is the classic text about the use of computational logic to solve problems. It is not specifically about logic programming, being concerned more with the use of logic for knowledge representation and knowledge processing in general, yet is firmly committed to the logic programming approach to such matters. Designed for newcomers to the field, it is especially helpful in explaining clausal-form logic and resolution theorem-proving, both of which are fundamental to most manifestations of classical logic programming. A great diversity of topics are covered within this framework. The book includes a generous quota of exercises and provides plenty of literature references, although some of these have since been superseded by new research.

"Introduction to Logic Programming"
Author: Christopher J. Hogger
Publisher: Academic Press, London (1984)
ISBN: 0-12-353092-4

This text does not dwell overmuch on logic *per se*, but does deal specifically with logic both as a programming language and as a specification language. It is perhaps most useful as an introduction to the *computational* concepts of logic programming, as an overview of logic programming research and as a guide to the topic of implementation, though other matters such as verification, knowledge-based applications and elementary theory are also discussed.

The book is intended primarily for computing science undergraduates and researchers new to the field. No exercises are included, but there are lots of literature references and historical summaries.

"Foundations of Logic Programming"
Author: John W. Lloyd
Publisher: Springer Verlag, Berlin (Second Edition, 1987)
ISBN: 3-540-18199-7

This presents a succinct and systematic development of the main strands of the *theory* of logic programming and is aimed strictly at those with mature backgrounds in discrete mathematics. It is currently the only such book available. It is concerned primarily with the semantics of logic programming and the correctness of its proof procedures, although there is much else besides. Some exercises are included, but without answers. It is an essential reference book for serious researchers.

"The Art of Prolog: Advanced Programming Techniques"
Authors: Leon Sterling and Ehud Y. Shapiro
Publisher: MIT Press, Cambridge, Mass. (1986)
ISBN: 0-262-19250-0

In my view this is the best book currently available about Prolog programming. It contains a substantial amount of material which is lucidly presented and richly illustrated with examples. Beginning with the elementary concepts needed for teaching Prolog to novices, it progresses to more sophisticated levels appropriate to the serious practitioner. The book does not say a great deal about either the logical foundations of Prolog or the wider possibilities of computational logic in general. It discusses a good many non-trivial case-studies in order to show how to get the most out of Prolog. It is a little thin on exercises and its selection of literature references is, in my view, a bit wayward. However, the authors thoughtfully include a number of sketches by Leonardo da Vinci to provide the reader with spiritual refreshment after plodding through all those clauses.

"A Profile of Mathematical Logic"
Author: Howard DeLong
Publisher: Addison-Wesley, Reading, Mass. (1970)
Library of Congress Catalog Card No: 75-109509

This book says nothing at all about logic programming, which had not come into being at the time of publication. Nevertheless it is a marvellous account of classical logic and sustains its clarity throughout even the most penetrating accounts of the more subtle issues. Besides its absorbing technical material it is well stocked with fascinating historical and anecdotal snippets, including a most gratifying proof that even a dog can reason logically.

"Logic, Programming and Prolog"
Authors: Ulf Nilsson and Jan Maluszynski
Publisher: John Wiley & Sons, Chichester (1990)
ISBN: 0-471-92625-6

This recent text gives a fine account of logic programming. It has three main sections. The first one presents the basic theory of definite-clause programming and the SLD paradigm, and goes on to discuss the finite failure extension. The second section describes various categories of application, including useful treatments of databases, meta-programming and grammars. The last one considers alternative logic programming schemes including constraint logic programming and concurrency. There are good exercises, but answers are given only to a selection of these. The book as a whole would perhaps be a little technical for a first course but of considerable value to more advanced students.

Exercises 2

1. Read the opening chapters of as many of the books cited in the Theme as you have access to.

Theme 3

Literature sources

The following sources of material relating to logic programming are certainly not exhaustive, but will provide a good introduction and pointers to other works.

Some journals covering Logic Programming

> Journal of Logic Programming
> New Generation Computing
> Logic and Computation
> Artificial Intelligence
> Machine Intelligence
> Knowledge Engineering Review
> Journal of Automated Reasoning
> Journal of the ACM
> Communications of the ACM
> Journal of Theoretical Computer Science
> Journal of Symbolic Logic
> Journal of Logic and Computation

Principal conferences covering Logic Programming

1976: First Int. Workshop on Logic Programming, London.
No published proceedings, but some ancient documentation held in the library of the Logic Programming Section, Department of Computing, Imperial College of Science, Technology and Medicine, London.

1980: Second Int. Workshop on Logic Programming, Debrecen.
Proceedings produced and edited by S.-A. Tarnlund at Uppsala University—subsequently republished as the following book:

"Logic Programming"
Editors: Keith L. Clark and S.-A. Tarnlund
Publisher: Academic Press, London (1982)
ISBN: 0-12-175520-7

1982: First Int. Conference on Logic Programming, Marseilles.
Faculté de Sciences de Luminy, Université d'Aix-Marseille II (*Ed.* M. Van Canaghem)—subsequently republished as the following book:

"Logic Programming and its Applications"
Editors: D. H. D. Warren and M. van Canaghem
Publisher: Ablex Publ., Norwood, New Jersey (1986)
ISBN: 0-89391-232-8

1983: Third Int. Workshop on Logic Programming, Albufeira.
Universidade Nova de Lisboa (*Eds*. L. M. Pereira, A. Porto, L. Monteiro and M. Filgueiras)

1984: IEEE Symposium on Logic Programming, Atlantic City.
IEEE Computer Society Press

1984: Second Int. Conference on Logic Programming, Uppsala.
Uppsala University Press (*Ed*. S.-A. Tarnlund)

1985: IEEE Symposium on Logic Programming, Boston.
IEEE Computer Society Press

1986: Third Int. Conference on Logic Programming, London.
Springer-Verlag (*Ed*. E. Y. Shapiro)

1986: IEEE Symposium on Logic Programming, Salt Lake City.
IEEE Computer Society Press

1987: Fourth Int. Conference on Logic Programming, Melbourne.
MIT Press (*Ed*. J.-L. Lassez)

1987: IEEE Symposium on Logic Programming, San Francisco.
IEEE Computer Society Press

1988: Fifth Int. Conference on Logic Programming, Seattle.
MIT Press (*Eds*. R. A. Kowalski and K. A. Bowen)

1989: Sixth Int. Conference on Logic Programming, Lisbon.
MIT Press (*Eds*. G. Levi and M. Martelli)

1990: Seventh Int. Conference on Logic Programming, Jerusalem.
MIT Press (*Eds*. D. H. D. Warren and P. Szeredi)

Some other conferences covering Logic Programming

North American Conference(s) on Logic Programming (**NACLP**)
Italian Conference(s) on Logic Programming (**GULP**)
Fifth Generation Computer Systems (**FGCS**)
Int. Joint Conference(s) on Artificial Intelligence (**IJCAI**)

Some useful Technical Reports and Newsletters

Technical Reports of the <u>Institute for New Generation Computer Technology</u> (**ICOT**), Tokyo.

Technical Reports of the <u>European Computer-Industry Research Centre</u> (**ECRC**), Munich.

Logic Programming Newsletters of the <u>Association of Logic Programming</u>. (**ALP**). Currently administered from the Logic Programming Section, Department of Computing, Imperial College of Science, Technology & Medicine, 180 Queen's Gate, South Kensington, London SW7 2BZ.

Exercises 3

1. Locate your own sources of the cited Conference Proceedings, as they will provide an extremely useful insight into the state of current research.

Theme 4

Selected papers

Foundational papers

The following papers are worth reading for their lucid exposition, foundational importance and historical significance.

"A machine-oriented logic based on the resolution principle" by J. A. Robinson.
Journal of the ACM **12**, 1965, pp.23–41.

"Computation and deduction" by P. J. Hayes.
Proc. of the 2nd Symposium on the Mathematical Foundations of Computer Science, Czechoslovak Academy of Sciences, 1973, pp.105–118.

"Predicate logic as a programming language" by R. A. Kowalski.
Proc. of IFIP-74, North Holland Publishing Company, Amsterdam, 1974, pp. 569–574.

"The semantics of predicate logic as a programming language" by R. A. Kowalski and M. H. van Emden.
Journal of the ACM **23**, 1976, pp.733–742.

"Programming in resolution logic" by M. H. van Emden.
In Machine Intelligence **8**, Ellis Horwood Ltd, Chichester, 1977, pp.266–299.

"A first order theory of data and programs" by K. L. Clark and S.-A. Tarnlund.
Proc. of IFIP-77, North Holland Publishing Company, Amsterdam, 1977, pp. 939–944.

"Negation as failure" by K. L. Clark.
In Logic and Data Bases (*Eds*. H. Gallaire and J. Minker), Plenum, New York, 1978, pp.293–322.

"Algorithm = logic + control" by R. A. Kowalski.
Comm. of the ACM **22**, 1979, pp.424–431.

Overview papers

The following overview papers have been selected for their breadth of coverage, tutorial style and technical accessibility.

"Logic programming" by R. A. Kowalski.
Invited Paper in Proc. of IFIP-83, North Holland Publishing Company, Amsterdam, 1983, pp.133–145.

"Prolog: a tutorial introduction" by R. A. Sammut and C. A. Sammut.
Australian Computer Journal **15**, 1983, pp.42–51.

"Logic programming" by M. R. Genesereth and M. L. Ginsberg.
Comm. of the ACM **28**, 1985, pp.933–941.

"An overview of automated reasoning and related fields" by L. Wos *et al.*
Journal of Automated Reasoning **1**, 1985, pp.5–48.

"Logic programming" by C. J. Hogger and R. A. Kowalski.
In Encyclopedia of Artificial Intelligence (*Ed.* S. C. Shapiro), John Wiley & Sons, New York, 1987, pp.544–558.

"The early years of logic programming" by R. A. Kowalski.
Comm. of the ACM **31**, 1988, pp.38–43.

Exercises 4

1. Read Kowalski's classic paper "Predicate Logic as a Programming Language" in the IFIP-74 Proceedings (cited in the Theme).

2. Read the Genesereth-Ginsberg paper in *Comm. of the ACM* (cited in the Theme).

3. If you already have some acquaintance with the theory of logic programming, read (or re-read) the Kowalski-van Emden paper in *Journal of the ACM* (cited in the Theme).

Theme 5

Logic programming—what it is

As a first approximation, *logic programming* is a computational formalism which combines these two central principles:

> it uses *logic* to express knowledge;
> it uses *inference* to manipulate knowledge.

In a problem-solving context, the first principle is concerned with representing assumptions and conclusions, whilst the second is concerned with establishing the logical connections between assumptions and conclusions. Roughly speaking, the general aim in any such context is to *infer* the desired conclusion from the given assumptions, and to do so in a manner which is computationally viable.

In concrete terms, the standard formalism uses a particular subset—*clausal-form logic*—of the (classical) first-order predicate logic as the language for knowledge representation, and uses a particular inference system—*resolution*—as the mechanism for knowledge manipulation.

Still more concretely, the logic programming formalism known as **Prolog** adds to the kernel logical system

clausal-form logic + resolution

a particular sort of **control strategy** in the pursuit of efficient implementation; the combination of these features alone is usually referred to as **pure Prolog** and is characterized by the fact that the *logical* analysis of programs written in it takes no account of behavioural considerations. However, the term 'Prolog' has another connotation besides its control strategy—namely, its addition to the pure kernel language of **non-logical primitives**, yielding a new formalism referred to as **impure Prolog**. Many of these primitives secure (supposedly beneficial) behavioural effects at the expense of corrupting the formalism's logical basis. That is, the conclusions computed from an impure Prolog program will not necessarily be logically inferrable from that program.

This distinction between purity and impurity raises for the logic programming discipline a fundamental dilemma which currently remains unresolved. Purity guarantees a great diversity of desirable properties which have the potential for raising the quality of programming methodology far above what is achievable with conventional formalisms. But up to the present time the use of logic programming for 'real-world' applications has had to rely heavily upon the sort of impure features found in Prolog. This dilemma reduces ultimately to the question of whether controlled, classical logical inference is entirely sufficient as an apparatus for practical computation, as many of us would like to believe. This is an important question for research, and is being explored along several avenues including meta-programming, control languages, machine architectures and non-classical logics, among others. What the end result of all these efforts will be is anybody's guess.

What does a logic program look like?—simply a set of **clauses** describing relations, as does the following example:

> likes(chris, Anyone) if buys(Anyone, this_book)
> buys(Anyone, this_book) if sensible(Anyone)
> sensible(you)

You may be able to infer from this program that chris likes you. In later Themes we will get down to the serious business of explaining why this is so, and why it matters.

Clausal-Form Logic

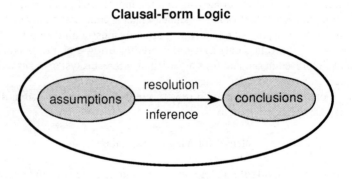

Figure 5.1. The essence of logic programming.

Exercises 5

The first three questions relate to the example in the Theme.

1. How *would* you infer that chris likes you?

2. Can you infer that chris is *not* sensible?

3. What elementary propositions can you infer altogether?

4. Taking your clues from the given example, try to compose a program which

expresses that

> "one's nephew is either one's brother's son or one's sister's son."

Each of your clauses must take one of the three following forms:

A
A if B
A if B_1 & ... & B_n for n>1

where A, B, B_1,... etc. are elementary propositions. You may use any names for relations (e.g. 'likes') and any names beginning with capital letters for variables (e.g. 'Anyone').

Theme 6

Logic programming—whence it came

Logic programming represents a point of convergence in the disciplines of logic, mechanical theorem-proving and computing science. Logic contributed, in particular, symbolic systems which enjoyed economy of syntax and for which the notions of *deriving* sentences and *interpreting* sentences could be independently articulated yet precisely related. For this we are indebted, in particular, to two famous logicians: Gottlob Frege, whose work led to what we now regard as the standard formulation of first-order logic; and Alfred Tarski, who clarified the long-standing semantic confusions between 'truth' and 'proof'.

The theory of clausal-form logic, and one central theorem in particular, we owe to another logician Jacques Herbrand. The discovery of resolution—a major step in the mechanization of clausal-form theorem-proving—is owed to J. Alan Robinson. The harnessing of these developments to the service of computer programming and, more broadly, of computing science and artificial intelligence, was pioneered by many individuals but especially by Carl Hewitt, Alain Colmerauer and Robert A. Kowalski.

Sketched out below is a potted chronology of key events during the last twenty-five years which have influenced the course of logic programming.

1965: J. Alan Robinson publishes his resolution principle for proving theorems in clausal-form logic.

1971: The Lighthill Report kindly advises the UK Government to reduce the level of funding for research into artificial intelligence.

1972: Robert A. Kowalski formulates the crucial programming-language interpretation of clausal-form logic.

1973: Alain Colmerauer, Philippe Roussel and others at the University of Aix-Marseille implement the first Prolog system.

1974: Robert A. Kowalski presents his seminal paper on predicate-logic programming to the IFIP-74 conference.

1976: The first International Workshop on Logic Programming is held at Imperial College, London and becomes the progenitor of the subsequent series of International Conferences on Logic Programming.

1977: Keith L. Clark publishes his key results linking negation and finite-failure, thereby laying a theoretical foundation for the support of default reasoning in Prolog.

1980: The second International Workshop on Logic Programming is held in Debrecen, Hungary (and provides the first evidence on film of Anglo-French cooperation on Prolog, convened in the swimming baths of Budapest—write to the author for details).

1981: William F. Clocksin and Christopher S. Mellish publish the world's first and best-selling book on Prolog ("Programming in Prolog", Springer-Verlag, Berlin, 1981, *ISBN*: 3-540-11046-1).

1981: Bombshell!—the Japanese Ministry of Trade and Industry announces the inauguration of the Fifth Generation Computer Systems Project, identifying logic programming as a key technology.

1983: The UK Government commits to funding the Alvey Programme for research into information technology, which includes a (modest) Logic Programming Initiative.

1984: The Journal of Logic Programming is initiated under the editorship first of J. Alan Robinson and subsequently of Jean-Louis Lassez.

1984: John W. Lloyd publishes the first, and highly influential, book on the theoretical foundations of logic programming.

1986: Inauguration of the Association of Logic Programming, whose remit includes organizing both the International and the North American Conferences on Logic Programming, as well as publishing regular Newsletters.

Exercises 6

1. Locate your own source of the *Journal of Logic Programming*.

2. If you feel like flexing your mathematical muscles, read the first chapter of John W. Lloyd's book (cited in Theme 2).

Theme 7

The alleged virtues

Many arguments have been advanced in favour of logic programming. The principal argument is that it enables one to express knowledge explicitly in a machine-independent manner, making programs more compact, flexible and intelligible. The thesis that the representation and derivation of knowledge is what computing is all about is not, at present, conceded by the majority of programmers, and even those who do concede it do not necessarily see logic programming as the natural way of realizing it. However this may be, the main strands of the thesis are as follows.

1. Logic programming can be regarded as the corner-stone of **knowledge based programming**. The expressiveness of logic enables one to formulate (encode) assumptions about the problem domain in a direct, implementation-independent manner. Conversely, one can readily decode such a formulation in order to recover its underlying assumptions. Furthermore, the conclusions computed from the formulation are exactly its logical consequences, and so are directly relatable to the assumptions.

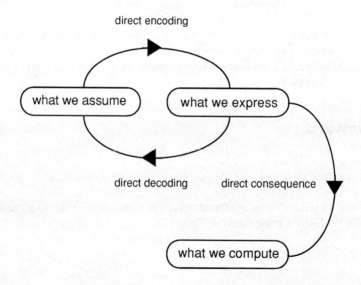

Figure 7.1. Desirable aspects of knowledge-based programming.

2. *It favours mathematical accountability*—giving precise and simple mathematical characterizations of the relationships between

> programs and the results computed from them
> programs and specifications
> programs and other programs.

3. *It separates knowledge from use*—one can vary the implementation details without affecting the program's logical competence: in particular one can vary either control strategies or machine architectures without necessarily having also to alter programs or their underlying language.

4. *It offers a uniform paradigm for software technology*—that is, one formalism serves for constructing and manipulating programs, specifications, databases and associated software tools.

5. *It can be modified or extended in natural ways* to support special forms of knowledge, such as meta-level or higher-order knowledge, as well as to reconstruct ostensibly non-logical formalisms.

6. Its main conceptual principles can be taught and understood without reference to computer technology—*it can contribute directly to other, non-computational disciplines* relying upon precise means of expression and reasoning.

7. *It works!*—that is, viable programming technologies have already been founded upon it.

Exercises 7

1. Reflect upon the extent to which these virtues are manifested in other programming formalisms already familiar to you.

Theme 8

The alleged deficiencies

Fifteen years ago logic programming was barely visible in the computing landscape. But during the ten years that followed its acclaim spread far and wide, and many of those working in the field felt there was quite a good chance that it would substantially displace older and supposedly less satisfactory formalisms. The Japanese had invested heavily in it for the purposes of their Fifth Generation Computer Systems Project, and the number of world-wide sites in which Prolog was used numbered tens—perhaps even hundreds—of thousands. There was a lot of interest in expert systems, many of which were written in Prolog. Industries in the UK and elsewhere in Europe readily joined with academia in various programmes of funded research and development, and numerous companies came into being as suppliers of logic programming technology.

Despite these excitements, logic programming did not make as much impact as had been hoped. Perhaps one reason was that, at first, insufficient investment was made in providing powerful environments, tools and language features, so that many potential users were inadequately served. In the early years, poor facilities for supporting arithmetic, mutable structures, types, input-output, graphics, file-handling and much else had a dissuasive effect upon large sections of the programming community. When such facilities were eventually provided it was often at the expense of the formalism's declarative semantics, leading to further embarrassments. Prolog came to be regarded—and used—by many as an overtly non-declarative language whose special attraction amounted to little more than the convenience of built-in unification and search.

The exaggerated association with the discipline of artificial intelligence also had damaging effects. Genuine problems at the heart of AI tended to be seen as problems peculiar to logic programming. For instance, the rather silly charge was often made that Prolog had a 'problem with negation'. In reality, its negation-by-failure facility was provided mainly for the benefit of those users requiring a built-in mechanism for default inference, the semantics of which had already been a matter of much debate long before logic programming was invented. Few other programming formalisms even attempted to support such a mechanism.

Besides extraneous matters of this sort, there were, arguably, inherent weaknesses in the language itself. No wholly satisfactory way has ever been found for representing those computational concepts which, in a conventional language, are supported directly through the built-in mechanisms of state variables and imperative actions. For instance, if one wishes to update a database then the only way of *fully* describing such an action in pure Horn-clause notation is to represent the database by a composite term—the direct implementation of which is impractical. To take another example, one might wish to mutate a large matrix iteratively until it reaches some goal state. In order to achieve this with Horn clauses in such a manner as to use memory economically, one must first struggle to find the correct recursive procedure for driving the iteration, and then adorn this with complicated and only half-convincing stories about invisible processes of tail-recursion and garbage-collection.

Logic programs *are* amenable to an operational interpretation which goes some way towards supporting concepts of state-oriented actions. Many logic programming idealists, including myself, have advocated the dual deployment of the declarative and operational interpretations in order that the programmer might harmoniously integrate his logical and computational insights during program construction. Unfortunately this ethos is often compromised by the fact that the customary operational interpretation reflects only the *single, general-purpose* proof procedure employed for program execution. My colleague Dov Gabbay has offered this analogy. A carpenter fashioning some object employs *multiple, special-purpose* tools in order to shape it effectively. Having laid out the appropriate tools he then picks them up and uses them as and when needed, to suit his natural instincts. Now suppose we confiscate all these tools and replace them by a single, fixed rotary saw mounted on the ceiling. Then in order to fashion the same object he must contrive perverse ways of holding it up against the saw so as to *simulate* the various actions previously achieved using the tools natural to his trade. The logic programming analogue of the rotary saw is the fixed proof procedure; the awkwardness of using the saw is the awkwardness of making that single proof procedure simulate a variety of computational actions; and the symptoms of that awkwardness are reflected in the convoluted logical structures needed in the program in order to induce those simulations. This analogy is, I believe, not a wholly fair one, but it nevertheless retains a certain potency which the promoters of logic programming would do well to think about.

The declarative style of programming is not to everybody's taste. There are many who simply prefer the overtly operational nature of machine-oriented programs—for them, there is more psychological satisfaction to be had in exercising active control over the 'moving parts' of a computation than there is in the seemingly more passive business of declaring what the computation is to achieve. This preference may persist whatever claims are made or substantiated about the virtues of (present-day) logic programming.

Deficiencies of a different sort are perceived even by some who do champion logic-based programming. Their complaints are mainly targeted upon the current fixation of logic programming with *first-order* logic. Their desire is to have executable logics in which one can directly express, for instance, nonmonotonic reasoning and modal concepts such as temporality and obligation. In their view, representing such concepts using, say, logic programming's metalogical features merely dodges the issue, depending again upon clumsy and artificial simulations of what the programmer really wants to express. A good deal of comparative study will be needed before this issue can be satisfactorily resolved.

Theme 9

The language of first-order logic

The language of **first-order predicate logic** is the set of all sentences constructible in accordance with the following (informal) grammar.

1. We assume some alphabet of **constant symbols** — a, b, c, ...
   some alphabet of **function symbols** — f, g, h, ...
   some alphabet of **variable symbols** — X, Y, Z, ...
   some alphabet of **predicate symbols** — likes, borrows, ...

   Note, in particular, that constant symbols begin with lower-case letters and that variable symbols begin with upper-case letters (as in Prolog).

2. A **term** is either a constant symbol or a variable symbol or a function symbol applied to a tuple of terms, as in these examples:

$$a \qquad X \qquad f(b, f(b,Y, Z), Y)$$

   Note—a **tuple** (or n-tuple) of n>0 items, where n is finite, is an ordered arrangement of those items. The three items b, Y and Z can be ordered, for instance, into the tuple <b, Y, Z>. Another possible 3-tuple is <Y, b, Z>, which is treated as being distinct from the previous one. The conventional tuple delimiters < and > are replaced by (and) in our logic language. A function symbol which applies to n-tuples for a specified value of n is said to be an n-ary function symbol or, equivalently, to have **arity** n. Thus, in the example above, 'f' is 3-ary.

3. An **atomic formula** is a predicate symbol applied to a tuple of terms, as in these examples:

$$\text{likes}(X, \text{mummy}(\text{chris})) \qquad \text{borrows}(\text{dov}, \text{book}, \text{chris})$$

   A predicate symbol which applies to n-tuples for a specified n is said to be an n-ary predicate symbol or, equivalently, to have arity n. In the examples just given, 'likes' is 2-ary and 'borrows' is 3-ary.

4. A **quantifier** is either of the constructs $(\forall X)$ and $(\exists X)$ where **X** is any variable symbol; the first kind is called a **universal quantifier** and the second kind an **existential quantifier**.

5. A **well-formed formula** is either an atomic formula or else takes one of the following seven forms, where **W**, **W1** and **W2** are any well-formed formulas and **(QX)** is any quantifier:

(W)	W1 & W2	W1 if W2
¬W	W1 or W2	W1 iff W2
(QX)W		

6. In a well-formed formula **(QX)W** the **scope** of the quantifier **(QX)** is defined as **W**. We say that **(QX)** *quantifies* every occurrence of **X** in **W** which occurs neither within any quantifer in **W** nor within the scope of any such quantifier. For example, in the formula (∀X)((∃X)A(X) if B(X)) the quantifier (∀X) quantifies only the occurrence of X in B(X).

7. An occurrence of a variable symbol **X** in a well-formed formula **W** is said to be **bound** if and only if

either   it lies within the scope of some quantifier **(QX)** which occurs in **W**,

or   it is in a quantifier **(QX)** which occurs in **W**.

8. In a well-formed formula **W**, an occurrence of a variable symbol which is not bound is said to be **unbound** (or **free**), as in this example where both occurrences of **X** are unbound:

$$(\exists Y)\text{father}(Y, X) \text{ if } \text{child}(X)$$

9. A **sentence** is a well-formed formula in which every occurrence of every variable symbol is bound, such as

$$(\forall X)((\exists Y)\text{father}(Y, X) \text{ if } \text{child}(X)) \quad \text{"every child has a father"}$$

Note that we have been rather casual in our language description as to the matter of **unique readability**. Our grammar so far permits such sentences as

$$A \text{ if } B \& C$$

In the absence of any other information, this sentence has two alternative readings

$$(A \text{ if } B) \& C \qquad A \text{ if } (B \& C)$$

There are two ways of eliminating such ambiguity. One way is to make the grammar more rigid by demanding that every well-formed formula be enclosed by parentheses. The more usual way is to operate a convention governing relative connecting strengths. We shall always use the following convention:

¬	connects more strongly than	& and 'or'
& and 'or'	connect more strongly than	'if'
'if'	connects more strongly than	'iff'

According to this, for example,

¬ A & B	reads uniquely as	(¬A) & B
A or B if C & D	reads uniquely as	(A or B) if (C & D)
A iff B if C	reads uniquely as	A iff (B if C)

Further conventions could be devised in order to disambiguate such sentences as

A or B & C   and   A if B if C

but, in order not to overtax the reader's memory, we shall supplement our main convention above with the use of parentheses whenever necessary.

Exercises 9

1. Express each of the following statements by a sentence of first-order logic (making liberal use of the quantifiers), using only the predicate symbols 'father', 'mother', parent', 'female' and 'child'.

Note—these predicate symbols may be either 1-ary or 2-ary, depending upon the context; for instance, take 'parent' as being 2-ary in (i) and (iii) but 1-ary in (ii) and (iv).

(i)   "if X is a father or X is a mother then X is someone's parent"
(ii) "if X is a parent and X is a female then X is someone's mother"
(iii) "if X is a father or X is a mother then someone is someone's parent"
(iv) "if everyone is a parent then someone is a child"

2. Using just the predicates likes(X, Y) and X=Y to express, respectively, that "X likes Y" and "X is identical to Y", compose sentences of first-order logic to express each of the following:

(i)   "everyone likes no one"
(ii)   "no one likes anyone"
(iii) "everyone likes themselves"
(iv)   "everyone likes every person except themselves"
(v)   "there is exactly one person who is liked by everyone"
(vi)   "no one likes anyone, except that chris likes himself "
(vii) "everyone either dislikes themselves or is disliked by someone"

Theme 10

More language definitions

1. A **literal** is either an atomic formula or a negated atomic formula, as in these two examples:

   likes(chris, mummy)   ¬likes(chris, suffering)

   The first kind is called a **positive literal** and the second kind is called a **negative literal**.

2. A **ground term** is a term containing no variables.
   A **ground formula** is a formula containing no variables.

   Note—henceforth, variable symbols and constant symbols will be referred to simply as **variables** and **constants**.

3. Atomic formulas are commonly called **predicates**.

4. The use of the word *atom* in many Edinburgh Prolog texts refers there to what we are calling a constant, not to what we are calling an atomic formula; this confusion of terminology is the fault of certain-persons-who-shall-not-be-named who sought to import LISP terminology into Prolog.

5. The symbols
$$\neg \quad \& \quad \text{or} \quad \text{if} \quad \text{iff}$$

   are called **connectives**; in other texts they may be rendered as

$$\sim \quad \wedge \quad \vee \quad \leftarrow \quad \leftrightarrow$$

6. A formula of the form ¬**W** is called a **negation**.
   A formula of the form (**W1** & **W2**) is called a **conjunction**.
   A formula of the form (**W1** or **W2**) is called a **disjunction**.
   A formula of the form (**W1** if **W2**) is called a **conditional**.
   A formula of the form (**W1** iff **W2**) is called a **biconditional**.

7. In a conditional formula (**W1** if **W2**), **W1** is called the **consequent** and **W2** is called the **antecedent**.

8. Let **W** be a formula some of whose unbound variables are $X_1, ..., X_n$ and let $t_1, ..., t_n$ be any terms. An **instance** of **W** is obtained by substituting, for each i, the term t_i for all occurrences of X_i in **W**. This instance is denoted by $W\{X_1/t_1, ..., X_n/t_n\}$. Each of the expressions X_i/t_i is called a **replacement** (or a **binding**). For example, one instance of this formula

$$W = \text{likes(chris, X)} \text{ if likes(X, Z)}$$

    is $W\{X/dad(Y)\} = \text{likes(chris, dad(Y))}$ if likes(dad(Y), Z)

9. A **ground instance** of a formula **W** is any instance of **W** that is ground. Thus, likes(chris, mummy) is a ground instance of likes(X, Y).

10. Let $(\forall X)W$ be a *sentence* such that no quantifier for **X** occurs in **W**, let **t** be any term and let $Y_1, ..., Y_m$ be the variables, if any, occurring in **t**. We assume that none of the latter variables occurs in the given sentence. Then the process of constructing the sentence $(\forall Y_1)...(\forall Y_m)(W\{X/t\})$ is described as (universally) **instantiating** the original sentence. This notion extends straightforwardly to the case where several variables in an original sentence $(\forall X_1)...(\forall X_n)W$ are replaced. For example, we might instantiate this sentence

$$(\forall X)(\forall U)(\forall Z)(\text{likes(U, X)} \text{ if likes(X, Z)})$$

    to obtain $(\forall Y)(\forall Z)(\text{likes(chris, dad(Y))}$ if likes(dad(Y), Z))

Exercises 10

1. For the formula

$$(\forall X)(((\forall X)p(X) \& (\forall Y)p(Y) \& q(X)) \text{ if } (p(X) \& q(Y)))$$

    (i)   identify the scope of each quantifier;
    (ii)   for each occurrence of a bound variable not within a quantifier, identify the quantifier which quantifies it;
    (iii)   identify any variables that are not bound by any quantifier.

2. Which instance of tree(t(Y, U)) gives the formula tree(t(t(U, X), X))?

3. Write out in full the formula which is denoted by the instance

    (has_niece(X) if $(\exists X)$daughter(X, Y) & sibling(X, Y)) $\{X/brother(Y)\}$

Theme 11

Elements of model theory

Model theory provides one way of attributing *meaning* to any given sentence of logic. Informally, the basic idea is to associate the sentence with some truth-valued statement about a chosen **domain**, a process known as **interpretation**. The domain is simply any set of our choice, for instance the set of natural numbers. Whatever truth-value that statement has is then bestowed upon the sentence.

The details are as follows. Assuming that a domain **D** has been chosen, an interpretation of the sentence under consideration is made by freely **associating**

> each constant symbol with some *element* of **D**,
> each n-ary function symbol with some *function* from $\mathbf{D}^n$ to **D**,
> each n-ary predicate symbol with some *relation* in $\mathbf{D}^n$.

Note— $\mathbf{D}^n$ denotes the n-fold **Cartesian Product** of **D** defined as follows:

$$\mathbf{D}^n = \{ <d_1, ..., d_n > \mid \text{each } d_i \in \mathbf{D} \}$$

Note also that it is common to write $\mathbf{D}^2$ as $\mathbf{D} \times \mathbf{D}$, $\mathbf{D}^3$ as $\mathbf{D} \times \mathbf{D} \times \mathbf{D}$, etc.

Example—take the simple ground sentence

> likes(chris, mummy)

and choose a domain consisting of just the two persons shown in Figure 11.1.

Figure 11.1. Choosing a domain.

In order to make an interpretation we must first associate the domain's elements with the sentence's constants 'chris' and 'mummy', and then associate some binary relation on the domain with the sentence's binary predicate symbol 'likes'. One way of making these associations is shown in Figure 11.2.

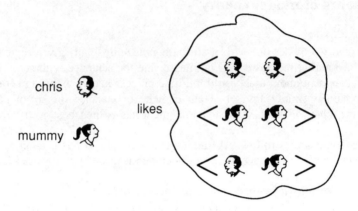

Figure 11.2. Interpreting the sentence's symbols.

Under this interpretation our sentence likes(chris, mummy) is read as a statement that the tuple

belongs to the domain relation. Since this statement is **true**, we say that the sentence takes the value **true** under this interpretation. On the other hand, if we associate the constants differently

but retain the same domain relation then, under this new interpretation, the sentence takes the value **false** (why?). Thus we see that, *in general*, a sentence may be evaluated either as **true** or as **false** depending upon how we interpret it. We have complete freedom to interpret it as we please, being permitted any choice of domain and any choice of associations.

Usually, of course, when we construct sentences of logic, as perhaps during the composition of a logic program, we already have some particular interpretation in mind—we are writing the program *for a purpose*, namely to represent whatever we are assuming about the problem domain. To say that our logic sentences *represent* the problem at hand is really to say that, *under their intended interpretation*, those sentences would each acquire the value **true.**

So far we have considered only the simplest sort of sentence—a ground atomic formula. Next we give the rules for interpreting more elaborate sentences containing variables, quantifiers and connectives. Together, these rules enable us to determine the truth-value of any sentence under a given interpretation.

Note—the symbols **W**, **W1** and **W2** below denote any well-formed formulas.

Rules for the quantifiers:

($\forall$X)W is **true** if and only if, for *every* domain element that we associate with those occurrences of **X** not bound by quantifiers within **W**, the statement then made by **W** is **true**;

($\exists$X)W is **true** if and only if, for *some* domain element that we associate with those occurrences of **X** not bound by quantifiers within **W**, the statement then made by **W** is **true.**

Rules for the connectives:

¬**W**	is **true**	if and only if	**W** is **false**;
W1 & **W2**	is **true**	if and only if	**W** is **true** and **W2** is **true**;
W1 or **W2**	is **true**	if and only if	either **W1** is **true** or **W2** is **true**;
W1 if **W2**	is **false**	if and only if	**W1** is **false** and **W2** is **true**;
W1 iff **W2**	is **true**	if and only if	either both **W1** and **W2** are **true** or both **W1** and **W2** are **false**.

Rule for parentheses:

(**W**)   is **true**   if and only if   **W** is **true.**

Exercises 11

1. For the sentence ¬(A iff (B or ¬C)) find an interpretation which makes it **true**; then find another one which makes it **false**.

2. Construct an informal argument which shows that the sentences

(A if B) if C   and   A if (B & C)

have the same values in any interpretation.

3. Referring to the example in the Theme, how many ways are there of associating the constants with the given domain? How many ways are there of choosing the relation associated with 'likes' over that domain? How many possible interpretations are there altogether over that domain?

4. For each of the sentences below, find an interpretation which makes it **true**:

    (i)   ($\forall$X)likes(chris, X)
    (ii)   ($\exists$X)likes(X, chris) if ($\forall$X)likes(X, X)
    (iii) $\neg$($\exists$X)likes(X, X)

5. For each of the sentences below, find an interpretation which makes it **false**:

    (i)   ($\forall$X)(even(X) or odd(X))
    (ii) $\neg$($\exists$X)(even(X) & odd(X))
    (iii) $\neg$($\exists$X)(0=s(X))
    (iv)   ($\forall$X)(even(X) if odd(s(X)))
    (v)   ($\forall$X)(even(X) iff $\neg$even(X))

Theme 12

More model theory definitions

1. An interpretation which gives the value **true** to a sentence is said to **satisfy** the sentence; such an interpretation is called a **model** for the sentence.

   Example—the interpretation first chosen in Theme 11 is a model for the sentence likes(chris, mummy).

   An interpretation which does *not* satisfy a sentence is called a **counter-model** for that sentence.

   By extension, we also have the notion of a model (or counter-model) for a *set* of sentences: an interpretation is a model for the set if and only if it is a model for each of the set's members.

2. A sentence which has *at least one model* is said to be **satisfiable**. A sentence which has *no models* is said to be **unsatisfiable**.

   Example— likes(chris, mummy) is satisfiable.
   Example— $(\exists X \exists Y)(\text{likes}(X, Y) \ \& \ \neg \text{likes}(X, Y))$ is unsatisfiable.

   By extension, we also have the notion of satisfiability of a *set* of sentences: the set is satisfiable if and only if each of its members is.

3. A sentence for which *every* interpretation is a model is said to be **valid**.

   Example— $(\forall X \forall Y)(\text{likes}(X, Y) \text{ or } \neg \text{likes}(X, Y))$ is valid.
   Example— likes(chris, mummy) is not valid.

4. We say that a sentence **S1 logically implies** a sentence **S2** if and only if every model for **S1** is also a model for **S2**. In this case we write, for short,

$$\text{S1} \models \text{S2}$$

   Alternatively, we say that **S2** is a **logical** (or **semantic**) **consequence** of **S1**. Note that the relation of logical implication is reflexive and transitive.

   Example— $(\forall X)\text{likes}(\text{chris}, X) \models \text{likes}(\text{chris, mummy})$

By extension, we have the notion of a *set* of sentences logically implying a sentence: the latter is satisfied by any model of the set.

5. Two sentences **S1** and **S2** are said to be **logically equivalent** when each one logically implies the other. In this case we write, for short,

$$S1 \equiv S2$$

Example— $(\forall X)\neg likes(X, misery) \equiv \neg(\exists X)likes(X, misery)$

6. Most of the sentences we shall be dealing with will not be valid yet will have many models. The meaning of any such sentence will vary from model to model. Often we will have some particular meaning in mind which corresponds to some particular model. However this may be, the point to be noted here is that the meaning is sought from amongst the models rather than from amongst the counter-models—one way or another the sentence is rendered meaningful through being read as some **true** statement about the domain.

Exercises 12

1. By constructing suitable models or counter-models show that

(i)   every ground atomic formula is satisfiable;
(ii)   no ground atomic formula is valid.

2. Construct an informal model-theoretic argument which establishes that

$$\{A, B\} \vDash C \quad \text{if and only if} \quad \{A\} \vDash (C \text{ if } B)$$

3. For the following formula

$$\neg(\forall X)(\forall Y)(\neg P(X) \text{ or } P(Y))$$

(i)   decide whether it is satisfiable on a domain with just one element;
(ii)   construct a model for it on a domain with just two elements.

4. This sentence s

$$(\forall X)(\text{ even}(s(X)) \text{ if } odd(X))$$

is *not* logically implied by this set **S** of four sentences

even(0)
odd(s(0))
($\forall$X)(even(s(s(X))) if even(X))
($\forall$X)(odd(X) if even(s(X)))

Prove that this is so by identifying an interpretation which is a model for **S** but a counter-model for **s**.

Hint—use the natural numbers {**0, 1, 2, 3**, ...} as the domain.

Theme 13

Useful equivalences and implications

When we know that two sentences are (logically) equivalent we know that they have identical meaning, since they must share the same models.

There are many contexts in which we wish to derive new sentences from given sentences in such a way as to preserve meaning. In the course of program transformation, for example, the intention is often to improve either the program's structure or its performance, but without altering the veracity of the statements it makes about the problem domain. The latter requirement can be enforced by transforming the program only into some equivalent one.

It is also important to be able to tell whether one sentence is implied by some others. For instance, if we can show that some sentence in a program is implied by the others then we know also (a) that it is computationally redundant and hence a source of inefficiency, and (b) that it can be safely deleted without affecting the program's logical meaning.

Besides its specific deployment in the logic programming context, the ability to demonstrate these properties is a general requirement in almost all logical and mathematical undertakings. In what follows we list some elementary and commonly-encountered equivalences and implications from which the more complex ones can be constructed as needed. **A**, **B** and **C** stand for any well-formed formulas.

Some equivalences

A	$\equiv$ (A)	
A	$\equiv$ A & A	idempotency of '&'
A	$\equiv$ A or A	idempotency of 'or'
A	$\equiv$ ¬¬A	idempotency of '¬'
A or B	$\equiv$ B or A	commutativity of 'or'
A & B	$\equiv$ B & A	commutativity of '&'
A iff B	$\equiv$ B iff A	commutativity of 'iff'
(A or B) or C	$\equiv$ A or (B or C)	associativity of 'or'
(A & B) & C	$\equiv$ A & (B & C)	associativity of '&'
A & (B or C)	$\equiv$ (A & B) or (A & C)	distributivity of '&'
A or (B & C)	$\equiv$ (A or B) & (A or C)	distributivity of 'or'

A if **B**	≡ **A** or ¬**B**	
(A if **B**) if **C**	≡ **A** if (**B** & **C**)	exportation law
A if (**B** if **C**)	≡ (**A** if **B**) & (**A** or **C**)	
A if (**B** or **C**)	≡ (**A** if **B**) & (**A** if **C**)	
(A & **B**) if **C**	≡ (**A** if **C**) & (**B** if **C**)	

A iff **B**	≡ (**A** & **B**) or (¬**A** & ¬**B**)	

¬(A & **B**)	≡ ¬**A** or ¬**B**	De Morgan's law
¬(A or **B**)	≡ ¬**A** & ¬**B**	De Morgan's law

¬(∀X)**A**	≡ (∃X)¬**A**	

(∀X)A(X)	≡ (∀Y)A(Y)	uniform renaming
(∃X)A(X)	≡ (∃Y)A(Y)	uniform renaming

(∀X)(∀Y)**A**	≡ (∀Y)(∀X)**A**	
(∃X)(∃Y)**A**	≡ (∃Y)(∃X)**A**	

(∀X)(A & **B**)	≡ (∀X)**A** & (∀X)**B**	distributivity of '∀'
(∃X)(A or **B**)	≡ (∃X)**A** or (∃X)**B**	distributivity of '∃'

Note—the next six equivalences hold provided that in each case there is no occurrence of **X** in **A** which is quantified by the outermost quantifier for **X**.

(∀X)A	≡ **A**	
(∃X)A	≡ **A**	
(∀X)(A & **B**)	≡ **A** & (∀X)**B**	
(∀X)(A or **B**)	≡ **A** or (∀X)**B**	
(∃X)(A & **B**)	≡ **A** & (∃X)**B**	
(∃X)(A or **B**)	≡ **A** or (∃X)**B**	

A & ¬**A**	≡ *False*	
A or ¬**A**	≡ *True*	

¬*True*	≡ *False*	
¬*False*	≡ *True*	

A & *True*	≡ **A**	
A or *True*	≡ *True*	

A & *False*	≡ *False*	
A or *False*	≡ **A**	

(... **A** ...)	≡ (... **B** ...) when **A** ≡ **B**	equivalence substitution

Some implications

A	⊨ **A or B**	
A	⊨ **A if B**	
A & B	⊨ **A**	
A & B	⊨ **A if B**	
A & B	⊨ **A iff B**	
(A if B) & (B if C)	⊨ **A if C**	transitivity of 'if'
B & (A if B)	⊨ **A**	
¬A & (A if B)	⊨ **¬B**	
(∀X)A	⊨ **(∃X)A**	for non-empty domain

Note—in the next implication, it is assumed both that Y_1, ... and Y_m are all the variables occurring in **t** and that none of those variables occurs in **A(X)**.

(∀X)A(X)	⊨ **(∀Y₁)...(∀Y_m)A(t)**	universal instantiation

where $(\forall Y_1)...(\forall Y_m)A(t)$

(∀X)A or (∀X)B	⊨ **(∀X)(A or B)**	
(∃X)(A & B)	⊨ **(∃X)A & (∃X)B**	

Note—for all the implications above, the converse implication does *not* hold.

Finally, note that implication is transitive:

$$\textbf{A} \vDash \textbf{C} \text{ whenever we have both } \textbf{A} \vDash \textbf{B} \text{ and } \textbf{B} \vDash \textbf{C}$$

Exercises 13

1. Using just the equivalences listed in the Theme, derive these:

  (i)   ¬(B iff C) ≡ (B or C) & ¬(B & C)
  (ii)   (A if B) iff (B if A) ≡ A iff B
  (iii) (A or B) iff ¬A ≡ ¬A & B
  (iv)   (∀X)(A if B(X)) ≡ A if (∃X)B(X)
  (v)   (∀Y)((∃X)A(X) if A(Y)) ≡ *True*
  (vi)   (∃X)(A(X) if B(X)) ≡ (∃X)A(X) if (∀Y)B(Y)

Note—in each case you will need to apply several basic equivalences in succession.

2. Using just the equivalences and implications listed in the Theme, derive these:

(i)   A & B ⊨ A if B

(ii)   (A or B) & (¬A or C) ⊨ B or C

(iii)   (A iff B) if C ⊨ B if (C & A)

Note—again, several steps will be needed in each case.

Theme 14

Clausal-form logic

Clausal form is one of the many **normal forms** of first-order logic and is the sublanguage in which pure logic programs are conventionally written. The common feature of all normal forms is that they make the structure of sentences more *regular*. Whatever sentences we might initially construct in arbitrary first-order logic in the course of formulating some problem, those sentences can always be converted into new clausal-form sentences without any loss of expressiveness.

We define a sentence to be in clausal form if and only if it takes the form

<universal-prefix >< matrix>

where the *universal-prefix* is a string of universal quantifiers, the *matrix* is a quantifier-free conjunction of formulas and each of those formulas is a disjunction of one or more literals.

Example—this sentence is in clausal form:

$$(\forall X \forall Y)(\ (likes(chris, X) \ \ or \ \ \neg likes(X, logic)) \ \&$$
$$(likes(chris, logic)) \ \&$$
$$(likes(bob, logic)) \ \&$$
$$(likes(X, Y) \ \ or \ \ \neg loves(X, Y))\ )$$

By virtue of the equivalence

$$(\forall X)(A \ \& \ B) \ \equiv \ (\forall X)A \ \& \ (\forall X)B$$

it is permissible to rewrite our clausal-form sentence as a *set* of *implicitly-conjoined* sentences called **clauses**—our example thus becomes a set of four clauses:

$$\{\ (\forall X)(\ likes(chris, X) \ \ or \ \ \neg likes(X, logic))$$
$$likes(chris, logic)$$
$$likes(bob, logic)$$
$$(\forall X \forall Y)(\ likes(X, Y) \ \ or \ \ \neg loves(X, Y))\ \}$$

Note that each clause is itself a sentence in clausal form.

Owing to the equivalence observed above, this rewriting is *consequence-preserving*—that is, every logical consequence of the original clausal-form sentence is a logical consequence of the corresponding set of clauses. This guarantees that any conclusions which may be inferrable from the former continue to be inferrable from the latter.

It is standard practice to organize a logic program as a set of clauses and to present them in a simplified style; the quantifiers are omitted and every occurrence of the connective sequence 'or ¬' is replaced by the equivalent 'if'. Doing this for the example above produces a logic program in conventional format:

likes(chris, X) if likes(X, logic)
likes(chris, logic)
likes(bob, logic)
likes(X, Y) if loves(X, Y)

This is very close to the way the program would be written in the notation of standard ('Edinburgh') Prolog:

likes(chris, X) :- likes(X, logic).
likes(chris, logic).
likes(bob, logic).
likes(X, Y) :- loves(X, Y).

There are several reasons why we may prefer to use clausal form rather than full first-order logic. The regular structure of clauses facilitates their storage in computer memory, reduces the number of inference rules required for problem-solving and makes it easier to assign computational significance to sentences by means of a procedural interpretation.

Exercises 14

1. Using just the predicates likes(X, Y) and X=Y to express, respectively, that "X likes Y" and "X is identical to Y", compose a clause-set to express each of the following:

   (i)   "everyone likes no one"
   (ii)   "no one likes anyone"
   (iii)   "everyone likes themselves"
   (iv)   "everyone likes every person except themselves"
   (v)   "no one likes anyone, except that chris likes himself"

2. Using just the three boldface phrases as predicate symbols, express the following in clausal form:

"**blessed** are the **pure in heart**, for they **shall see** God."

What extra clause(s) would be needed to ensure that *only* the pure in heart shall see God?

3. Using just the three boldface words as predicate symbols, express the following in clausal form:

"everyone is either ones's **friend** or one's **enemy**; friends are exactly those who **like** one another, whilst enemies are exactly those who dislike one another."

4. Using, in each case, just the boldface words as predicate symbols, express each of the following in clausal form:

(i)   "not all that **glitters** is **gold**"
(ii)   "all's **well** that **ends-well**"
(iii)   "no **man** is an **island**"
(iv)   "the **end justifies** the **means**"

Theme 15

Classifying clauses

Clauses may be classified according to the number of positive and negative literals they contain.

A **definite clause** contains exactly one positive literal and zero or more negative literals.
Example— happy(chris) or ¬eating(chris, apple_crumble)

A **positive unit clause** is a definite clause containing no negative literals.
Example— happy(chris)

A **negative unit clause** is a negative clause with exactly one negative literal.
Example— ¬desirable(pop_music)

A **unit clause** is either a positive unit clause or a negative unit clause, as in the last two examples.

A **negative clause** contains zero or more negative literals and no positive literals.
Example— ¬happy(chris) or ¬eating(chris, sheep's_brains)

The **empty clause** is a negative clause containing no literals and is denoted conventionally by the special symbol □.

An **indefinite clause** is a clause containing at least two positive literals.
Example— happy(chris) or unhappy(chris)

Alternative classifications of clauses

Indefinite clauses are called **non-Horn clauses**. All other clauses are called **Horn clauses**.

In the logic programming context, positive unit clauses are also called **assertions**. All other definite clauses are called **conditional clauses**. Negative clauses are called either **queries** or **goal clauses**.

In the Prolog context, positive unit clauses are called **facts**. All other definite clauses are called **rules**. Negative clauses are called either **queries** or **goal clauses**.

Classifying sets of clauses

In the logic programming and Prolog contexts, a set of non-negative clauses may be termed a **program**, a **database**, a **knowledge base** or a **rule base**.

A set of definite clauses whose positive literals all share the same predicate symbol is referred to either as a **definition** or as a **procedure** for that symbol.

Example— the following set of definite clauses

> likes(chris, X) if likes(X, logic)
> likes(chris, logic)
> likes(bob, logic)
> likes(X, Y) if loves(X, Y)

would be called a definition (or a procedure) for 'likes'.

A program all of whose clauses are definite is called a **definite program**, as is the case with the example just given. Any other program is called an **indefinite program**.

The most fundamental (and theoretically sufficient) class of logic programs is the class of definite programs. Indefinite programs are also of considerable importance, but both their theory and their implementation are much more complicated (and more interesting).

Exercises 15

1. Classify the following clauses according to whether they are definite, indefinite or negative:

    (i)   definite(X) or indefinite(X) or negative(X) or ¬clause(X)
    (ii)   ¬happy(chris) or ¬unhappy(chris)
    (iii)   happy(chris) or ¬happy(chris) or indifferent(chris)
    (iv)   ¬perfect(X)
    (v)   likes(X, Y) or ¬friends(X, Y)

2. Classify the same clauses above according to whether they are Horn or non-Horn.

3. Classify the same clauses above according to whether they are rules, facts or queries.

4. Give an example of a pair of clauses, one definite and one indefinite, which are logically equivalent to one another.

5. Express that every clause is either Horn or non-Horn

    (i)   by means of a non-Horn clause;

    (ii)   by means of a Horn clause.

Theme 16

Moving literals within clauses

The classical representation of a clause is a disjunction of literals. However, any such clause can be rewritten, with no loss of equivalence, as a sentence in **conditional format** having the form

disjunction of literals   if   conjunction of literals

Thus a clause such as

A or B or ¬C or ¬D or ¬E

can be rewritten, for example, in this conditional format

A or B   if   C & D & E

Starting with the classical format, we obtained this new format by disjoining, on the left of an 'if', all the positive literals and by conjoining, on the right of the 'if', all the *atomic parts* of the negative literals. That the two versions are equivalent is owed solely to the logical interpretations of the connectives:

$$\begin{array}{ll} & \text{A or B or } \neg\text{C or } \neg\text{D or } \neg\text{E} \\ \equiv & \text{A or B or } \neg(\text{C \& D \& E}) \\ \equiv & \text{A or B} \quad \text{if} \quad (\text{C \& D \& E}) \end{array}$$

   A useful property of this format is that one may then freely transport any literal from either side of the 'if' to the other, *provided one simultaneously negates it*, to yield a further equivalent rewriting. Thus the clause above could be further rewritten as any of the following equivalent forms:

A   if   ¬B & C & D & E
B   if   ¬A & C & D & E
A or B or ¬C   if   D & E
A or B or ¬C   if   C & E
¬C or ¬D or ¬E   if   ¬A & ¬B

among others. Although these new sentences are not strictly clauses, we shall henceforth loosely refer to them as clauses.

Moving literals around in this manner allows the special case where no literals remain on the right-hand side of the 'if'. In this case it is useful to insert there a special literal *True* whose value is **true** in all interpretations, noting that any formula **W** is equivalent to (**W** if *True*). Thus our original clause above could also be rewritten in conditional format as

$$\text{A or } \neg\text{C or } \neg\text{D or B or } \neg\text{E} \quad \text{if} \quad True$$

Analogously, in the special case where no literals remain on the left-hand side of the 'if', it is useful to insert there a special literal *False* whose value is **false** in all interpretations, noting that any formula $\neg$**W** is equivalent to (*False* if **W**). Thus our clause above could also be rewritten in conditional format as

$$False \quad \text{if} \quad \neg\text{A \& } \neg\text{B \& C \& D \& E}$$

We impose a convention whereby *True* may occur only as the unique antecedent of a conditional, and *False* only as the unique consequent of a conditional. Ignoring the relative order of literals, it is then the case that any clause having n>1 literals when written in classical format (having no 'if') must have (n!+2) structurally distinct rewritings in conditional format (having one 'if'). In the special case where n=0 we have the **empty clause** $\square$ whose unique rewriting in conditional format shows that it must be **false** in all interpretations:

$$False \quad \text{if} \quad True$$

The significance of these rewritings lies in the fact that they correspond to distinct problem-solving formulations. Logic programming treats the sentence

$$\text{A} \quad \text{if} \quad \neg\text{B}$$

as saying that in order to show that A holds it suffices to show that B does not. By contrast, it treats this rewriting of it

$$\text{B} \quad \text{if} \quad \neg\text{A}$$

as saying that in order to show that B holds it suffices to show that A does not. These formulations are operationally inverse to one another, yet they have identical logical content; revealed in classical format, this is simply

$$\text{A or B}$$

The process of moving one or more literals from either side of a conditional clause to the other can be regarded as the application of an inference rule which we shall henceforth refer to as **transportation of literals**. We shall find some use for this rule later on when we begin to explain the resolution principle.

Exercises 16

1. Rewrite each of the following clauses as a sentence in conditional format:

    (i)   ¬six_legs(X) or insect(X)
    (ii)   evergreen(X) or ¬tree(X) or deciduous(X)
    (iii)   vertebrate(X) or invertebrate(X)
    (iv)   omniscient(god)
    (v)   ¬*True*

   Note—some of these have several alternative answers.

2. Rewrite each of the following sentences as a clause in standard (disjunctive) format:

    (i)   ¬weed(X) if ¬plant(X)
    (ii)   *False* if lunch(X) & free(X)
    (iii)   I've_seen(X) if I've_seen(Y) & elephant(Y) & flies(Y)
    (iv)   will_be_saved(X) or ¬repents(X) if *True*

Theme 17

Converting sentences to clausal form

In many cases when we set out to formulate some problem with the eventual aim of solving it using a logic program it is convenient to write down the assumptions directly in clausal-form logic. Sometimes, however, it may be more natural to write them down initially in unrestricted first-order logic and subsequently convert them into clausal-form.

There is a simple algorithm for converting any sentence of first-order logic to a set of clauses. It is assumed throughout that, besides the steps shown below, free use is made of the commutativity and associativity properties of & and 'or', as well as the removal of superfluous parentheses. We also ensure, by suitably renaming variables, that no two quantifiers in the initial sentence refer to the same variable. The algorithm is then as follows:

1. First, rewrite every subformula

$$\textbf{W1 iff W2} \quad as \quad \textbf{(W1 if W2) \& (W2 if W1)}$$

2. Next, rewrite every subformula

$$\textbf{W1 if W2} \quad as \quad \textbf{W1 or } \neg\textbf{W2}$$

3. Next, maximally distribute all occurrences of $\neg$ by rewriting

$$
\begin{array}{lcl}
\neg(\exists X)\textbf{W} & as & (\forall X)\neg\textbf{W} \\
\neg(\forall X)\textbf{W} & as & (\exists X)\neg\textbf{W} \\
\neg(\textbf{W1 or W2}) & as & \neg\textbf{W1 \& } \neg\textbf{W2} \\
\neg(\textbf{W1 \& W2}) & as & \neg\textbf{W1 or } \neg\textbf{W2} \\
\neg\neg\textbf{W} & as & \textbf{W}
\end{array}
$$

4. Next, maximally distribute all occurrences of 'or' by rewriting

$$
\begin{array}{lcl}
\textbf{W or (W1 \& W2)} & as & \textbf{(W or W1) \& (W or W2)} \\
\textbf{W1 or } (\forall X)\textbf{W2} & as & (\forall X)(\textbf{W1 or W2}) \\
\textbf{W1 or } (\exists X)\textbf{W2} & as & (\exists X)(\textbf{W1 or W2})
\end{array}
$$

noting that, in the latter two cases, X cannot occur in **W1** because of our assumption that no two quantifiers refer to the same variable.

In applying these distributions, give priority to the first case above before attempting to apply the other two.

5. Next, maximally distribute all occurrences of $\forall$ by rewriting

$$(\forall X)(W1 \; \& \; W2) \quad as \quad (\forall X)W1 \; \& \; (\forall X)W2$$

If, at this stage, the sentence contains no existential quantifiers then the conversion process is virtually complete—omit Step **6** and proceed to Step **7**.

6. Otherwise, replace each closed subformula (having no unbound variables) of the form

$$(\forall X_1)...(\forall X_n)(\exists Y)W(Y)$$
$$\text{by} \quad (\forall X_1)...(\forall X_n)W(f(X_1, ..., X_n))$$

where **f** is any function symbol *alien* to the current state of the sentence. This process is called **Skolemization** and the newly-introduced function symbol is called a **Skolem function**. In the special case where n=0 we simply replace

$$(\exists Y)W(Y)$$
$$\text{by} \quad W(c)$$

where **c** is any constant symbol *alien* to the current state of the sentence and is called a **Skolem constant**.

7. If further applications of Step **5** are now possible then carry them out. The sentence will now be a conjunction of clauses. In order to present it as a *set* of implicitly-quantified clauses, delete all universal quantifiers and all occurrences of &.

Note on Skolemization

Skolemization is merely the process of providing a *name* for something that exists. If the thing that exists potentially depends upon certain variables then the name has to reflect this by taking those variables as parameters (otherwise there may be some loss of information content in the conversion). This is the rationale behind the details of Step **6**.

Example—a conversion presented in 7 steps as above; the initial sentence happens to be the standard definition of the subset relation (here named 's').

$$(\forall X)(\forall Y)[\quad s(X, Y) \; \text{iff} \; (\forall U)(U \in Y \; \text{if} \; U \in X) \;]$$

(∀X)(∀Y)[(s(X, Y) if (∀U)(U∈Y if U∈X))

      & ((∀U)(U∈Y if U∈X) if s(X, Y))]   after Step **1**.

(∀X)(∀Y)[(s(X, Y) or ¬(∀U)(U∈Y or ¬U∈X))

      & ((∀U)(U∈Y or ¬U∈X) or ¬s(X, Y))]   after Step **2**.

(∀X)(∀Y)[(s(X, Y) or (∃U)(¬U∈Y & U∈X))

      & ((∀U)(U∈Y or ¬U∈X) or ¬s(X, Y))]   after Step **3**.

(∀X)(∀Y)[(∃U)((s(X, Y) or ¬U∈Y) & (s(X, Y) or U∈X))

      & (∀U)(U∈Y or ¬U∈X or ¬s(X, Y))]   after Step **4**.

    (∀X)(∀Y) (∃U)((s(X, Y) or ¬U∈Y) & (s(X, Y) or U∈X))

& (∀X)(∀Y) (∀U)(U∈Y or ¬U∈X or ¬s(X, Y))   after Step **5**.

    (∀X)(∀Y) ((s(X, Y) or ¬f(X, Y)∈Y) & (s(X, Y) or f(X, Y)∈X))

& (∀X)(∀Y) (∀U)(U∈Y or ¬U∈X or ¬s(X, Y))   after Step **6**.

Finally, Step **7** yields a set of clauses, presented here in conditional format:

s(X, Y) if f(X, Y)∈Y

s(X, Y) if ¬f(X, Y)∈X

U∈Y if U∈X & s(X, Y)

Steps **1-5** and **7** of the conversion algorithm are **equivalence-preserving** since their rewritings respect standard logical equivalences of first-order logic. So if those steps *alone* suffice to complete the conversion then the conjunction **C** of the resulting clauses is equivalent to the initial sentence **S**—that is, we shall have

C ≡ S

However, if *any* Skolemization by Step **6** is needed then this equivalence will *not* prevail: we shall then have only the weaker properties

(i)   **C** is satisfiable if and only if **S** is satisfiable, and

(ii)   **C ⊨ S**.

Later on we shall see that these are good enough for our purposes.

The failure of Skolemization to preserve logical equivalence can be demonstrated by this simple example:

convert (∃X)p(X) to p(a)

Consider an interpretation over the domain {**0**, **1**} whereby 'a' is associated with

0 and 'p' is associated with the relation $\{X : X>0\}$. This is a model for $(\exists X)p(X)$ but not for p(a). Therefore the sentences cannot be equivalent. Less formally, to say that a proposition holds for some element in the domain does not imply that it holds for an arbitrarily selected element in the domain; on the other hand, the converse must hold, whatever the domain and whatever the proposition—hence property (ii) must always prevail.

Exercises 17

1. Exercise 9 asked you to express each of the statements below in unrestricted first-order logic:

    (i)   "if X is a father or X is a mother then X is someone's parent"
    (ii)   "if X is a parent and X is a female then X is someone's mother"
    (iii)   "if X is a father or X is a mother then someone is someone's parent"
    (iv)   "if everyone is a parent then someone is a child"

    Convert each of your answers for Exercise 9 into a set of clauses.

2. Confirm the following equivalences by converting to clausal form the formulas on each side of the ≡ symbol:

    (i)   A if (A if B) ≡ A or B
    (ii)   (A if B) if C ≡ A if (B & C)
    (iii) $(\forall X)(A$ if $B(X))$ ≡ A if $(\exists X)B(X)$
            where A contains no occurrences of X.

Theme 18

Some useful conversions

In the logic programming context some species of conversion are particularly common. To perform these conversions it is easier to follow pre-defined schemata than to work through all the stages of the algorithm previously described.

Each schema below provides for the conversion of a given conditional sentence into a set of simpler conditional sentences which are more clause-like. As usual, **W**, **W1**, ... etc. denote arbitrary formulas; in the special case where they are all atomic, the conversion yields a set of clauses.

In all cases, where the given sentence has outermost universal quantifiers $(\forall X_1)...(\forall X_n)$, these are (a) not shown explicitly below, in order to simplify the presentation, and (b) inherited by the new sentences to which they are converted. We assume, as in Theme 17, that no two quantifiers refer to the same variable.

$$\mathbf{W} \text{ if } (\mathbf{W1} \,\&\, \mathbf{W2}) \;\Rightarrow\; \text{unchanged}$$

$$\mathbf{W} \text{ if } (\mathbf{W1} \text{ or } \mathbf{W2}) \;\Rightarrow\; \begin{array}{l}\mathbf{W} \text{ if } \mathbf{W1} \\ \mathbf{W} \text{ if } \mathbf{W2}\end{array}$$

$$\mathbf{W} \text{ if } (\mathbf{W1} \text{ if } \mathbf{W2}) \;\Rightarrow\; \begin{array}{l}\mathbf{W} \text{ if } \mathbf{W1} \\ \mathbf{W} \text{ if } \neg\mathbf{W2}\end{array}$$

$$\mathbf{W} \text{ if } (\mathbf{W1} \text{ iff } \mathbf{W2}) \;\Rightarrow\; \begin{array}{l}\mathbf{W} \text{ if } \mathbf{W1} \,\&\, \mathbf{W2} \\ \mathbf{W} \text{ if } \neg\mathbf{W1} \,\&\, \neg\mathbf{W2}\end{array}$$

$$(\mathbf{W} \text{ or } \mathbf{W1}) \text{ if } \mathbf{W2} \;\Rightarrow\; \mathbf{W} \text{ if } \neg\mathbf{W1} \,\&\, \mathbf{W2}$$

$$(\mathbf{W} \,\&\, \mathbf{W1}) \text{ if } \mathbf{W2} \;\Rightarrow\; \begin{array}{l}\mathbf{W} \text{ if } \mathbf{W2} \\ \mathbf{W1} \text{ if } \mathbf{W2}\end{array}$$

$$(\mathbf{W} \text{ if } \mathbf{W1}) \text{ if } \mathbf{W2} \;\Rightarrow\; \mathbf{W} \text{ if } \mathbf{W1} \,\&\, \mathbf{W2}$$

$$\mathbf{W} \text{ if } (\exists Y)\mathbf{W1}(Y) \;\Rightarrow\; \begin{array}{l}(\forall Y)(\mathbf{W} \text{ if } \mathbf{W1}(Y)) \\ \text{noting that } \mathbf{Y} \\ \text{cannot occur in } \mathbf{W}.\end{array}$$

$$(\forall Y)W(Y) \text{ if } \mathbf{W1} \quad \Rightarrow \quad (\forall Y)(W(Y) \text{ if } \mathbf{W})$$

Note—in the above, the **Y** variables do not occur in **W1**.

$$\mathbf{W} \text{ if } (\forall Y)\mathbf{W1}(Y) \quad \Rightarrow \quad \mathbf{W} \text{ if } \mathbf{W1}(f(X_1, ..., X_n))$$

Note—in the above, **f** is a Skolem function; recall that X_1, ...and X_n are the variables assumed bound by the sentence's implicit outermost quantifiers.

$$(\exists Y)W(Y) \text{ if } \mathbf{W} \quad \Rightarrow \quad W(f(X_1, ..., X_n)) \text{ if } \mathbf{W1}$$

Note—in the above, **f** is a Skolem function; recall that X_1, ...and X_n are the variables assumed bound by the sentence's implicit outermost quantifiers.

Two more general conversion rules which are often useful are the following:

1. A conjunction of sentences W_1 & ... & W_n converts to the set

$$C_1 \cup ... \cup C_n$$

where each C_i is the set of sentences obtained by converting W_i.

2. If a sentence **W if W1** converts to a set of sentences

$$\{\mathbf{W} \text{ if } \mathbf{B_i} \mid i = 1, ..., n\}$$

then the sentence **W if (W1 & W2)** converts to the set of sentences

$$\{\mathbf{W} \text{ if } (\mathbf{B_i} \text{ \& } \mathbf{W2}) \mid i = 1, ..., n\}$$

Example—a conversion using the earlier schemata:

"All happy families are alike, but an unhappy family is unhappy after its own fashion." [From Tolstoy's *Anna Karenina*.]

$(\forall Y)(\text{alike}(X, Y) \text{ if } \text{happy}(Y)) \text{ if } \text{happy}(X)$
$(\forall Y)(\neg\text{alike}(X, Y) \text{ if } \neg\text{happy}(Y) \text{ \& } \neg Y=X) \text{ if } \neg\text{happy}(X)$

$\Rightarrow \quad (\text{alike}(X, Y) \text{ if } \text{happy}(Y)) \text{ if } \text{happy}(X)$
$\qquad (\neg\text{alike}(X, Y) \text{ if } \neg\text{happy}(Y) \text{ \& } \neg Y=X) \text{ if } \neg\text{happy}(X)$

$\Rightarrow \quad \text{alike}(X, Y) \text{ if } \text{happy}(Y) \text{ \& } \text{happy}(X)$
$\qquad \neg\text{alike}(X, Y) \text{ if } \neg\text{happy}(Y) \text{ \& } \neg Y=X \text{ \& } \neg\text{happy}(X)$

Exercises 18

1. Using just the binary predicate 'likes', express in clausal form the following statements:

    (i)   "chris likes everyone"
    (ii)   "chris likes someone"
    (iii)   "everyone likes everyone"
    (iv)   "everyone likes someone"
    (v)   "someone likes everyone"
    (vi)   "someone likes someone"
    (vii)   "no one likes chris"
    (viii) "no one likes no one"
    (ix)   "no one likes anyone"
    (x)   "no one likes everyone"

2. Using just the binary predicates 'likes' and '=', express in clausal form the following statements:

    (i)   "chris likes himself and no one else"
    (ii)   "no one likes anyone except himself"
    (iii) "everyone likes everyone except himself"

3. Convert to clausal form the sentence

        A iff (B & (C iff D))

4. Convert to clausal form each of the following sentences:

    (i)   path(X, Y) iff (go(Y) if go(X))
    (ii)   empty(X) iff ¬(∃U)U∈X
    (iii) function(F) iff (∀X)(∀Y)(∀Z)(Y=Z if maps(F, X, Y) &
                                     maps(F, X, Z))

Theme 19

Elements of proof theory

Whereas model theory considers the assignment of meaning to sentences, **proof theory** considers the generation of sentences from other sentences. Later on we shall see that proof theory yields a precise framework in which to articulate the computational features of the logic programming formalism, whilst model theory yields precise information about the formalism's semantics.

We have seen that the language **L** of first-order logic is just a set of sentences constructible from a particular grammar. We have also seen that, using the notion of truth-value, certain model-theoretic relations of interest can be defined upon the language. For our purposes, the most important of these is the relation of **logical implication** between sets of sentences and individual sentences, that is:

$$\vDash \ = \ \{<S, s> \ | \ S \text{ is a subset of } \mathbf{L}, s \text{ is a member of } \mathbf{L} \text{ and}$$
$$\text{every model for } \mathbf{S} \text{ is a model for } \mathbf{s}\}$$

Proof theory defines relations upon the language by quite different means. Instead of considering the truth-value of a sentence in the context of some interpretation, it considers the **derivability** of the sentence in the context of some **set of rules** for sentence-derivation.

Putting logic aside for a moment, imagine that we have *any* language **L**—for instance, the set of all sentences which are strings constructible from just the characters **a** and **b**. We might then freely invent *any* set **R** of rules each taking the schematic form

"from a set of sentences of *that* kind,
derive a sentence of *this* kind."

e.g.   "from the set of strings {**aX**, **abX**}, where X is any string,
derive the string **ababX**."

We might then take *any* initial set **S** of sentences in **L** and, by applying various rules in **R**, eventually derive some new sentence **s** from **S** and/or other derived sentences. The totality of all such exercises conducted within the given language constructs a **derivability relation** characterized by **R**:

$$\vdash \ = \ \{<S, s> \ | \ S \text{ is a subset of } \mathbf{L}, s \text{ is a member of } \mathbf{L} \text{ and}$$
$$s \text{ is derivable from } \mathbf{S} \text{ using } \mathbf{R}\}$$

Whether or not such an exercise serves any *purpose* must depend entirely upon both the use being made of **L** and the particular choice of rule-set **R**.

In the logic context, the sentences initially given are called **axioms**, the derived sentences are called **theorems** (or **syntactic consequences**) and the derivation rules in **R** are called **inference rules**. The best-known and most frequently used inference rule is *modus ponens*:

$$\{(A \text{ if } B), B\} \vdash A$$

Together, the axioms and **R** constitute an **inference system**. We define a **proof** drawn from such a system as a sequence

$$< s_1, s_2, ..., s_n >$$

such that each s_i is either an axiom or else is derivable using **R** from some subset of the preceding members of the sequence. The sequence is said to be a proof of the theorem s_n. Proofs of this sort are also variously referred to as **derivations** or **deductions**.

The axioms together with all the theorems derivable using **R** constitute a **theory**. A theory is said to be **consistent** if and only if there is no sentence **s** such that the theory contains both **s** and ¬**s**. A theory which is not consistent is said to be **inconsistent**.

Note that all the concepts above are wholly *syntactical*, in that they are based upon consideration of sentences' syntax alone, paying no regard to the notion of interpretation.

The sort of inference systems we employ in logic programming are ones employing so-called **non-logical axioms** (or *hypotheses*). Here the axioms are just any sentences of logic which we freely compose in order to express our assumptions about the problem at hand, such as

$$\text{likes(chris, X)} \text{ if } \text{likes(X, logic)}$$

The theorems we derive from such systems are then called **non-logical theorems**.

It is important not to confuse these systems with ones employing only so-called **logical axioms**, which are selected **valid sentences** of logic. Such systems serve the purpose of defining, in a generative manner, *all* the valid sentences (**logical theorems**) of logic. For first-order logic a typical system has a few logical axioms, such as

$$(U \text{ if } V) \text{ if } U$$
$$((W \text{ if } U) \text{ if } (V \text{ if } U)) \text{ if } ((W \text{ if } V) \text{ if } U)$$
$$(U \text{ if } V) \text{ if } (¬V \text{ if } ¬U)$$
$$\vdots$$

etc.

and *modus ponens* as its principal inference rule. Here we shall not dwell further upon systems of this kind, since logic programming does not engage in the *explicit* manipulation of valid sentences. Presently, however, we shall observe important connections between logic programming's **non-logical** framework and the **logical** frameworks just discussed.

Exercises 19

1. Consider the following inference system which operates upon the language of strings defined over the alphabet {**a**, **b**, **c**}:

   Axiom: just the unit string **a**.
   Rules of inference:

   1. from any theorem X ending with **a**, infer the string X**ba**;
   2. from any theorem X, infer the string obtained by replacing any one substring **bab** of X by **c**.

   (i)   Exhibit a proof of the string **acabaca**.
   (ii)   Give an indication of the theory determined by this system.

2. Using just the inference rule *modus ponens* and the axioms

                     A if B
                     B if C
                     B if D
                     C if E
                     D if E
                     D
                     E

   (i)   exhibit a proof of A;
   (ii)   determine the set of all atomic theorems.

3. Using just the inference rule *modus ponens* and the axioms

                     ¬A if B
                     B if C
                     A if C
                     C if D
                     D

   show that the resulting theory is inconsistent.

Theme 20

Problem solving and logical implication

Our overall approach in any problem-solving exercise will be to supply as input some set **S** of sentences expressing our *assumptions* about the problem domain, and to require the problem solver to yield as output some sentence **s** expressing a *conclusion* about the problem domain.

Our *minimal requirement* of the relationship between **S** and **s** is that the following shall hold:

> *if*   **S** correctly expresses the assumptions
> *then* **s** correctly expresses the conclusion.

Here the phrase 'correctly expresses' indicates that we have in mind some *intended interpretation* **I** associating particular objects and relations in the problem domain with particular terms and predicate symbols occurring in the sentences. So, in model-theoretic terms, what we are minimally requiring is that

> for *this* intended interpretation **I**,
> *if*   **I** is a model for **S**
> *then* **I** is a model for **s**.

Despite the reasonableness of this minimal requirement it turns out that we cannot construct on a computer a problem solver capable of deriving **s** from **S** so as to satisfy exactly that requirement *and no more*. Such a problem solver would either have to be internally engineered so as to take account of just the intended interpretation or else it would need to have the details of that interpretation conveyed to it as input data. But the intended interpretation will typically concern objects in the 'real world', whereas the computer can never know about anything other than syntactic objects. Any attempt to encode real-world requirements in the computer must ultimately entail their translation into symbols and hence only contribute further to the computer's internal syntactic world.

In any case, we may not wish to be hampered by a commitment to any particular real-world interpretation. For instance, consider the following sentences:

> **S** = { likes(harry, logic)
>   likes(chris, X) if likes(X, logic) }
>
> **s** =   likes(chris, harry)

We may not wish to be in the position whereby our problem solver can derive s from S when we interpret 'harry' and 'chris' as real-world males *Harold* and *Christopher*, but not when we interpret them as real-world females *Harriet* and *Christine*.

The way we avoid such discrimination in practice is to aim for *more* than the minimal requirement. One way of escaping commitment to any particular interpretation is to require:

> for *every* possible interpretation **I**,
> *if*   **I** is a model for **S**
> *then* **I** is a model for **s**

that is, the stronger relation of logical implication, **S ⊨ s**. For the example above this relation does in fact prevail, so that both of the interpretations mentioned above are covered, as well as all others: if the stronger relation holds, then the minimal one certainly does. We can certainly construct on the computer a problem solver which fulfils this requirement. Presently we shall see that such a problem solver does not, in fact, need to consider *every* interpretation—it can accomplish its task by considering just one special interpretation defined over syntactic objects. In order to discuss how it does this we shall make use of the proof-theoretic (syntactic) notions introduced earlier.

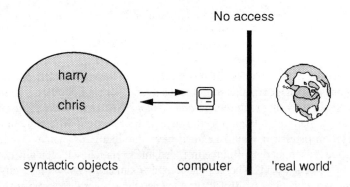

Figure 20.1. The computer's world *versus* the 'real world'.

Exercises 20

1. Using just one unary predicate symbol 'p', one unary function symbol 's' and one constant '0', compose a logic program having just two clauses which computes

the natural numbers $\{0, 1, 2, \ldots\}$
and   the even numbers $\{0, 2, 4, \ldots\}$
and   the prime numbers $\{2, 3, 5, \ldots\}$.

2. Assuming a language having no function symbols, give a condition under which the following holds:

> for the interpretation I_1 it is the case that
> if I_1 is model for **S** then I_1 is a model for **s**

> if and only if

> for the interpretation I_2 such that $I_2 \neq I_1$ it is the case that
> if I_2 is model for **S** then I_2 is a model for **s**.

3. Given the assumptions

> likes(X, logic) if X=harry
> likes(Y, X) if likes(X, logic) & Y=chris

what further assumptions, not referring to 'likes', should be added to establish that 'christine' likes 'harriet' yet not establish that 'christopher' likes 'harold'?

Theme 21

Problem solving and theorem proving

The problem-solving mechanism of logic programming is fundamentally a theorem proving (inferential) mechanism. As indicated earlier in the course, our aim is to characterize computation as the inference-driven manipulation of knowledge. More concretely, the **interpreters** that we employ to execute logic programs are just **automated theorem provers**, so that we might expect proof theory to tell us something about their capabilities and limitations.

Consider, therefore, a problem solver which applies deductive inference rules in order to derive a sentence (theorem) s expressing the answer to a problem from a set **S** of other sentences (axioms) expressing the assumptions. We have previously argued that we would like s to be *logically implied* by S in order to be sure of the answer's correctness in the intended interpretation yet without us having to characterize that particular interpretation.

However, whether or not this implication requirement is met depends entirely upon which inference rules are used. Inference rules which *do* meet it are said to be **sound**. In other words, the derivability relation which they determine is a subset of the logical implication relation:

$$\text{for all S and s,} \quad S \vDash s \quad \text{if} \quad S \vdash s$$

Inference using only sound rules is referred to as **sound inference** or **valid inference**. Inference rules which are sound include

$$\textit{modus ponens} \qquad \{B, \quad A \text{ if } B\} \vdash A$$
$$\text{and} \quad \textit{modus tollens} \qquad \{\neg A, \quad A \text{ if } B\} \vdash \neg B$$

whilst the following inference rule is unsound (despite its popularity):

$$\textit{modus mistakens} \qquad \{A, \quad A \text{ if } B\} \vdash B$$

We also want our problem solver to have *sufficient inferential power* to be able to derive s from S whenever S implies s. Otherwise, problems might have correct answers which the problem solver was unable to derive. Hence we also want this to hold:

$$\text{for all S and s,} \quad S \vdash s \quad \text{if} \quad S \vDash s$$

If it does, we say that the inference rules are (jointly) **complete**. For an inference system which is both sound and complete, the relations of derivability and logical implication *coincide*, so that we then have

for all S and s,   S ⊢ s   if and only if   S ⊨ s

Do such complete inference systems exist? The answer depends upon the language under consideration. For instance,

for propositional logic, the answer is *yes*;
for first-order predicate logic, the answer is *yes*;
for second-order predicate logic, the answer is *no*.

These important results from proof theory, known as the **completeness theorems**, were established many decades ago by the great logician Kurt Gödel. That which pertains to first-order logic is clearly the one of greatest concern to us here and establishes many vital links between the model theory and the proof theory of that logic.

Languages for which the answer is *yes*, such as first-order logic, are said to be **deductively complete**. Moreover, if a language is deductively complete then so are all of its subsets. Hence we know that if we choose to work exclusively in the clausal-form subset of first-order logic then there must exist a complete inference system for it. This gives us one of several essential assurances as to the viability of making a *comprehensive* problem-solving formalism out of clausal-form logic.

However, merely possessing a complete inference system is not enough: we shall also require an assurance that algorithms exist capable of *generating* all those derivations which solve our problems. Note that an inference system by itself is *not* an algorithm—it says which rules are available but prescribes no *strategy* for applying them. The coupling of an inference system with a strategy yields an algorithm called a **proof procedure**. Whether or not such a proof procedure is complete depends upon both of its components. Finally, there is the question of whether the entire apparatus of complete inference systems and algorithms for applying them is able to compute the whole range of theoretically-computable functions and relations. We will examine these questions later on, in Theme 39.

Exercises 21

1. Determine whether each of the following inferences is sound:

(i)   {A, B} ⊢ A if B
(ii)   {(A if C), (B if C)} ⊢ A if B
(iii)   {(A or B), (¬A or C)} ⊢ B or C

2. Show that *modus mistakens* is unsound.

3. Show that, for propositional logic, any problem which is solvable by using *modus ponens* is solvable by using *modus tollens*.

   Hint—rewrite the assumptions so that they refer to new propositions which name the *negations* of the original ones.

Theme 22

Implication and validity

Recall that there are some sentences in our language which are **valid**—that is, are **true** in all interpretations. The simplest such sentences take the form

(**A** if **A**) where **A** denotes any atomic formula

We remarked earlier that logic programming does not normally make explicit use of valid sentences. Indeed, for the most part such sentences are a nuisance when they occur (typically inadvertently) within logic programs, for they tend to plunge execution into infinite loops.

Nevertheless, for first-order logic there is a close link between validity and the logical implications that we seek amongst the (typically non-valid) sentences from which logic programs are built. This link, determined by the underlying model theory, can be easily revealed by exploiting this theorem about logical implication:

for any sentence-set $S=\{s_1, ..., s_n\}$ and any sentence s,
$S \vDash s$ if and only if $S-\{s_i\} \vDash (s \text{ if } s_i)$ [for any i]

We can easily prove the 'if' part of this theorem, namely

$S \vDash s$ if $S-\{s_i\} \vDash (s \text{ if } s_i)$ [for any i]

Firstly, assume that the implication on the right holds—so that every model for $S-\{s_i\}$ is also a model for (s if s_i). Secondly, assume that there exists some interpretation **I** which is a model for **S** but not for **s**. Then **I** must be a model for $S-\{s_i\}$, since a model for a set of sentences must be a model for any of its subsets. But, by the first assumption above, **I** must be a model for (s if s_i)—in which case, since **I** is assumed not to be a model for **s**, neither can it be a model for s_i. Then it cannot be a model for **S** either, since $s_i \in S$. This contradicts the second assumption, which must now be revoked—thus we conclude that every model for **S** is also a model for **s**, so completing the proof. It is equally easy to prove the theorem's 'only-if' part by a similar line of argument.

In effect the theorem tells us that an implication is preserved when we remove any assumption from its left-hand side and make it a *condition* of the sentence on the right-hand side. By repeated applications of this process we can remove *all* of the assumptions from the left-hand side; the nested-conditional sentence which evolves on the right-hand side is then logically equivalent to the sentence

$$(s \text{ if } s_1 \& \dots \& s_n)$$

since, in general, $((\mathbf{A} \text{ if } \mathbf{B}) \text{ if } \mathbf{C})$ is equivalent to $(\mathbf{A} \text{ if } (\mathbf{B} \& \mathbf{C}))$. So we have

$$S \vDash s \quad \text{if and only if} \quad \emptyset \vDash (s \text{ if } s_1 \& \dots \& s_n)$$

By convention, all interpretations are models for the empty set $\emptyset$ and therefore the sentences implied by $\emptyset$ are exactly the valid sentences; so we also have

$$S \vDash s \quad \text{if and only if} \quad (s \text{ if } s_1 \& \dots \& s_n) \text{ is } \textbf{valid}$$

Thus every assertion that some logical implication holds is equivalent to an assertion that some associated sentence is valid. For example, (A if (A if B) & B) can be shown to be valid as follows:

trivially	$\{B, (A \text{ if } B)\} \vDash A$
therefore	$\{B\} \vDash (A \text{ if } (A \text{ if } B))$
therefore	$\emptyset \vDash ((A \text{ if } (A \text{ if } B)) \text{ if } B)$

Note further that a sentence is valid if and only if its negation is unsatisfiable and hence inconsistent. The significance of these various observations is twofold. Firstly, they will assist us presently in explaining the connection between the way logic programming is organized and the logical foundation upon which it relies— Herbrand's Theorem, which makes an important statement about inconsistent sets of clauses. Secondly, there are important decidability results about validity which tell us about the limitations of our implication-oriented problem solvers.

Exercises 22

1. Prove the 'only-if' part of the theorem discussed in the Theme:

$$S \vDash s \quad \text{only if} \quad S-\{s_i\} \vDash (s \text{ if } s_i) \qquad \text{[for any i]}$$

2. Show, by using standard equivalences, that

$$((A \text{ if } B) \text{ if } C) \text{ if } D \equiv A \text{ if } (B \& C \& D)$$

3. By convention, $\emptyset$ is satisfied by all interpretations. Show that if this were not so then no sentence-set would be satisfied by all interpretations.

Theme 23

The Herbrand domain

When we compose a logic program we do so with some 'real-world' domain in mind. But, as remarked earlier, the computer cannot (normally) operate directly upon that domain—instead, its workings are confined to its own internal domain comprising just the *symbols* representable within it. In the logic programming context that domain is called the **Herbrand domain** (or **Herbrand universe**), and is determined wholly by the language (set of sentences) **L** in which we formulate our programs and queries. Accordingly, we denote it either by H_L or—when the choice of language is clear in the current context—by just **H**.

What does H_L consist of? Simply all those **ground terms** that can be constructed using the constant symbols and function symbols available in the alphabets of **L**. These terms can be viewed as the fundamental *data* upon which logic programs and queries operate.

Consider a simple case where **L**'s alphabets provide just one constant symbol '0' and two function symbols 's' and 'p'. In this language we might write the following program:

$$int(0)$$
$$int(s(X)) \text{ if } int(X)$$

as well as other sentences that we might attempt to prove using that program, such as

$$int(s(s(0)))$$
$$\text{and} \quad int(p(p(0)))$$

Here the Herbrand domain H_L is the infinite set

$$\{0, s(0), p(0), s(s(0)), s(p(0)), p(s(0)), p(p(0)), \ldots\}$$

and can be viewed as comprising all the ground terms that the language makes available to the program interpreter in its attempts to construct those proofs. In fact, no terms beyond s(s(0)) are needed in order to prove int(s(s(0))), whereas int(p(p(0))) is unprovable no matter how many terms we might use in trying to prove it.

For the example above, it might well be that the 'real-world' domain we had in mind was the set of integers

$$Z = \{\ldots, -2, -1, 0, +1, +2, \ldots\}$$

with the intended interpretation being:

1. associate '0' with **0**

2. associate 's' with the function from **Z** to **Z** taking x∈Z to x+1
associate 'p' with the function from **Z** to **Z** taking x∈Z to x–1

so that, for instance, s(0)   is interpreted as **+1**
and   p(0)   is interpreted as **-1**
and   p(s(0)) is interpreted as **0**

3. associate 'int' with the relation **Z**.

The computer knows nothing about these intentions in the mind of the programmer. When analysing the properties and behaviour of a logic program we can for many purposes (but not for all) ignore the programmer's *real-world intentions* and concentrate instead only upon the way in which the program operates upon the Herbrand domain. In this way we avoid issues which are extraneous to the formalism. So we shall take a rather narrow, but mathematically convenient, view of any computer executing a logic program: it is just a **Herbrand-symbol-cruncher**.

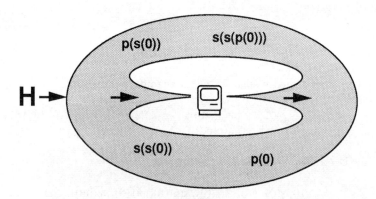

Figure 23.1. A computer crunching Herbrand symbols.

It will be useful at this stage to comment upon the reason why we have chosen to define the Herbrand domain solely in terms of some pre-specified language **L**. In some other texts you will find that a Herbrand domain is defined instead with respect to a given program **P** and that the alphabets of **L** are assumed to contain only those symbols appearing in **P**. This latter assumption, however, is unduly restrictive in the logic programming context. In order to see why, consider the standard 'append' program for appending lists:

> append(nil, W, W)
> append(U•X, Y, U•Z) if append(X, Y, Z)

In later Themes we shall discuss certain classes of **ground atoms** having special significance. One such class comprises those atoms **q** which can be proved from a given program **P** (equivalently, those atoms **q** for which the query ?**q** can be solved by that program). Jointly, those classes constitute some *overall* set of atoms within the language **L**. Thus we must ensure that **L** is large enough to contain all the atoms in which we are potentially interested. However, if we were to identify **L** as the language constructed solely from the alphabets of **P** then—in most practical cases—we would exclude many such atoms.

For example, it is plausible that we might wish to prove either of these two atoms using the 'append' program:

> **q1**: append(nil•nil, nil•nil, nil•nil•nil)
> **q2**: append(a•b•nil, c•d•nil, a•b•c•d•nil)

Since both of these are provable it seems reasonable that both should belong to the overall set of interest. In this case our language's alphabet of constants ought to contain 'a', 'b', 'c' and 'd' (which do not appear in the program) as well as 'nil' (which does). Atoms like **q1** which use only 'nil' are, in fact, the least likely ones we would wish to prove, whilst those like **q2** are much more likely. There will be yet other atoms which cannot be proved but which may well be queried, and these may also contain constants or function symbols not in the program. In order to be *realistic* about the way we use programs, we must make **L**'s alphabets of constants and function symbols large enough to construct *all* the terms that might appear in the atoms of interest. The Herbrand domain H_L is then constructed from these two alphabets.

Given some program **P** and a pre-specified language **L**, we can then define the set of ground atoms in which we are interested. The largest possible such set is the so-called **Herbrand base** of **L** which is simply the set of all ground atoms in **L**. Notice, however, that this set may contain some atoms whose predicate symbols do not appear in **P**. Such atoms are unlikely to be of much interest, since we *know in advance* that they cannot be proved using **P**. It is hard to imagine, for example, that we would query any atom of the form

> **q3**: silly(...)

using the 'append' program, even if 'silly' did happen to belong **L**'s alphabet of predicate symbols. In order to exclude atoms of this sort, we shall use instead the so-called **Herbrand base** of **P** and define this to be the set of all ground atoms whose predicate symbols appear in **P** and whose arguments belong to H_L.

These ideas will now be illustrated for a simpler program **P** written in a language **L** whose alphabet of constant symbols is {you, chris, this_book} and whose alphabet of function symbols is empty:

likes(chris, Anyone) if buys(Anyone, this_book)
buys(Anyone, this_book) if sensible(Anyone)
sensible(you)

Since we have no function symbols, the domain H_L={you, chris, this_book} is finite. The set of predicate symbols in the program is {likes, buys, sensible}. The Herbrand base of **P** is denoted by **B(P)**, in which the assumption of a pre-specified language **L** is left implicit. Then **B(P)** must be the following finite set of ground atoms:

{   likes(chris, chris)   buys(chris, chris)
    likes(chris, you)   buys(chris, you)
    likes(chris, this_book)   buys(chris, this_book)

    likes(you, chris)   buys(you, chris)
    likes(you, you)   buys(you, you)
    likes(you, this_book)   buys(you, this_book)

    likes(this_book, chris)   buys(this_book, chris)
    likes(this_book, you)   buys(this_book, you)
    likes(this_book, this_book)   buys(this_book, this_book)

    sensible(chris)
    sensible(you)
    sensible(this_book) }

Some of these atoms, such as likes(chris, you), are soundly provable from the program. Most of them, however, are not; for instance, likes(chris, this_book) is not soundly provable—due, it might be argued, to the program offering no evidence that this_book is sensible.

Exercises 23

1. Give an indication of the Herbrand domain when the language has

   (i)   two constants 'a' and 'b' and two 1-ary function symbols 'f' and 'g';
   (ii)   one constant 'a' and one 2-ary function symbol 't';
   (iii)   no constants but one 1-ary function symbol 'f'.

2. Using *modus ponens*, prove the proposition int(s(s(0))) from the 'int' program in the Theme and identify the ground terms involved in the proof.

3. For the same 'int' program, suggest an interpretation of it based upon the domain of all strings whose members belong to {**a**, **b**}.

Theme 24

Inference systems for clausal form

In this Theme we take a preliminary look at the issue of how one might set up an automated problem solver capable of investigating problems formulated in clausal-form logic.

It is worth observing straightaway that clausal-form logic can be approximated by the much simpler system of propositional (variable-free) logic. The approximation is facilitated by recognizing that only the Herbrand domain **H** need be considered. This is because any model for a clause-set over some real-world domain necessarily has an isomorphic (structurally-identical) model over **H**—in effect, those two models are just renamings of one another. According to the approximation, any clause of the form

$$(\forall X_1)...(\forall X_n)W(X_1, ..., X_n)$$

is shorthand for a set of implicitly-conjoined **ground clauses**

$$\{W(t) \mid t \in H^n\}$$

In particular, suppose we have a program **P** consisting of a set of clauses. Then we define the **ground instantiation** of **P** as the set of all the ground instances of all its clauses and denote it by **G(P)**.

Example—if **P** is the program

> likes(chris, X) if likes(X, logic)
> likes(bob, logic)

then, taking **H**={chris, bob, logic}, **G(P)** is the ground program

> likes(chris, chris) if likes(chris, logic)
> likes(chris, bob)   if likes(bob, logic)
> likes(chris, logic) if likes(logic, logic)
> likes(bob, logic)

Since **G(P)** is wholly ground it is essentially propositional. Without any loss of problem-solving capability we could rename all of its atoms by structureless proposition names, as follows:

LIKESCC if LIKESCL
LIKESCB if LIKESBL
LIKESCL if LIKESLL
LIKESBL

The significant point here is that, for propositional logic, particularly simple inference systems are available. For instance, if we confine ourselves to definite programs and seek only to derive atomic consequences then *modus ponens* together with *transportation of literals* is sufficient for the task. In the example just shown the only atomic consequences are LIKESBL and LIKESCB, the first of which is a given axiom whilst the second is derivable by one step of *modus ponens* applied to the second and fourth clauses.

A major drawback of inference based upon repeated application of *modus ponens* is that its use does not inherently focus upon any particular answer—it just derives whatever it can and may therefore derive much that is irrelevant. But in general we have, at the start, a pretty good idea of what we want to derive, and all we require of the inference system is *confirmation* that what we want is indeed a logical consequence. In view of this, a better inference system is that which instead makes use of *modus tollens* in order to construct a so-called **proof by contradiction**.

At this point it is useful to recall the property of implication presented in Theme 22:

$$S \vDash s \quad \text{if and only if} \quad S - \{s_i\} \vDash (s \text{ if } s_i) \qquad [\text{for any } i]$$

Suppose we have a program **P** with a conjectured answer **A** and take the specific case where $S = P \cup \{\neg A\}$ and $s = \square = False$. We shall then have

$$P \cup \{\neg A\} \vDash \square \quad \text{if and only if} \quad P \vDash (False \text{ if } \neg A)$$

that is, $\quad P \cup \{\neg A\} \vDash \square \quad \text{if and only if} \quad P \vDash A$

that is, $\quad P \cup \{\neg A\} \vdash \square \quad \text{if and only if} \quad P \vdash A$

assuming, as always, that the inference system we employ is both sound and complete. To summarize, instead of directly deriving **A** from **P** we may equivalently derive a contradiction from **P** and ¬**A**.

In the case where **P** is ground definite and **A** is ground atomic, *modus tollens* together with *transportation of literals* is a sufficient inference system for this new approach. Here is a reminder of what the *modus tollens* rule says:

$$\{\neg A, (A \text{ if } B)\} \vdash \neg B$$

Note the special case where **B** is *True*—the rule then reduces to the simplest way of showing a contradiction:

$$\{\neg A, A\} \vdash \square$$

To illustrate its use, consider again the task of confirming that LIKESCB is an answer to our propositional program. Starting with the *negation* of this conjectured answer, we can derive a contradiction by two steps of *modus tollens*:

$$\{\neg\text{LIKESCB}, (\text{LIKESCB if LIKESBL})\} \vdash \neg\text{LIKESBL}$$
$$\{\neg\text{LIKESBL}, \qquad\qquad \text{LIKESBL}\} \vdash \square$$

This derivation is concerned only with contradicting the particular proposition ¬LIKESCB initially given. Although the derivation can be viewed as a *proof*

$$< \neg\text{LIKESCB}, \neg\text{LIKESBL}, \square >$$

in the sense defined in Theme 19, it is accorded the special title of **refutation** by virtue of terminating with the contradiction $\square$. Loosely speaking, we have used the assumptions in **P** in order to *refute* the proposition ¬LIKESCB, rather than to *affirm* the proposition LIKESCB as we did previously using *modus ponens*.

Refutational, rather than affirmational, theorem proving is the underlying principle in most manifestations of logic programming and will serve as our staple reasoning technique in many of the later Themes.

Exercises 24

1. Give an indication of **G(P)** for this clause-set **P**:

   $$\text{last}(f(U, \text{nil}), U)$$
   $$\text{last}(f(U, Z), V) \text{ if } \text{last}(Z, V)$$

   assuming that the language has just two constants 'nil' and 'a', and just one 2-ary function symbol 'f'.

2. Taking **G(P)** from the exercise above, construct a proof, using *modus ponens* only, of the proposition

   $$\text{last}(f(a, f(a, \text{nil})), a)$$

3. By making appropriate use of the special atom *True*, show that the **reflexivity property** of ⊢, namely

   $$\text{for all } A, \{A\} \vdash A$$

   can be cast as a special case of *modus ponens*.

Theme 25

Herbrand procedures

In the early days of automated theorem proving much use was made of the principles discussed in the last Theme:

> replace the given clause-set by its ground instantiation;
> then seek a contradiction.

The formal justification for this approach relies upon a profound and highly important result in proof theory known as **Herbrand's Theorem**. There are many ways of expressing and specializing this theorem, but the specialization of it which follows is perhaps the one best-suited to our present context:

> a contradiction $\square$ can be derived
> from a set of clauses $\mathbf{P} \cup \{\neg A\}$
>
> if and only if
>
> it can be derived from some finite subset
> of the ground instantiation $\mathbf{G}(\mathbf{P} \cup \{\neg A\})$.

The crucial word here is *finite*, for it ensures the existence of an effective procedure (**algorithm**) by which one can demonstrate a contradiction and hence, indirectly, that A is a consequence of $\mathbf{P}$. It overcomes the *infinitistic* aspect of our fundamental requirement of showing that $\mathbf{P}$ implies A, that is:

> each of the (*infinitely many*) models for $\mathbf{P}$ is a model for A.

In other texts you may come across a similar theorem posed in terms of *unsatisfiability* rather than in terms of derivability:

> a set of clauses $\mathbf{P} \cup \{\neg A\}$
> is unsatisfiable
>
> if and only if
>
> some finite subset of $\mathbf{G}(\mathbf{P} \cup \{\neg A\})$
> is unsatisfiable.

This is the theorem conventionally used for proving that the inference system known as *resolution* is complete; it is called the **Skolem-Herbrand-Gödel Theorem** and can be derived from Herbrand's Theorem together with the assumption that Gödel's Completeness Theorem holds for clausal-form logic (which it does). It can also be viewed as a variant of the **Compactness Theorem** for first-order logic, which holds that a set of sentences is satisfiable if and only if every finite subset of it is satisfiable.

The most naive algorithm based upon Herbrand's Theorem is as follows. First, order the ground clauses constituting $G(P \cup \{\neg A\})$ into some sequence

$$< g_1, g_2, \ldots >$$

Note that this sequence will be infinite if and only if the language contains at least one function symbol and $P \cup \{\neg A\}$ contains at least one non-ground clause. Then for $k = 1, 2, \ldots$ etc. seek a contradiction amongst the (finite) subsequence

$$< g_1, g_2, \ldots, g_k >$$

This latter test can always be decided (using truth-tables, for instance) in a finite time, since there are only a finite number of connectives and ground propositions to consider. If the original clauses *are* contradictory then, by Herbrand's Theorem, there *must* exist some k such that, after k steps, a contradiction is detectable.

Algorithms of this kind are variously referred to as **Herbrand procedures** or as **saturation procedures**. In practice they do not, of course, first construct explicitly the (possibly infinite) ground instantiation. Rather, they retain the original clauses and, from them, construct and accumulate successive ground-instances until a contradiction (if it exists) is found. Even so, such algorithms are hopelessly inefficient for the routine requirements of theorem proving and computer programming. The search for better algorithms led eventually to the discovery of resolution inference which, whilst in some sense based upon Herbrand's Theorem, is nevertheless a much more sophisticated realization of it than are the naive procedures outlined above. Nearly all instances of automated reasoning now acknowledged as 'logic programming' are driven by resolution.

Exercises 25

1. Given this clause-set **P**:

> arc(a, b)
> arc(b, c)
> path(X, Z) if arc(X, Z)
> path(X, Z) if arc(X, Y) & path(Y, Z)

together with this clause **C**:

        path(a, c)

(i)   write out **G(P ∪ ¬C)** on the assumption that **H**={a, b, c};
(ii)   indicate how a saturation procedure might show, for this particular
            example, that **G(P ∪ ¬C)** is unsatisfiable.

Theme 26

Resolution for propositional logic

Resolution comprises a single inference rule applicable to clausal-form logic. Briefly, from any two clauses having an appropriate form, resolution derives a new clause as their consequence. It is best explained by first showing how it works in the special case of propositional clausal form.

Therefore suppose that we have any set of propositional clauses. A **resolution step** entails first selecting any two of these clauses, called the **parents** for this step, constrained only by the requirement that some literal A in one parent be complementary to some literal ¬A in the other parent (two literals are **complementary** when one is the negation of the other). Thus the parents must take the forms:

A or more-literals   and   ¬A or yet-more-literals

The resolution step then infers a new clause, called the **resolvent** of the parents, which consists of the disjunction of all the parents' literals other than the complementary pair:

more-literals or yet-more-literals

Example—a single resolution step eliminating complementary 'father' literals:

parents   mother or father or ¬parent
                    male or ¬father

resolvent   mother or male or ¬parent

The rationale of the resolution step becomes more apparent when clauses are written in conditional format. For then the parent clauses can be written as

yet-more-literals if A   and   A if ¬more-literals

and the resolvent as

yet-more-literals if ¬more-literals

Clearly, all we are doing here is exploiting the transitivity of 'if':

$$\{B \text{ if } A, A \text{ if } C\} \vdash B \text{ if } C$$

Thus our former example can be paraphrased as follows:

from   male if father
and   father if parent & ¬mother

infer   male if parent & ¬mother

In this case there is only one possible resolvent because the parents have only one complementary pair. More generally, a given pair of parents may afford several alternative steps yielding distinct resolvents.

Resolution possesses the following important properties, which apply to the clausal forms of both propositional logic and predicate logic:

1. resolution is **sound**—every resolvent is implied by its parents;

2. a resolvent is the empty clause □ if and only if both its parents are unit clauses—in which case one parent is simply an atom **A** and the other is the complement ¬**A**;

3. for any set of **Horn clauses**, the empty clause □ is derivable by resolution if that set is unsatisfiable; by virtue of this we describe resolution as being **refutation-complete**.

The usual way of employing resolution for Horn-clause logic programming is thus as follows. The assumptions are formulated as a set **P** of definite clauses and the desired answer (or target conclusion) **A** is formulated as a negative clause ¬**A**; resolution is then applied with the aim of generating a proof of □, that is, a refutation. We then know that

$$\mathbf{P} \vDash \mathbf{A} \quad \text{if and only if} \quad \mathbf{P} \cup \{\neg\mathbf{A}\} \text{ is unsatisfiable;}$$
$$\text{so} \quad \mathbf{P} \vDash \mathbf{A} \quad \text{if and only if} \quad \mathbf{P} \cup \{\neg\mathbf{A}\} \vdash \square \quad \text{using resolution.}$$

due to the soundness and refutation-completeness properties.

For the cases where **P** ∪ {¬**A**} contains one or more **non-Horn** (indefinite) clauses, resolution must be supplemented with an additional rule called **factoring** in order to guarantee refutation-completeness; this is discussed more fully in Theme 39.

The efficiency of resolution as an inference system does not depend primarily upon the propositional structure of the resolution step as described above. Instead, it depends upon the particularly economic method by which resolution deals with clauses containing variables, this being a far more efficient method than the Herbrand procedures discussed previously.

Exercises 26

1. Show that the resolvent of any two Horn clauses is necessarily a Horn clause.

2. Use resolution to establish the validity of the sentence ((A if B) if A).

3. Using just the refutation-completeness property of resolution, show that the inference {A, A if B} ⊢ B is unsound.

4. Show that resolution is not affirmation-complete by virtue of the logical implication {A, B} ⊨ A if B.

   Note—an inference system is **affirmation-complete** if it can derive **Q** from **P** whenever **Q** is implied by **P**.

Theme 27

Applying and composing substitutions

When resolution is used for clausal-form predicate logic, the task of constructing a resolvent generally requires substituting certain terms for variables in the literals which the resolvent inherits from its parents. Later on we shall say exactly how this is done, but in the meantime it will be useful first to make precise what we mean by 'substitutions' and then to consider some of their properties.

A **substitution** is a restricted finite set of **replacements** each one of which takes the form **U/t** where **U** is a variable and **t** is a term. Thus any non-empty substitution σ takes the form

$$\sigma = \{U_1/t_1 , ..., U_m/t_m\}$$

The **application** of σ to any formula **W** is the act of simultaneously replacing, for all $i \in \{1, ..., m\}$, every free occurrence of U_i in **W** by t_i. The result is called a **substitution instance** of **W** and is denoted by **Wσ**.

Example—consider the formula W=likes(X, Y). The result of applying to W the substitution $\sigma 1$={X/chris, Y/logic} is the substitution instance Wσ1=likes(chris, logic). The result of applying to W the substitution $\sigma 2$={X/Y, Y/logic} is the substitution instance Wσ2=likes(Y, logic), and the result of applying $\sigma 2$ to the latter is (Wσ2)σ2=likes(logic, logic). Note carefully that, when carrying out any individual replacement, we pay no regard whatever to either the content or the impact of any other replacements.

Not all sets of replacements are legal substitutions. For example, the set {X/chris, Y/logic, Y/suffering} is not a legal substitution because the replacement of Y is not prescribed uniquely. We therefore insist that for any legal substitution $\{U_1/t_1, ..., U_m/t_m\}$ all the U_i variables shall be distinct; this requirement is called the **functionality** property.

We also prefer that any legal substitution σ shall be **idempotent**, which means that for any formula **W** we have **Wσ=(Wσ)σ**. This in turn requires that for any substitution $\{U_1/t_1, ..., U_m/t_m\}$ no U_i variable shall occur in any t_j term. By this criterion the example $\sigma 2$ above is not strictly a legal substitution.

The most important operation on substitutions is that of composition; informally, composing two substitutions means constructing a single set of replacements whose application has the same effect as applying the former two replacements in succession.

Thus suppose we have two functional, idempotent substitutions

$$\sigma 1 = \{U_1/t_1, ..., U_m/t_m\}$$
$$\sigma 2 = \{V_1/s_1, ..., V_n/s_n\}$$

The **composition** of $\sigma 1$ with $\sigma 2$ is denoted by the expression $\sigma 1 \circ \sigma 2$ and is defined as

$$\{U_1/t_1\sigma 2, ..., U_m/t_m\sigma 2\} \cup \{V_j/s_j \mid V_j \notin \{U_1, ..., U_m\}\}$$

This definition is easily explained. Applying $\sigma 1$ to any formula **W** entails replacing all (free) variables U_i occurring in **W** by terms t_i, yielding the instance $W\sigma 1$. Then there are just two ways in which the application of $\sigma 2$ must impinge upon $W\sigma 1$: it must replace all V_j variables occurring in those t_i terms which $\sigma 1$ introduced into **W**; and it must also replace all (free) V_j variables in **W** which were *not* replaced by $\sigma 1$. These two requirements are met respectively by the two parts of the above definition.

Not all compositions are themselves strictly legal substitutions, since they are not all idempotent. Nevertheless, they always possess the following three properties:

(i) $\quad \sigma 1 \circ \sigma 2$ is functional

(ii) $\quad W(\sigma 1 \circ \sigma 2) = (W\sigma 1)\sigma 2$ $\qquad$ [for any formula **W**]

(iii) $\quad (\sigma 1 \circ \sigma 2) \circ \sigma 3 = \sigma 1 \circ (\sigma 2 \circ \sigma 3)$ $\qquad$ [associativity of $\circ$]

But note that composition is *not*, in general, commutative.

Due to the associativity property we can dispense with parentheses when expressing the results of successively-applied substitutions. Given a sequence of substitutions $< \sigma 1, \sigma 2, ..., \sigma k >$, we express their cumulative application to **W** as $W\sigma 1\sigma 2 ... \sigma k$.

Example—some simple compositions:

$$W = p(U1, g(V1), V2)$$
$$\sigma 1 = \{U1/f(V1)\}$$
$$\sigma 2 = \{V1/a, V2/b, U1/c\}$$

then $\qquad W\sigma 1 = p(f(V1), g(V1), V2)$

and $\qquad W\sigma 1\sigma 2 = p(f(a), g(a), b)$

whereas $\qquad W\sigma 2 = p(c, g(a), b)$

and $\qquad W\sigma 2\sigma 1 = p(c, g(a), b)$

whilst the composition of $\sigma 1$ with $\sigma 2$ is

$$\sigma1 \circ \sigma2 = \{U1/f(a) \} \cup \{V1/a, V2/b\}$$
$$= \{U1/f(a), V1/a, V2/b\}$$

and $W(\sigma1 \circ \sigma2) = p(f(a), g(a), b) = W\sigma1\sigma2$

Exercises 27

1. Determine, in each case, the result of applying the given set of replacements to the given formula:

(i)   apply $\{X/mum(Y), Y/chris\}$ to likes(X, dad(Y))
(ii)   apply $\{X/mum(chris), Y/chris\}$ to likes(X, dad(Y))
(iii)   apply $\{X/t(U, U), Y/U\}$ to tree(t(X, t(Y, Y)))
(iv)   apply $\{X/elizabeth\}$ to $(\exists X)$wife(X, Y) if man(Y) & married(Y, X)

2. Comment upon the legality of the following as substitutions:

(i) $\{X/mum(Y), Y/chris\}$
(ii) $\{X/X\}$
(iii) $\emptyset$
(iv) $\{X/2, X/3\}$
(v) $\{X/2, X/2\}$
(vi) $\{X/Y, Y/X\}$
(vii) $\{X/2, Y/2, Y/X\}$
(viii) $\{f(X)/f(Y)\}$

3. Given the set of replacements

$$\sigma = \{X/f(a, Y), Y/f(b, Z), Z/c\}$$

determine the least value of n>0 for which σ^n is idempotent.

4. Evaluate the composition $\sigma^* = \sigma1 \circ \sigma2$ where

$$\sigma1 = \{X/f(a, Y), W/f(U, Z)\}$$
$$\sigma2 = \{X/f(a, a), Y/b, V/c\}$$

and confirm that $W\sigma^* = (W\sigma1)\sigma2$ when $W = p(V, X, Y, W)$.

Theme 28

Extending resolution to predicate logic

In order to deal with clauses of predicate logic, the propositional resolution inference rule described in Theme 26 must be supplemented by the implicit use of a further sound inference rule known as **universal instantiation**:

$$(\forall X)W(X) \vdash (\forall Y_1)...(\forall Y_m)W(X)\{X/t\} \quad \text{for any term } t$$

where $Y_1, ...$ and Y_m are the variables, if any, occurring in t.

Here is a simple example, in which the clauses' assumed outermost universal quantifiers are, as usual, omitted from the presentation. Given the parent clauses

¬likes(chris, Y) or ¬female(Y) or ¬aunt(Y, Z)
likes(X, mum) or ¬loves(X, mum)

resolution acts as though it first instantiated both of them via the substitution

$$\theta = \{Y/\text{mum}, X/\text{chris}\}$$

so as to make their 'likes' literals complementary:

¬likes(chris, mum) or ¬female(mum) or ¬aunt(mum, Z)
likes(chris, mum) or ¬loves(chris, mum)

before continuing exactly as in the propositional case to yield the resolvent

¬female(mum) or ¬aunt(mum, Z) or ¬loves(chris, mum)

This resolvent is bound to be implied by the original parents because both stages making up the inference step are sound.

Suppose that the Herbrand domain in this case is

$$H = \{\text{chris, mum, dad}\}$$

The 'likes' literals that we wish to make complementary by applying the substitution then refer respectively to two subsets of $H \times H$. The substitution θ effectively identifies the *intersection* of these two subsets, and it is this that is then referred to by the complementary 'likes' literals, as indicated in Figure 28.1.

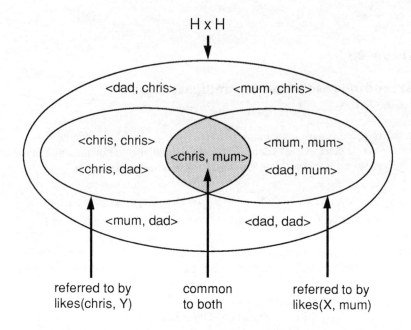

Figure 28.1. Identifying the common meaning of two predicates.

In order to ensure that the *whole* intersection is obtained it is necessary, in general, to choose the *most-general* substitution which makes the literals complementary. In so far as its application makes the atomic parts of those literals identical (or 'unified'), that substitution is then referred to as their **most-general unifier**. Formally, a **unifier** of two formulas **W1** and **W2** is any substitution θ such that **W1**θ = **W2**θ; it is their most-general unifier if and only if, for every other unifier σ of **W1** and **W2**, **W1**σ is a substitution instance of **W1**θ.

Informally, what is going on here is this: one parent says something about the 'likes' relation and the other parent says something else about it; in constructing their resolvent we want the latter to utilize whatever the parents say in common about 'likes'. If this were not the case then the resolvent would be a weaker consequence than otherwise, which might diminish what we were able ultimately to infer from the original clauses.

Here is a simpler example which shows why it is desirable that our chosen unifiers should be most-general. Initially we have the clause-set {C1, C2, C3} shown below:

C1 : ¬p(X)
C2 : p(Y) or ¬q(Y)
C3 : q(a)

This clause-set is unsatisfiable, so by the refutation-completeness property we know that the empty clause must be derivable. Using only most-general unifiers, there are exactly two ways of deriving □; these are shown in Figure 28.2 as two **resolution graphs** in which each resolvent **R**i is placed directly beneath its two parents.

In principle it is possible to construct a resolution theorem prover which investigates all possible ways of resolving clauses in its attempt to derive □. If the given clauses are unsatisfiable then we know that the attempt is bound eventually to succeed, and in fact this holds good irrespective of whether the chosen unifiers are most-general or not.

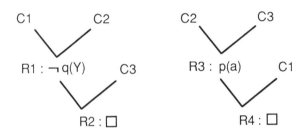

Figure 28.2. Resolution graphs demonstrating unsatisfiability.

In practice, however, such an approach is highly inefficient—the sort of resolution theorem prover actually used for executing logic programs is quite selective in the way it chooses parent clauses and literals to resolve upon. Given the clause-set above, it would typically generate only the graph shown on the *left* of the figure. The unifier used in the first step there is {X/Y}, which is the most-general one. Apart from a single exception (what is it?) every *less-general* unifier for that step, such as {X/b}, would yield a resolvent that was not itself resolvable with C3, thus making □ underivable.

To summarize, we use most-general unifiers in order to preserve refutation-completeness in the cases where selection criteria are imposed upon resolution inference. Later on we shall describe the algorithm typically used for constructing the unique most-general unifier of any two unifiable atoms.

Exercises 28

1. Use resolution to refute ¬likes(chris, chris) given the assumption

    likes(chris, X) if ¬likes(X, chris)

2. Show that resolution alone is incapable of demonstrating the unsatisfiability of the sentence

$$\text{likes(chris, X) iff }\neg\text{likes(X, chris)}$$

3. In a caring world, everyone helps all those who do not help themselves.

   Show that such a world is also a self-serving one by using resolution to show that everyone helps themselves.

4. Convert to conditional-format clausal form the sentence

$$\text{path(X, Y) iff (go(Y) if go(X))}$$

   Then use resolution in refutational mode to show, in turn, that the 'path' relation is (i) reflexive and (ii) transitive.

5. Add to the clauses from Exercise 4 the clauses

$$\text{go(c) if go(b)}$$
$$\text{go(b) if go(a)}$$

   and then use resolution to refute $\neg$path(a, c).

6. Convert the following set of sentences to clausal form:

$$\text{subset(X, Y) iff }(\forall U)(U \in Y \text{ if } U \in X)$$
$$U \in a \text{ iff } U=1$$
$$U \in b \text{ iff } U=1 \text{ or } U=2$$

   Using the resulting clauses, apply resolution in order to refute $\neg$subset(a, b).

7. A certain binary relation R is antisymmetric; compose a clause which expresses this property, referring only to the relations R and '='. The relation '=' is symmetric; compose a clause which expresses this property. Another relation S is defined by

$$\text{S(X, Y) iff ((R(X, Y) or X=Y)}$$

   Convert this definition to a set of clauses. Using all the above clauses, apply refutational resolution to prove that S is also antisymmetric.

Theme 29

Resolution in logic programming

We shall now start bringing together various ideas from the preceding Themes in order to explain how resolution is typically adapted for the purpose of logic programming.

The first matter to discuss is the way in which **programs** and **queries** are presented. In the case of programs, these are simply sets of clauses—typically definite clauses—written in conditional format with their outermost universal quantifiers omitted. This is the way in which we would present, for example, the definite program customarily used for appending two lists:

> C1 :   append(nil, W, W)
> C2 :   append(U•X, Y, U•Z) if append(X, Y, Z)

Here any predicate of the form append(L1, L2, L3) expresses that the result of appending list L2 onto the end of list L1 is the list L3. Any term of the form U•L denotes a list whose first element is U and whose remainder—its *tail*—is the list L. The symbol '•' is a function symbol used in *infix* mode; in the more orthodox *prefix* mode we would write the term as •(U, L). The constant 'nil' denotes the empty list. The labels C1 and C2 are *not* parts of the program—they are merely our means of referring to its clauses.

The query is conventionally a **negative clause**. The simplest sort of query we can pose to this program takes the form

$$? \text{ append}(t1, t2, t3)$$

where $t1$, $t2$ and $t3$ are any terms. The question mark is syntactic sugar for the connective ¬. In the case where $t1$, $t2$ and $t3$ are all ground, the query is read as the ground negative clause

$$\neg \text{append}(t1, t2, t3)$$

In the case where $t1$, $t2$ and $t3$ jointly contain variables $X_1, ..., X_n$ the query is read as the non-ground negative clause

$$(\forall X_1) ... (\forall X_n)\neg\text{append}(t1, t2, t3)$$

equivalently, $\neg(\exists X_1) ... (\exists X_n)\text{append}(t1, t2, t3)$

At this point it is useful to introduce two new pieces of terminology. Given any formula W having unbound variables $X_1, ..., X_n$ we define

the **universal closure** of W as the sentence $(\forall X_1)...(\forall X_n)W$ and denote it, for short, by $\forall W$;

the **existential closure** of W as the sentence $(\exists X_1)...(\exists X_n)W$ and denote it, for short, by $\exists W$.

Then we read any query $?\ A_1\ \&\ ...\ \&\ A_n$

as $\neg\exists(A_1\ \&\ ...\ \&\ A_n)$

The query's negation symbol anticipates the use of resolution to demonstrate a contradiction. Given a logic program P, resolution seeks to show that

$$P \cup \{\neg\exists(A_1\ \&\ ...\ \&\ A_n)\} \vdash \square$$

Using the 'append' program above, let us see what resolution can do with the query

$$Q1 :\ ?\ append(V{\cdot}L1, L2, V{\cdot}a{\cdot}nil)$$

Clearly, Q1 cannot be resolved with program clause C1 since there is no substitution which unifies 'nil' with $V{\cdot}L1$. Q1 can, however, be resolved with C2 using the most-general unifier (m.g.u.)

$$\theta 1 = \{U1/V, X1/L1, Y1/L2, Z1/a{\cdot}nil\}$$

where the new variables U1, X1, Y1 and Z1 are *renamings* of C2's original variables U, X, Y and Z.

Note straightaway, then, the convention that, whenever a program clause is about to be used as a parent in a resolution step, new (previously unused) names are first given to all of its variables—technically, a **renaming substitution** is first applied to it. If this were not done then we might easily become confused when (i) *repeated uses* of some clause resulted in *distinct substitutions* for its variables, or (ii) when the parent clauses in some step had some variable in common.

Having found the m.g.u. $(\theta 1)$ which enables us to eliminate both the negative literal of one parent (Q1) and the complementary positive literal of the other parent (C2), that m.g.u. has to be applied to the remaining literals in the parents—in this case, just the negative literal of C2; this yields the resolvent

$$Q2 :\ ?\ append(L1, L2, a{\cdot}nil)$$

The rest of the story is summarized in Figure 29.1. The graph shown there contains all the possible steps which use resolution in the style of *'modus tollens'*—that is, using some negative clause as a parent in each step.

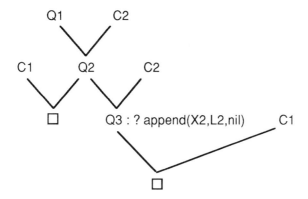

Figure 29.1. Resolution graph for solving the 'append' problem.

It is common to use an even simpler diagram called a **search tree** whose nodes, other than the root node, are just the resolvents. Each edge then signifies a resolution step; if space permits, we may label the edge with the step's associated unifier. Figure 29.2 shows the tree for our example. Such a tree contains sufficient information to determine exactly which answers, if any, are computed in response to the root node. Henceforth we shall always represent logic program executions by trees of this sort.

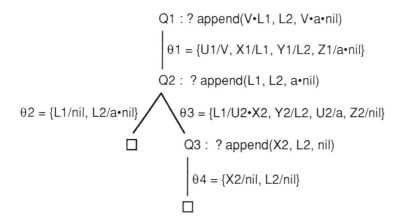

Figure 29.2. Search tree for solving the 'append' problem.

Exercises 29

1. The following query is posed to the 'append' program shown in the Theme:

   Q : ? append(a•X•nil, Y•nil, Z)

   (i)   rewrite Q in standard clause notation, showing all the relevant
           quantifiers;
   (ii)   sketch a resolution graph which solves Q;
   (iii)   say what answer you think should be computed for Q.

2. The query Q : ? sub(a•X, a•b•nil) is posed to this program:

   S1 : sub(X, Y) if pre(X, Y)
   S2 : sub(X, U•Y) if sub(X, Y)
   P1 : pre(nil, Y)
   P2 : pre(U•X, U•Y) if pre(X, Y)

   (i)   sketch a resolution graph which solves Q;
   (ii)   say what answer(s) you think should be computed for Q;
   (iii)   write an alternative program which defines 'sub' in terms only of
           'append'.

Theme 30

Computations and answers

Various species of derivation may evolve from a query at the root of a search tree. Let us take another look at the tree obtained using the 'append' program for the query

$$Q1 : ? \; append(V{\cdot}L1, L2, V{\cdot}a{\cdot}nil)$$

The tree, previously encountered in Theme 29, is reproduced here in Figure 30.1.

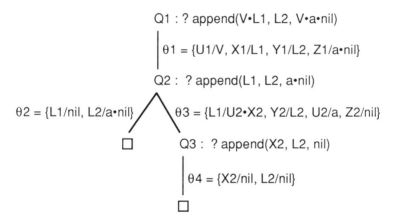

Figure 30.1. Search tree for solving the 'append' problem.

In any such tree, a derivation beginning with the **root query** (Q1) is called a **computation** from that query. In general, a tree may contain both **finite computations** and **infinite computations** ('loops').

Finite computations are of two kinds. A **successful computation** must end with □, and is thus a refutation. A **finitely failed computation** must end with some non-empty query which fails to resolve with any program clause; it is customary in this case to emphasize the failure by adding the special symbol ■ to the end of the computation. This definition of a finitely failed computation requires qualification when some selection policy is in force (recall the discussion at the end of Theme 28). Typically such a policy constrains the choice of literal resolved upon in one or other of the parent clauses. In this event we must define a computation to be finitely failed when the terminating query resolves with no program clause *under the constraint of that selection policy.*

A **finite tree** is a tree having a finite number of computations, each one of which has a finite length. A **finitely failed tree** is a finite tree each of whose computations is finitely failed.

A query at the root of a tree **succeeds** (is solved) if and only if the tree contains at least one successful computation. Otherwise the query **fails** (is unsolved). In the example, Q1 succeeds (in two ways).

Every successful computation yields some **answer** (to the root query) which is constructed using the sequence $<\theta_1, ..., \theta_k>$ of m.g.u.s associated respectively with steps 1 to k of that computation. Let θ^* denote the composition $(\theta_1 \circ ... \circ \theta_k)$. The root query has the form

$$\neg\exists(A_1 \& ... \& A_n)$$

Then the fact that this has been *refuted* using a program **P** determines, *at the least,* that we have

$$P \vDash \exists((A_1 \& ... \& A_n)\theta^*)$$

In our example tree, therefore, the rightmost computation there determines that

$$P \vDash \exists((\text{append}(V \bullet L1, L2, V \bullet a \bullet nil))\theta^*)$$

$$\text{where} \quad \theta^* = \theta1 \circ \theta3 \circ \theta4$$

We need only apply the *significant subset* of θ^* which contributes to the final values of the root query's variables V, L1 and L2; this turns out to be {L1/a•nil, L2/nil}. Hence we have

$$P \vDash (\exists V)\text{append}(V \bullet a \bullet nil, nil, V \bullet a \bullet nil)$$

The significant subset Φ of θ^* is called the **computed answer substitution** for the computation and is the smallest subset of θ^* satisfying

$$(A_1 \& ... \& A_n)\Phi\theta^* = (A_1 \& ... \& A_n)\Phi$$

In general, $(A_1 \& ... \& A_n)\Phi$ may be non-ground, as in our example. In this case the most general answer is this formula's *universal* closure, which is also implied by **P**. Thus our final **answer** is

$$(\forall V)\text{append}(V \bullet a \bullet nil, nil, V \bullet a \bullet nil)$$

In effect this is a theorem summarizing a whole class of tuples in the 'append' relation, each one of which is a solution to the initial query.

Exercises 30

1. For each of the following queries Q posed to the 'append' program given in Theme 29, say whether the search tree generated from Q is finite and successful, or infinite and successful, or finitely failed or infinitely failed:

   (i)   ? append(a•X•nil, Y•nil, Z)
   (ii)   ? append(a•X, Y, Z)
   (iii)   ? append(a•X, Y, b•Z)
   (iv)   ? append(X, a•Y, b•Z)
   (v)   ? append(X, nil, X•nil)
   (vi)   ? append(X, a•b•nil, Z) & append(a•b•nil, X, Z)
   (vii)   ? append(a•X, Y, Z) & append(Z, V, b•W)

   Note—there is a trap in part (v).

2. Sketch the search tree for solving the query

   $$Q: \ ? \ append(a•X•nil, Y•nil, Z)$$

   using the same 'append' program and mark upon it all the m.g.u.s generated along the successful computation. Construct their composition and hence the computed answer. What is the universally-closed form of the answer?

3. Suppose a query ?R(Y) is solved using a program **P** yielding the answer substitution $\Phi=\{Y/X\}$. Then we know, at the least, that the existential closure $\exists(R(Y)\Phi)$ is an answer, that is

   $$\mathbf{P} \vDash (\exists X)R(X)$$

   Justify the remark made at the end of the Theme which states that we may conclude that the universal closure $\forall(R(Y)\Phi)$ is also an answer, that is

   $$\mathbf{P} \vDash (\forall X)R(X)$$

   even though $(\exists X)R(X)$ does not imply $(\forall X)R(X)$.

Theme 31

SLD-resolution

An unsatisfiable set of input clauses will typically afford numerous ways of deriving the empty clause by resolution: there may be *many ways of choosing* parent clauses, while for each choice of parents there may be *many ways of resolving* them according to the various literals available for resolving upon. The history of research into **resolution proof procedures** (coupling the *resolution principle* with certain *strategies*) has been largely concerned with determining how to restrict these choices—in the interests of efficiency—without sacrificing completeness. In this context, note that for our purposes it is not sufficient merely to be assured that the empty clause be derivable—we usually want to derive it in every way that yields some *distinct new answer* to the problem.

The species of restricted resolution normally used for executing negative-clause queries with definite-clause logic programs is called **SLD-resolution**.

The 'L' stands for **linear**, indicating that each resolution step uses as one parent (the **centre clause**) the most-recent resolvent, and uses either some earlier resolvent or one of the input clauses as the other parent (the **side clause**). However, the choice of an earlier resolvent as a side-clause parent is precluded whenever the derivation begins with a query; for then, every resolvent must also be a query, and no query can be resolved with any other query.

The 'D' stands for **definite**, indicating that all the program clauses are definite.

The 'S' stands for **selection**, indicating that some fixed selection rule—usually called a **computation rule**—is applied in each resolution step in order to *select a particular literal* to resolve upon in the centre clause.

Resolution remains refutation-complete under the SLD restriction. Moreover, it admits the derivation of all distinct answers to the root query *whichever* selection rule is employed for choosing the literals resolved upon; this property is customarily referred to as **the independence of the computation rule** and is an important feature of our formalism.

Example—consider the following query and definite program:

> Q1 : ? grandparent(amelia, Z)

> C1 :   grandparent(X, Z) if parent(X, Y) & parent(Y, Z)
> C2   parent(amelia, chris)
> C3 :   parent(chris, brendon)
> C4 :   parent(chris, emlyn)

(a)

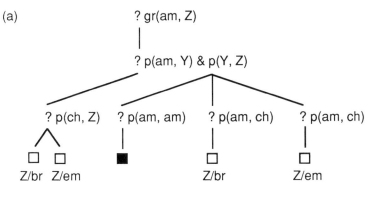

(b)

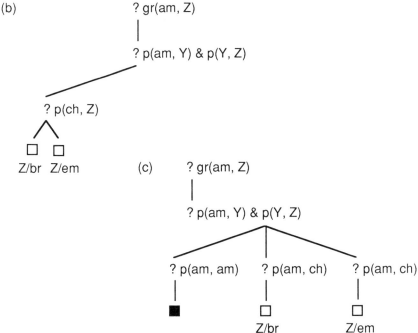

Figure 31.1. Search trees for the 'grandparent' problem.

Figure 31.1 shows various search trees for solving the 'grandparent' problem. Predicate symbols and constant symbols have been abbreviated. Figure 31.1(a) shows the search tree that would be obtained if *all* resolvable literals in each centre-clause were resolved upon (thus *not* using SLD). This is clearly a highly redundant policy in that each answer would be computed more than once.

The other two trees employ SLD-resolution and so are termed **SLD-trees**. Figure 31.1(b) shows the SLD-tree for that computation rule which always selects from the centre clause the *leftmost literal* as the one resolved upon, whilst Figure 31.1(c) is the SLD-tree for that computation rule which always selects the *rightmost literal*. In both cases the complete set of correct answers

$$\{\text{grandparent(amelia, brendon), grandparent(amelia, emlyn)}\}$$

is obtained, in accordance with *the independence of the computation rule*. For Prolog, this corresponds to the fact that whatever the *text-order* in which C1's calls are written, the answer set remains the same. Note, however, that the first SLD-tree (b) is more efficient than the second one (c)—the choice of computation rule affects only the *efficiency* of execution.

In all three trees the sub-derivations from branch-nodes are displayed in correspondence with the first-to-last text-order of their associated side parent clauses C1–C4 within the program.

It will be useful now to summarize what is involved in any SLD computation step. One parent will be a query containing $n>0$ calls

$$\mathbf{Q} : \ ? \ \mathbf{A}_1 \ \& \dots \& \ \mathbf{A}_i \ \& \dots \& \ \mathbf{A}_n$$

First, the chosen computation rule is applied in order to select some call $\mathbf{A}_i$ from the query; note that what is really happening here is the selection of a *negative* literal from the *classical* form of the query

$$\neg\mathbf{A}_1 \ \text{or} \dots \text{or} \ \neg\mathbf{A}_i \ \text{or} \dots \text{or} \ \neg\mathbf{A}_n$$

Next, some program clause containing $m \geqslant 0$ calls

$$\mathbf{C} : \ \mathbf{A} \ \text{if} \ \mathbf{B}_1 \ \& \dots \& \ \mathbf{B}_m$$

is selected whose (unique) *positive* literal $\mathbf{A}$ can be unified with $\mathbf{A}_i$. Before determining the m.g.u. θ, the variables of $\mathbf{C}$ are renamed as necessary such that the renamed version shall have no variables in common with $\mathbf{Q}$.

Finally, the resolvent is constructed by forming another query containing $(n-1+m)$ calls:

$$\mathbf{Q'} : \ ? \ (\mathbf{A}_1 \ \& \dots \mathbf{A}_{i-1} \ \& \ \mathbf{B}_1 \ \& \dots \mathbf{B}_m \ \& \ \mathbf{A}_{i+1} \ \& \dots \& \ \mathbf{A}_n)\theta$$

The logical connections between the clauses involved are:

(i) $\{\mathbf{Q}, \mathbf{C}\} \vDash \mathbf{Q'}$;
(ii)   if $\mathbf{Q'}$ can be solved (refuted) then so can $\mathbf{Q}$;
(iii)   in the case where $n=1$ and $m=0$, $\mathbf{Q'}$ is $\square$.

Exercises 31

1. The following clause **s**

$$even(s(X)) \ if \ odd(X)$$

is *not* logically implied by the following program **P**

$$even(0)$$
$$even(s(s(X))) \ if \ even(X)$$
$$odd(s(0))$$
$$odd(X) \ if \ even(s(X))$$

Prove that this is so by converting ¬s to its clausal form **C** and then applying SLD-resolution to the combined clause-set **P** ∪ **C** (show that no SLD refutation can be derived).

2. The following program can be used to compute certain lists containing alternating ones and zeros:

$$one\text{-}and\text{-}zero(X) \ if \ ones(X) \ \& \ zeros(X)$$

$$ones(nil)$$
$$ones(1 \bullet U \bullet Y) \ if \ ones(Y)$$

$$zeros(nil)$$
$$zeros(U \bullet 0 \bullet Y) \ if \ zeros(Y)$$

   (i)   Show the SLD-tree for the query ? one-and-zero(1•0•1•0•nil) under the computation rule which selects the leftmost literal. Would the computation rule which selects the rightmost literal be more efficient for the same query?

   (ii) Which of those two computation rules is least efficient for executing the query ? one-and-zero(1•2•1•0•nil), and why?

   (iii) If the interpreter can easily access and compare the lengths of arguments in calls, what new computation rule can you suggest which deals satisfactorily with both the above queries?

Theme 32

Resolution versus Herbrand procedures

It is instructive to see what would be involved in using a Herbrand procedure in order to solve the 'grandparent' problem presented in the last Theme:

Q1 : ?   grandparent(amelia, Z)

C1 :   grandparent(X, Z) if parent(X, Y) & parent(Y, Z)
C2 :   parent(amelia, chris)
C3 :   parent(chris, brendon)
C4 :   parent(chris, emlyn)

Such a procedure would operate upon the **ground instantiation** of these clauses. Taking the Herbrand domain here to be

H = {amelia, chris, brendon, emlyn}

the ground instantiation would then comprise 71 ground clauses, indicated below in an abbreviated form:

¬gr(am, am)
¬gr(am, ch)
¬gr(am, br)
¬gr(am, em)

gr(am, am) if p(am, am) & p(am, am)
:
gr(am, br) if p(am, ch) & p(ch, br)
:
gr(em, em) if p(em, em) & p(em, em)

p(am, ch)
p(ch, br)
p(ch, em)

According to the Herbrand Theorem, the ground instantiation is contradictory (inconsistent) if and only if it includes some finite, contradictory subset. One such subset consists of the four clauses shown above in bold face. It is trivial to derive a contradiction □ from them by using elementary propositional inference rules. This particular subset corresponds to our computed answer

grandparent(amelia, brendon)

In order to get the other answer

grandparent(amelia, emlyn)

it suffices to use almost the same subset of the ground instantiation but with all its occurrences of **br** replaced by **em**. Note that, since the derivation of a contradiction requires at least two clauses, the search for a contradiction in this example potentially ranges over 2^{71}–72 subsets of the ground instantiation. In practice, of course, various other structural considerations about the clauses available can be brought to bear in order to reduce the search. For example, at least one negative clause must be involved in obtaining a contradiction—this fact eliminates 2^{67} subsets from our consideration, and so reduces the total number of potentially relevant subsets to 2^{71}–2^{67}–4 (since the figure of 2^{67} includes 68 subsets having fewer than two clauses, and these have already been counted amongst the 72 identified above). However, this amount of reduction is still negligible compared with the original total. In fact, we cannot achieve much more reduction without making a detailed analysis of the clauses' arguments.

Such a detailed analysis is exactly what resolution does. Consider what SLD resolution achieves in the first computation step, where the parent clauses are Q1 and C1. The m.g.u. for this step contains the replacement X/amelia, effectively concentrating attention upon only those ground instances of C1 whose 'grandparent' literals have 'amelia' as their first argument; there are only 16 of these, compared to the total number 64 of all ground instances of C1. Thus we see that the unifiability requirement behaves as an implicit filter for the selection of *relevant* instances, and moreover *represents* its selection very economically through the device of the m.g.u. This is why resolution is so much more efficient than explicit Herbrand procedures, and hence why J. Alan Robinson's discovery of resolution in the early Sixties is acknowledged as a major landmark in the development of automated proof procedures for clausal-form logic.

Exercises 32

1. Taking the 'grandparent' example from the Theme, confirm that the ground instantiation *is* inconsistent by

    (i)   deriving □ using propositional inference rules;
    (ii)   identifying a counter-model.

2. The arguments given in the Theme establish, for the 'grandparent' example, that no more than $2^{71}-2^{67}-4$ subsets of the ground instantiation need be considered in the search for a contradiction. What further reduction arises from observing that any contradiction must involve at least one ground clause for 'grandparent' and at least one ground clause for 'parent'?

Theme 33

The unification algorithm

There are many different species of algorithms available for computing most-general unifiers. The one most commonly employed in logic program interpreters is known as **Robinson's Algorithm** (named after the discoverer of resolution). Its task is as follows. Given as input two atoms of the form

$$P(r_1, ..., r_n) \quad \text{and} \quad P(t_1, ..., t_n)$$

in which the r_i and t_i are any terms, its aim is to decide whether the atoms are unifiable and—if they are—to deliver as output their most-general unifier; if they are *not* unifiable then the output is the message "failure".

In the initial set-up, all the term-pairs $< r_i, t_i >$ are stored on a stack **S**. Another stack θ, initially empty, is made available for accommodating those **bindings** (called 'replacements' in earlier Themes) which the algorithm will construct in the course of comparing each pair of terms on **S**. These two stacks are the only data structures required.

Example—Figure 33.1 shows the initial stacks for an attempt at unifying atoms p(a, W, X, f(f(X))) and p(Z, g(Y), g(Z), f(Y)).

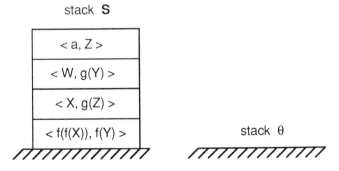

Figure 33.1. Initial stacks for the unification algorithm.

The unification algorithm consists essentially of one main cycle in each iteration of which a term-pair is popped from **S** and its two component terms syntactically compared in the context of θ. This comparison may result in the algorithm terminating with "failure", or it may modify both S and θ in readiness for the next iteration. The algorithm in full is shown below.

The Unification Algorithm

repeat cycle

if S is empty **then** terminate and output θ as the m.g.u.
else begin comparisons

> pop the next term-pair $< s_1, s_2 >$ from S
> and construct $< e_1, e_2 > = < s_1\theta, s_2\theta >$

> **if** e_1 and e_2 are distinct constants
>   **then** issue "failure" and terminate

> **else if** e_1 and e_2 are functional terms
>   with distinct principal function symbols
>   **then** issue "failure" and terminate

> **else if**   either of e_1 and e_2 is a constant
>   and the other is a functional term
>   **then** issue "failure" and terminate

> **else if** e_1 and e_2 are functional terms with
>   identical principal function symbols
>   **then** push pairs of all their corresponding
>   arguments onto S

> **else if** e_1 and e_2 are both variables
>   **then** push the binding e_1/e_2 onto θ

> **else if**   either of e_1 and e_2 is a variable
>   which occurs *strictly within* the other
>   **then** issue "failure" and terminate

> **else if** e_1 is a variable
>   **then** push the binding e_1/e_2 onto θ

> **else if** e_2 is a variable
>   **then** push the binding e_2/e_1 onto θ

> **end comparisons**
end cycle

This algorithm always succeeds in constructing the m.g.u. of the given atoms if they are unifiable. A proof that the algorithm *always terminates*, whether successfully or not, is an important component of any proof that a concrete implementation of resolution is refutation-complete.

Figure 33.2 shows how the algorithm continues with our example.

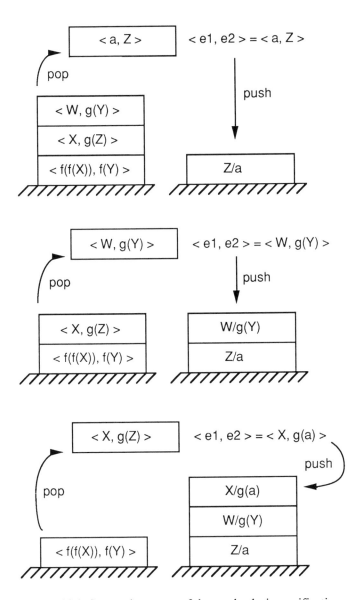

Figure 33.2. Successive states of the stacks during unification.
(*continued overleaf*)

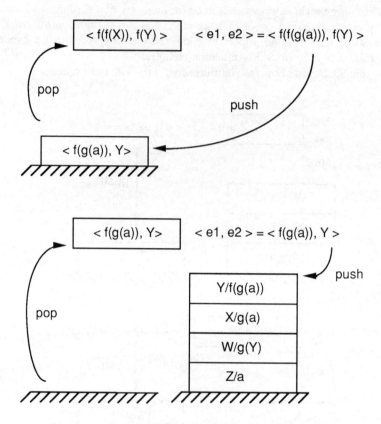

Figure 33.2. Successive states of the stacks during unification.

In the final state the stack **S** is empty, hence the stack θ now represents our m.g.u. which consists of

$$\{Z/a, W/g(Y), X/g(a), Y/f(g(a))\}$$

The algorithm as described above does not guarantee, upon successful termination, that θ will be an **idempotent** m.g.u. There are several alternative modifications we can make in order to ensure idempotency. One way is to arrange that, rather than merely pushing each new binding e_1/e_2 onto θ, we first *apply* it to θ—in other words, we update θ to $\{e_1/e_2\} \cup (\theta \circ \{e_1/e_2\})$. Another way is to take the output θ of the algorithm as it stands and then determine the smallest n for which

$$\theta^n = \theta^{n+1}$$

whereupon θ^n will be the unique idempotent m.g.u.

In practice the algorithm as first given is the one actually used. The reason for this is that the idempotency property is not a precondition for the correctness of resolution; its only potential benefit is in saving us from having to do any extra work when it comes to outputting the final, fully-dereferenced form of some computed answer. When about to perform an individual resolution step, the interpreter has no way of knowing whether the current computation will succeed or fail. In the event of the computation failing, prior enforcement of idempotency would have been a waste of effort.

Observe that the m.g.u. computed in our example is not idempotent—this is because the algorithm did not propagate the final binding Y/f(g(a)) to the occurrence of Y in the second binding W/g(Y). However,

$$\theta 2 = \theta 3 = \{Z/a, W/g(f(g(a))), X/g(a), Y/f(g(a))\}$$

gives the fully-dereferenced and idempotent form of the m.g.u.

Besides the matter of idempotency, unification in any case imposes a significant run-time overhead upon the performance of any logic program interpreter. A typical interpreter will perform a pre-execution analysis of both the program and the query in order to compile some of the anticipated unification into object-code, thereby reducing the work that remains to be done at run-time. Moreover, some Prolog dialects enable one to place **type** and/or **mode** declarations within one's programs in order to facilitate this compilation. Thus the algorithm as expressed above should be viewed only as an *abstraction* of the way unification is actually carried out in serious implementations.

Exercises 33

1. Give an informal explanation of why the unification algorithm as described in the Theme is bound always to terminate.

2. For each of the following pairs of atoms, determine whether or not they can be unified; if they can, state both (the idempotent form of) their m.g.u. and, if possible, some less-general unifier for them:

   (i)   p(a, X) and p(Y, b)
   (ii)   p(X, X) and p(Y, Z)
   (iii)   p(X, Y) and p(Y, X)
   (iv)   p(t(X, t(X, b))) and p(t(a, Z))
   (v)   p(t(X, t(X, b))) and p(t(a, t(Z, Z)))
   (vi)   p(X, f(Y)) and p(f(Y), X)
   (vii)   p(X, f(X)) and p(f(Z), f(Z))

Theme 34

The occur-check

The unification algorithm presented in the previous Theme includes in its comparison cycle the following test:

> **else if** either of e_1 and e_2 is a variable
> which occurs *strictly within* the other
> **then** issue "failure" and terminate

This test is called the **occur-check** and its purpose is to disallow self-referential bindings such as X/f(X). Here is a simple example in which that binding would arise in the unifier if the occur-check were to be omitted:

> unify the atoms   p(f(X), f(f(X)))   and   p(W, W)

The binding X/f(X) effectively assigns to X the **infinite term** f(f(f...)), whereas all expressions in our language are presumed to be syntactically *finite*. In particular, although the Herbrand domain might well be an infinite set of terms, the terms themselves are presumed to be finite.

The temptation to omit the occur-check from the unification algorithm is very strong, owing to the high processing cost of including it; it is the only test in the comparison cycle which has to scrutinize the inner content of terms, whereas all the other tests examine only the terms' principal (outermost) symbols. Consequently, most logic programming interpreters omit the occur-check from their unification algorithms.

The price of this omission is potential loss of soundness. Take the simple example of executing the query

> ? p(f(X), f(f(X)))

using the assertion p(W, W). Then we find that—with the occur-check suppressed—an apparent refutation is obtained together with the computed answer

> p(f(X), f(f(X)))θ where $\theta = \{X/f(X)\}$

Nevertheless, the query and the assertion are *not* jointly unsatisfiable: one simple model for them is the following:

let the domain be the set of natural numbers $N = \{0, 1, 2, ...\}$;
associate 'f' with the function $N \rightarrow N$ taking $X \in N$ to $X+1$;
associate 'p' with the equality relation on $N \times N$.

Thus the computed answer cannot here be a logical consequence of the program. Worse still, an attempt to output the final, fully-dereferenced form of the answer would typically plunge an interpreter into an infinite loop—there is no n such that $\theta^n = \theta^{n+1}$.

In practice, for normal problem-solving purposes over domains represented by finite terms, it is moderately unusual for logic programs to contain clauses which would require operation of the occur-check in order to guarantee that all answers were sound. In the case of standard Prolog (which omits the test) the programmer is expected to take responsibility for avoiding such programs. Some versions of Prolog include the occur-check as an option that can be enabled by the programmer, whilst others provide built-in primitives that can be invoked within the program text in order to perform sound unification. Besides these possibilities, however, there are other logic languages—such as Alain Colmerauer's Prolog II—which are specifically engineered for the correct handling of self-referential bindings in order to provide for problem solving over domains represented by infinite terms.

Exercises 34

1. With the occur-check suppressed, the unification algorithm can compute exactly one result when it is presented with the atoms $p(f(X), f(f(X)))$ and $p(W, W)$ and compares their arguments from left to right. Is the same true when it is presented instead with the atoms $p(X, f(X))$ and $p(W, W)$?

2. A **difference-list** is a term of the form $\text{diff}(e_1 \bullet ... \bullet e_n \bullet X, X)$ where X is a variable and $n \geq 0$, and is viewed as an abstract representation of the concrete list $e_1 \bullet ... \bullet e_n \bullet \text{nil}$. The term $\text{diff}(a \bullet b \bullet X, X)$, for instance, represents the list $a \bullet b \bullet \text{nil}$.

   An element can be appended to the end of a list in a single step provided that the given list is represented by a difference-list. In particular, the following query

   $$? \text{ put\_on\_end}(c, \text{diff}(a \bullet b \bullet X, X), L)$$

   can be solved to give the output binding $L/a \bullet b \bullet c \bullet \text{nil}$ by invoking a single assertion of the form

   $$A : \text{ put\_on\_end}(U, ?, L)$$

What do you suggest the assertion's second argument should be in order to produce this outcome? Investigate whether your suggested assertion also correctly solves the queries

Q1 : ? put_on_end(c, diff(X, X), Y)
and Q2 : ? put_on_end(X, diff(X, X), Y)

when the occur-check is in force. What happens when it is not?

3. The following two sentences make intuitively correct statements about the 'append' relation:

A1 : $(\forall U)(\exists V)$append(V, U, U)
A2 : $(\exists V)(\forall U)$append(V, U, U)

Use resolution to decide (i) whether A1 implies A2, and (ii) whether A2 implies A1. Would different conclusions be obtained if the occur-check were suppressed?

Theme 35

Search strategy

Given any program **P** and any query **Q**, the choice of some computation rule determines a unique SLD-tree rooted at **Q**. This tree represents all the SLD-computations that can be derived using that computation rule. In general, different computation rules applied to a given input set {**P**, **Q**} will determine different SLD-trees, although—as observed previously—all those trees will agree upon the computed answer set.

A typical interpreter implements some fixed computation rule, although there are some interpreters which allow the user to choose a rule from a range of alternatives. A common way of specifying one's own computation rule without considering the interpreter is to define that rule via a meta-program **M** interposed between the interpreter and the object program {**P**, **Q**}; the interpreter then executes **M** using its own rule, and this action in turn drives the execution of the object program in accordance with the defined rule. Whichever such arrangement is made, however, we always know that some unique SLD-tree has to be incrementally constructed by the interpreter in order that it may **search** for answers.

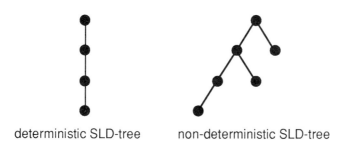

deterministic SLD-tree   non-deterministic SLD-tree

Figure 35.1. Various SLD-trees.

The search for answers is simplest when the SLD-tree contains no branch nodes, for there is then just one computation in the tree and this circumstance makes the execution process **deterministic**. In general this is *not* the case; a tree will typically contain a number of branch nodes and hence a number of distinct computations, making the execution process **non-deterministic**—it is this circumstance that raises the need for a **search strategy**.

Such a strategy, presented with various alternative computations, determines the manner of their exploration. The need to search amongst alternatives is a characteristic of **relational** formalisms (such as logic), distinguishing them from **functional** formalisms. If we have a query, say ?p(X), at some node and if that node has two or more immediate descendant nodes, then the latter property signifies that the program contains two or more clauses for 'p'; often, though not always, this in turn signifies that there are two or more distinct answers to ?p(X)—in other words, that 'p' names a relation rather than a function. It remains a possibility, nevertheless, that 'p' *does* name a function but that the program provides two or more distinct ways of evaluating it.

There are, of course, innumerable ways of searching (equivalently, constructing) a tree. The broad options include sequential *versus* parallel search and top-down *versus* bottom-up search. The standard search strategy used by logic program interpreters on single-processor machines is **sequential, top-down, depth-first search** with **backtracking**. This strategy can be summed up as follows.

1. Each node in the tree is

> **either** the empty query □
> **or** a non-empty query having no immediate descendants
> **or** a query having one or more immediate descendants.

Nodes of the first two kinds are called **leaf nodes** and nodes of the third kind are called **non-leaf nodes**.

2. For each non-leaf node, each of its immediate descendants is assigned a distinct **priority** relative to its siblings.

3. The search begins by **generating** the tree's **root node**.

4. A **search step** from a non-leaf node **generates** whichever one of that node's so-far-ungenerated immediate descendants has the highest priority; the next search step is from that descendant.

5. A search step from a leaf node identifies that node's most-recently-generated ancestor, if any, having so-far-ungenerated immediate descendants, and the next search step is from that ancestor; if there is no such ancestor then the whole tree has been generated.

Steps **3** and **4** of this strategy are responsible for the top-down, depth-first nature of the search; loosely, their effect is to drive the search down some particular computation, ignoring all other computations until the current one has been completely generated.

Step **5** is responsible for the backtracking nature of the search, always seeking the most-recently-encountered alternative to the current computation once the latter has been conclusively searched.

Step **2** embodies the so-called **search rule** which determines the relative order in which computations are generated; it is equivalent to prioritizing, for each relation queried during the search, those program clauses which define that relation.

Figure 35.2 indicates the progress this search strategy would make through a typical SLD-tree. The tree has been drawn according to the standard convention that each group of siblings is displayed such that their relative priorities for generation decrease from left to right.

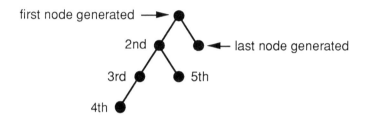

Figure 35.2. Standard search of an SLD-tree.

Observe that the standard strategy as described above is not guaranteed always to terminate. It will certainly terminate if the tree has finite depth, but equally it will certainly *not* terminate if the tree has infinite depth—in other words, if there is at least one infinite computation. This much is true of any strategy committed to **exhaustive search**. Note also that we do not here consider the possibility of a tree having infinite *breadth*, since we are assuming (at present) that our program does not have an infinite number of clauses.

Does it matter which search strategy is used? If the tree is finite and our intention is to search it exhaustively, then

(a) the choice of search rule is logically inconsequential, and

(b) depth-first search will be optimal in memory utilization whilst fully realizing the completeness of SLD-resolution.

What this means is that *all* correct answers will be discovered and that the choice of search rule affects only the *relative order* of their discovery.

However, if the tree is infinite then depth-first search may result in *effective* incompleteness. This is because the exploration of an infinite computation may—depending upon one's choice of search rule—defer indefinitely the exploration of some alternative computation capable of yielding a correct answer. By contrast, a breadth-first strategy would in all cases ensure effective completeness in that every correct answer would be discovered after some finite time (although with an infinite tree the search would thereafter still continue indefinitely). In general, breadth-first search is too expensive in memory utilization to be practicable. Besides the two strategies just considered there are, of course, many other possibilities—but we shall not discuss these here.

Exercises 35

1. The skeletal meta-program **M** below, when used to execute the meta-query

> ? **solve**(Query)

under the standard strategy, *simulates* the execution of Query using a given object program under some other strategy whose details depend upon the way in which '**select**', '**reduce**' and '**combine**' are defined in **M**:

> **solve**(Query) if **empty**(Query)
> **solve**(Query) if **select**(Query, Call, Others) &
>   **reduce**(Call, New_calls) &
>   **combine**(New_calls, Others, New_query) &
>   **solve**(New_query)

This says that in order to **solve** Query it suffices

> either to show that it is **empty**
> or to

>> **select** a call from it,
>> **reduce** it to a set of new calls
>>   (*by invoking some object clause*),
>> **combine** the new calls with the others in the query and
>> **solve** the resulting new query.

(i)   Assuming that Query is represented by a list of calls, compose suitable definitions of '**select**' and '**combine**' which simulate

(a) the standard computation rule;
(b) the computation rule which selects the query's last call.

Hint—define both the '**select**' and '**combine**' relations in terms of 'append'.

(ii)   For the case of (i)(a), give a rough indication of the simulated execution by **M** of the query

? one-and-zero(1•0•1•0•nil)

using the object program given in Exercises 31.

2. Using a style similar to the Theme's semi-formal definition of the sequential, top-down, depth-first search strategy, define a **sequential, top-down, breadth-first strategy** which generates each layer of the tree in turn.

Theme 36

Varying the selection rules

Given a query and a program, the choice of **computation rule** determines a corresponding SLD-tree. Assuming that the search procedure is top-down and depth-first, the choice of **search rule** determines only the order in which the tree's computations are generated. Below we sketch some SLD-trees generated from a simple path-finding problem (seeking paths commencing at node 'a').

computation rule: select leftmost literal of query.
search rule: select clauses in text-orders shown below.

> p(X, Z) if a(X, Z)
> p(X, Z) if a(X, Y) & p(Y, Z)

> a(a, b)
> a(b, c)

SLD-tree:

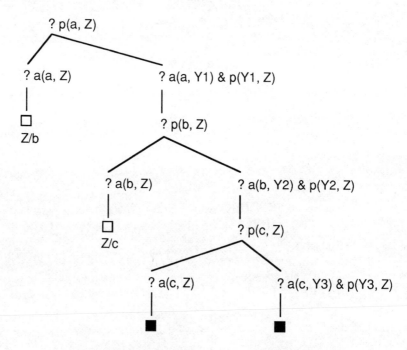

Figure 36.1. First choice of selection rules.

Figure 36.1 shows the tree given by the standard selection rules of Prolog. All of its computations are of finite depth. Note that the clauses for 'p' will be selected in the traditional order whereby non-recursive ('base') clauses take priority over recursive clauses. Here, as elsewhere, we follow the usual convention of displaying the computations from left-to-right across the page in correspondence with their chronological order of generation.

computation rule: select rightmost literal of query.
search rule: select clauses in text-orders shown below.

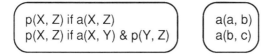

SLD-tree:

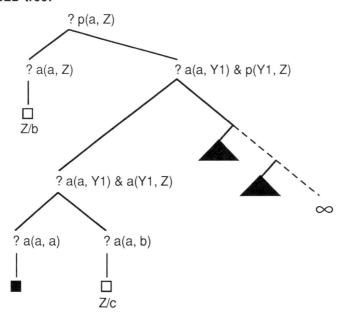

Figure 36.2. Second choice of selection rules.

Figure 36.2 shows that a radically different tree is obtained when we select the right-most literal in each query rather than the leftmost literal. The search rule remains the same as in Figure 36.1. In accordance with the independence of the computation rule we find that the same answers as before—namely path(a, b) and path(a, c)—are computable. However, we now also have an infinite (right-most) computation subtended from which there are an infinite number of finitely-failed subtrees. All the answers to the problem will be computed before the search becomes committed indefinitely to the exploration of the infinite region of the tree.

computation rule: select leftmost literal of query.
search rule: select clauses in text-orders shown below.

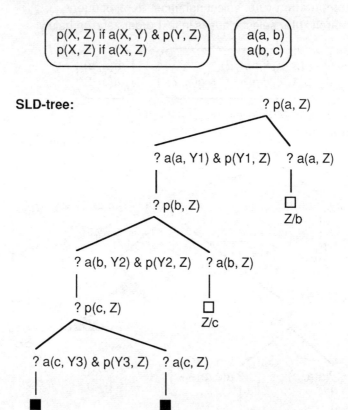

Figure 36.3. Third choice of selection rules.

Figure 36.3 restores the standard computation rule, but now alters the search rule such that selection of recursive clauses takes priority over that of non-recursive clauses. The tree is (topologically) identical to that in Figure 36.1, but now has to be presented as the mirror image in order to represent the new chronological ordering of the computations. The result now is that the failed computations are generated first, after which the same answers are computed but in the opposite order to their generation in Figure 36.1.

The worst possibility, not displayed here, would be the case which combined the computation rule of Figure 36.2 with the search rule of Figure 36.3, for then the search would lock straightaway into an infinite computation and so never discover any answers at all.

Exercises 36

1. The naive program for reversing a list is as follows:

> reverse(nil, nil)
> reverse(U•X, Y) if reverse(X, W) & append(W, U•nil, Y)
>
> append(nil, Z, Z)
> append(V•X, Y, V•Z) if append(X, Y, Z)

For each of the queries below state which computation rule is better—that which always selects the query's leftmost literal, or that which always selects the query's rightmost literal.

(i)   ? reverse(a•b•c•nil, Y)
(ii)   ? reverse(X, c•b•a•nil)
(iii)   ? reverse(a•b•c•nil, c•b•a•nil)

2. Referring to the example program used in the Theme, sketch the SLD-tree obtained by combining the computation rule of Figure 36.2 with the search rule of Figure 36.3.

Theme 37

The procedural interpretation

Writing down clauses is a process of defining relations. On what grounds does such a process deserve to be called *programming* rather than merely *defining*? Arguably, it becomes a programming process when—and only when—the particular composition of the clauses reflects a particular way of solving the queries posed to them. One way of conferring such a property upon clauses is to assign to them a **procedural interpretation**. Under such an interpretation clauses acquire procedural significance, complementing the definitional (or declarative) significance conferred upon them by their logical interpretation. By providing an interpretation which reflects the computational machinery used for problem solving we acquire a basis on which to choose computationally-effective clauses; without it, our programs' efficacies would be subject wholly to the mercy of our (unintelligent) interpreter. A computational interpretation is the essential difference between a *logic* and a *computational logic*.

The procedural meaning of a program can be characterized in terms of how the program behaves in a particular computational setting. For the logic programming paradigm we can envisage, at the simplest, an abstract SLD-resolution engine controlled by the sort of selection rules we examined in the last Theme. We know exactly how this engine works—specifically, how it generates computations, how it determines the order of their generation and how it uses their associated bindings to construct computed answers. A procedural interpretation is obtained by associating the structural features of our programs with these sorts of mechanism.

Let us first consider a query

$$? \, q_1 \, \& \, q_2 \, \& \, ... \, \& \, q_n$$

We can interpret the individual q_j as **calls** to procedures. Under the given computation rule we read the query as some sequence

$$< C_1, C_2, ..., C_n > \quad \text{where each } C_i \text{ is some } q_j$$

of calls **scheduled** (according to some computation rule) for activation. A **procedure-calling step** initiated by activating a call C_i begins by selecting some clause from the **procedure** (clause-set) supplied for whichever relation C_i refers to; we say that the clause is **invoked** by the call C_i. It will take the general form

$$C \text{ if } B_1 \text{ \& } \ldots \text{ \& } B_m$$

where C is interpreted as a **procedure heading** and $(B_1 \text{ \& } \ldots \text{ \& } B_m)$ is interpreted as a **procedure body**. The clause is invoked subject to two preconditions:

(a) the call C_i and the heading C must unify, in which case we say that the clause is **invokable** by the call, and

(b) this clause has highest priority amongst all the other untried clauses invokable by the call.

In general the unifier may bind variables occurring in the call as well as variables occurring in the clause's body. We can imagine that the unifier is correspondingly partitioned into two sets of bindings θ_{in} and θ_{out}. The completion of the procedure-calling step entails

(a) applying θ_{in} to the clause's body—interpreted as passing **input data** from the call to the clause;

(b) applying θ_{out} to the current query via the call—interpreted as passing **output data** from the clause to the query;

(c) adding the substituted body calls into the current schedule of query calls in accordance with the computation rule—interpreting the latter as a **scheduling policy**.

A successful computation can now be viewed as a sequence of procedure-calling steps sufficient to execute *all* the calls in the query (that is, the calls originally posed together with those subsequently introduced). The output data passed back to the query by those steps cumulatively construct the values of the original query variables, and hence determine the final form of the computed answer.

Using notions of this sort we can more easily perceive how our programs manipulate data, and hence more readily assess their computational merits.

Exercises 37

1. Given the following procedure for 'append'

A1 : append(nil, Z, Z)
A2 : append(U•X, Y, U•Z) if append(X, Y, Z)

identify θ_{in} and θ_{out} in respect of the following invocations:

(i)   ? append(a•T•nil, b•V, W)   invoking A2;
(ii)   ? append(W, a•X, V•b•nil)   invoking A1.

Pruning the search using 'cut'

The **cut** (denoted in most Prolog dialects by either ! or /) is a control device which caters for dynamic curtailment (or **pruning**) of the search process. For ease of implementation, and to provide for simple user-control over its activation, a cut is both expressed in the program text and scheduled for execution just like any other call.

Executing a cut prevents some part of the tree from being searched—we say that it **prunes** the tree. This is how it works. Suppose a call to **A** invokes a clause of the form

A if calls & ! & more-calls

When executed, the cut shown in this clause immediately prunes out

all *untried* ways of executing **A** and
all *untried* ways of executing **calls**.

Example—suppose we wish to compute the least number Z of two numbers X and Y, using the predicate least(X, Y, Z). Assume that our implementation provides the two built-in primitives > and = for comparing numbers and that we have to define 'least' in terms of these. The intuitive specification of the predicate least(X, Y, Z) is then

if X greater_or_equal Y **then** Z=Y **else** Z=X

We can approximate this with a definite-clause program as follows:

least(X, Y, Z) if greater_or_equal(X, Y) & Z=Y
least(X, Y, Z) if Y>X & Z=X

greater_or_equal(X, Y) if X>Y
greater_or_equal(X, Y) if X=Y

This program will always produce correct answers no matter how it is queried. For instance, Figure 38.1 shows the SLD-tree obtained by querying which of 3 and 2 is the least. The leftmost computation gives the unique and correct solution Z/2. The rightmost computation correctly fails but is redundant, since we know that if the query

? greater_or_equal(3, 2) & Z=2

succeeds then the query

? 2>3 & Z=3

is bound to fail and so need not be generated. Likewise, the middle computation
is redundant since we know that if the query

? 3>2 & Z=2

succeeds then the query

? 3=2 & Z=2

is bound to fail and so need not be generated.

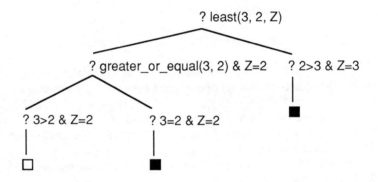

Figure 38.1. Using SLD alone to solve the 'least' problem.

Our perception of these redundancies is owed to *our own knowledge* about
the relations > and =, knowledge which is not available to the interpreter.
Moreover, there is no way of conveying that knowledge in definite-clause logic:
in order to express, for example, that X>Y and X=Y are mutually exclusive we
need to use a negative clause such as

¬X>Y or ¬X=Y

Essentially, our program fails to capture logically the notion of *exclusivity*
underlying these two uses of **else**:

if greater_or_equal(X, Y) **then** Z=Y **else** Z=X

> **if**   X>Y **then** greater_or_equal(X, Y)
> **else if**   X=Y **then** greater_or_equal(X, Y)

Using a single cut, however, we can deal with the first of these in an operational manner, thus:

> least(X, Y, Z) if greater_or_equal(X, Y) & ! & Z=Y
> least(X, Y, Z) if Y>X & Z=X
>
> greater_or_equal(X, Y) if X>Y
> greater_or_equal(X, Y) if X=Y

With this modification we can be sure that if the first clause's call greater_or_equal(X, Y) succeeds then there is no point in trying also to use the second clause for 'least'. When the cut is eventually executed it prunes out the use of the latter clause, and moreover also prunes out whichever clause for 'greater_or_equal' is redundant.

   If we had some larger program which included the program above then it might be the case that there were other ways of invoking the clauses for 'greater_or_equal' without first encountering a cut. In that case we would still not have eliminated those clauses' own redundancy. In order to do so we would have to insert into them a cut of their own, as follows:

> greater_or_equal(X, Y) if X>Y & !
> greater_or_equal(X, Y) if X=Y

However, in the original context this modification would result, unnecessarily, in the execution of two cuts in succession.

   Figure 38.2 shows the SLD-tree obtained when using just the single cut first mentioned.

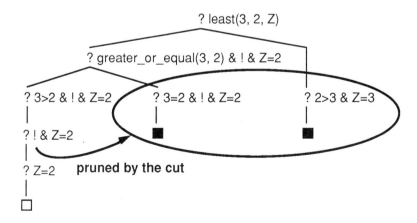

Figure 38.2. Using SLD and **cut** to solve the 'least' problem.

In general, cuts are used in order to prune out computations which either produce no answers or else produce unwanted answers. The latter case arises in a variety of circumstances: the program may determine distinct answers of which only certain ones are required, or it may redundantly determine some particular answer in more than one way. More specialized uses of cut include approximating default reasoning, forcing the evaluation of certain relations to be strictly functional and forcing determinism in order to facilitate the implementation of tail-recursion.

A significant problem owed to the availability of cut in formalisms such as Prolog is that it encourages sloppy programming style. Below is a simple illustration based on the problem of determining the lowest common multiple Z of two given positive integers X and Y.

Example—to find the lowest common multiple Z of 12 and 15:

> ? lcm(12, 15, Z)
>
> lcm(X, Y, Z) if positive-int(Z) & X divides Z & Y divides Z & !
> positive-int(1)
> positive-int(Z) if positive-int(W) & Z=W+1

The query is solved here—yielding the correct output (Z/60)—by generating progressively larger choices of Z until finding the first one which is exactly divisible by each of the given numbers X and Y. As soon as this has been found, the cut prunes out further choices of Z. In fact this program *always* correctly computes the lowest common multiple when X and Y are given and Z is initially unknown. Unfortunately the program may compute incorrect output for other query modes. For example, in response to the query

> ? lcm(12, 15, 120)

it will incorrectly answer 'yes'.

Some commentators have distinguished between so-called 'green cuts' and so-called 'red cuts', the first of which *never* cause incorrect answers and the second of which *sometimes* do. My own view is that this characterization is misleading. The fundamental defect of the program above is that the *logical* content of its first clause

> lcm(X, Y, Z) if positive-int(Z) & X divides Z & Y divides Z

is not a correct statement about lowest common multiples in the intended interpretation. That clause actually defines only common multiples, but without enforcing the requirement of 'lowest'. It just so happens that, in the first mode, the cut defends against the computation of higher common multiples; yet it can offer no defence against it in the second mode. In summary, it is not the clause's *cut* which is 'red', but its *logic*.

As a final comment upon the matter of correctness, we can say that whenever a program's logic is correct (that is, is **true** in the intended interpretation), the insertion of cuts into its text never leads to the computation of wrong answers; the worst penalty is *incompleteness*, in that we may accidentally prune out answers that *are* required.

Exercises 38

1. The interchange-sort program below is suitable for executing **standard queries** of the form ? sort(**list**, Y) where **list** denotes any ground list:

> S1 : sort(Y, Y) if ord(Y)
> S2 : sort(X, Y) if append3(X1, U•V•nil, X2, X) & V<U &
> append3(X1, V•U•nil, X2, Z) &
> sort(Z, Y)

It works by repeatedly seeking disordered pairs of adjacent elements of the current list and correcting them. Here, ord(Y) means that Y is a list of numbers arranged in strictly ascending order, whilst append3(L1, L2, L3, L) means that L is the result of appending L3 to the result of appending L2 to L1. Assume that 'ord', 'append3' and '<' are defined correctly by further clauses supplementing S1 and S2. The intended meaning of sort(X, Y) is that Y is some permutation of X for which ord(Y) holds.

Comment upon the efficiency of this program for executing the standard query ? sort(3•1•4•2•nil, Y) under the standard strategy.

For the same query comment upon the correctness and efficiency of each of the three following adaptations of the above program:

(i)   a cut inserted immediately *before* the call V<U;
(ii)   the cut inserted instead immediately *after* the call V<U;
(iii)   as in (ii) but with S1 deleted and a new clause

> S3 : sort(Y, Y)

placed *after* the clause S2.

Are there any **standard queries** which adaptation (iii) would solve incorrectly relative to the intended meaning?

2. The 'least' program with the cut discussed in Theme 38 can be modified further as follows:

least(X, Y, Y) if greater_or_equal(X, Y) & !
least(X, Y, X)

greater_or_equal(X, Y) if X>Y
greater_or_equal(X, Y) if X=Y

(i)   what is the motivation behind this modification?
(ii)   confirm that for both the queries ? least(2, 3, Z) and ? least(3, 2, Z)
         this program works correctly.
(iii)   does the program work correctly for all queries to 'least' whose first
         two arguments are ground?

3. Automating the insertion of cuts into programs might be aided by the
    availability of an algorithm capable of deciding, for any given program **P**,
    whether any given query ? **q** could be solved in exactly one way. Such an
    algorithm would, in effect, always correctly solve the meta-query

    ? one-way(**P**, **q**)

    What does the following instance of **P** tell you about the existence of
    algorithm **A**?

    q if one-way(**P**, **q**)
    q

Theme 39

Adequacy of the SLD paradigm

In previous Themes we have described the basic workings of a computational formalism founded upon the following principles:

> the language is **Horn-clause logic**,
> a program is a set of **definite clauses**,
> a query is a **negative clause**,
> a computation is an **SLD-derivation**, and
> an execution is an **exhaustive search** of an SLD-tree.

What is the technical capability of this formalism? Such a question raises other, more fundamental ones such as:

1. what problems can we represent?
2. what problems can we solve?
3. what is the significance of the restriction to Horn-clause logic?
4. can we fully realize the soundness of SLD-inference?
5. can we fully realize the completeness of SLD-inference?
6. what can the formalism *not* achieve, and does it matter?

The scope of the present course permits only a brief consideration of these issues; moreover, we must leave many other important issues wholly unaddressed.

1. The representable problems

A definite-clause program determines, for each m-ary predicate symbol **p** appearing in it, some relation $\mathbf{R_p}$ which is a subset of $\mathbf{H}^m$ where $\mathbf{H}$ is the Herbrand domain of the language. Now consider any *function* **f** mapping $\mathbf{H}^n$ to $\mathbf{H}$ where $n>0$. Clearly every such function **f** can be trivially represented by a corresponding $(n+1)$-ary relation $\mathbf{R_p}$ satisfying

$$< x_1, ..., x_n, x_{n+1} > \in \mathbf{R_p} \quad \text{if and only if} \quad f(x_1, ..., x_n) = x_{n+1}$$

In particular, every **partial recursive function** can be so represented. It has been proved that for every partial recursive function **f** there exists a definite-clause program which determines the corresponding relation $\mathbf{R_p}$, and moreover that every request to evaluate **f** is expressible by some negative clause querying **p**.

2. The computable problems

The notion of effective computability was made precise more than half a century ago by Alan Turing: the effectively computable functions are, *by definition*, those functions computable by a **Universal Turing Machine**. At about the same time, it was conjectured by Alonzo Church that these were the *only* functions that could be computed by *any* sort of machine; this conjecture— known as **Church's Thesis**—has not so far been refuted, and almost certainly never will be. Furthermore, the class of partial recursive functions was then defined in a machine-independent manner by Stephen Kleene and proved to be identical to the class of Turing-computable functions. Thus, since we know that Horn-clause logic is adequate for defining all the partial recursive functions, it must also be adequate for defining all those functions capable of evaluation by computers, and hence for representing all effectively-solvable problems.

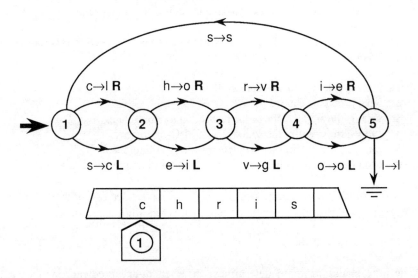

Figure 39.1. Turing machine computing that which chris loves.

3. The restriction to Horn-clause logic

Since Horn-clause logic is capable, in theory, of expressing all computational problems, the main questions remaining about its adequacy are

> is it *convenient* for expressing problems?
> is it *practical* for solving problems?

The first of these can be explored at various levels. First, we might consider how appropriate it is to use *any* sort of logic rather than, say, an imperative or object-oriented language. Next, we might consider the significance of choosing classical first-order logic rather than some non-classical logic. Then there is the choice of using either full first-order logic or just a subset such as clausal form. Finally, we have built our formalism so far upon an even smaller subset, Horn-clause form.

The way people feel about these choices is inevitably determined by their own particular perspective—by what vision they hold as to how their own preferences might be located and realized within the broad landscape of computational problem-solving. If I were a logician with a passionate interest in mechanizing, say, temporal epistemic logic, ought I to feel obliged—on behalf of the wider community—also to work out how to integrate my particular logic with someone else's modal action logic, and how to integrate my theorem-prover with theirs? Ought I also to consider how well my logic will stand up to the demands of the software engineers who will want to know—amongst much else—what techniques I can offer for analysing, verifying and transforming the programs which I write in that logic?

The fundamental issue here is whether one's preferred formalism is intended to service only one's own specialized needs or to service the highly variegated needs of others. In the latter case the main options are these: either we end up with a wide range of co-existing formalisms *and* the means of integrating them when necessary, or we fuse all together to produce one gigantic universal formalism, or we choose just a few of them as *base formalisms* in which the *concepts* of the others can be *encoded*. It is the last of these—the pursuit of broadly acceptable base formalisms—that has so far characterized the general thrust of programming language development.

Currently the most popular base formalism for logic programming is (impure) Prolog. This reflects the fact that some problems seem not to be conveniently representable in pure definite-clause logic, especially those which require

> reasoning about non-atomic goals,
> reasoning about action, time and change and
> reasoning nonmonotonically.

The first of these, in particular, reflects the difference between full first-order logic and Horn-clause logic. Although first-order logic is able to represent all computable problems, not all of its subsets are: for instance, any subset which fails to include at least one n-ary function symbol for n>0 cannot be Turing-complete. What about general clausal form? We have seen earlier in the course that if we construct in first-order logic an expression **A** of our assumptions about the problem domain, then the conversion of **A** to its clausal-form **C** preserves logical equivalence except in the case where Skolemization is needed. It turns out that such a conversion does not compromise expressiveness. Suppose that **a** is some answer to the problem, so that **A** implies **a**. Then, since the conversion at least guarantees that **C** implies **A** it follows that **C** implies **a** by transitivity. Hence any problem solvable in first-order logic must be solvable in clausal form.

The further restriction to Horn-clause logic is more serious: there is no *direct* method of converting non-Horn clauses to Horn clauses. If we want to reason about negated atoms or disjunctions of atoms and yet remain within the realm of Horn-clause logic, then one option is to *encode* those formulas using functional terms and then write a special Horn-clause program which processes them so as to *simulate* some reasoning process for non-Horn-clause logic. For example, suppose we start with some assumption set **C** and some query ?a, both written in non-Horn-clause logic. We know that there exist sound and complete theorem-provers for this logic and—from what has been said earlier—that any one of these *algorithms* must itself be encodable as some Horn-clause program **P**. Given a term-representation **T** of **C** and a term-representation **t** of **a**, **P** can solve a Horn-clause query of the form ? solve(**T**, **t**) whenever **a** is solvable using **C**. Thus the original non-Horn-clause formulation {**C**, ?a} has become *encoded* as a computationally-equivalent Horn-clause formulation {**P**, ? solve(**T**, **t**)}.

Questions about the *convenience* and *practicality* of Horn-clause logic when deployed as a general base formalism then become questions about the convenience and practicality of such encodings and simulations, and the answers to them have both subjective and objective components. In the end we can judge the worth of a language only by its capacity to satisfy its intended users.

4. Realizing sound SLD-inference

Only one comment need be made here: the occur-check is too expensive to implement with a permanently-enabled status. In practice we usually omit or disable it and just do the best we can to avoid those circumstances where it would be needed in order to defend against unsound inference.

5. Realizing complete SLD-inference

People speak loosely of resolution being 'complete'. In order to give precision to this statement we have to make more qualified statements which distinguish between Horn-clause logic and general-clause logic, between refutational and affirmational modes of inference and between fair and unfair search strategies.

(a) for Horn-clause logic, resolution (including SLD-resolution) is refutation-complete in all situations;
(b) for Horn-clause logic, resolution is affirmation-complete for the case where the target conclusions are atoms or conjunctions of atoms;
(c) for general-clause logic, resolution is refutation-complete provided it is supplemented by a second inference rule called **factoring**;
(d) for general-clause logic, resolution is not affirmation-complete whether we have factoring or not.

Note that these are all properties of resolution *inference*, taking no account of *search strategy*.

Reasoning in general-clause logic becomes important when we want to reason about program properties or specifications using resolution-based technology. Often these will have their most 'natural' expression in unrestricted first-order logic, which we must first convert to clausal form; this conversion may produce non-Horn clauses and hence prompt the need for factoring. The factoring rule simply says that from any clause of the form

L1 or **L2** or **other_literals**

such that the literals **L1** and **L2** have an m.g.u. θ, one may soundly infer the simpler clause

(L1 or **other_literals)**θ

For example, from the clause

likes(mrs_thatcher, X) if supports(X, Y) & ¬likes(Y, socialism)

["mrs_thatcher likes supporters of those who dislike socialism"]

we may infer, by factoring, the improbable conclusion

likes(mrs_thatcher, socialism) if supports(socialism, mrs_thatcher)

The need for factoring is one of several impediments (which also include ancestor-resolution) to efficient theorem-proving in general clausal-form logic, as there is a high overhead entailed in scanning clauses for opportunities to apply the rule.

The comments above refer only to the completeness of resolution inference. We also need to know the consequences of choosing any particular search strategy. When the strategy is *unfair*—as with depth-first search—then the completeness of the resulting proof procedure can no longer be guaranteed. Conversely, it *is* guaranteed by the use of a *fair* strategy such as breadth-first search. Unfortunately, fair strategies have proved too expensive to implement on standard machine architectures: in practice we have to employ unfair strategies and do the best we can to ensure that our search-trees contain no infinite computations.

6. What we cannot achieve

From what has been said already we know that any *solvable* computational problem can be solved by applying resolution to clausal-form logic. Equivalently, any logical implication that holds can be confirmed using this method. Equivalently, the validity of any valid sentence can be confirmed using this method. But how does the method respond if we submit as input a computational problem that is *unsolvable*, or an implication that does *not* hold, or a sentence that is *not* valid? Can the method be relied upon to *tell* us that these situations prevail?

The answer to this is provided by the fact that, for first-order logic, the validity property is only **semi-decidable**. By this we mean that it is impossible to construct an algorithm which is capable of *perfectly* distinguishing valid from non-valid sentences. The best we can do is to construct an algorithm which can confirm the validity of any valid sentence but which may either finitely-fail or loop when given a non-valid sentence. When we transfer this limitation into the logic programming framework, it tells us that we can never construct a logic interpreter which is complete yet guaranteed not to loop when applied to a given program and query. Thus, when a program logically affords no solution to the query, we cannot, *in general*, rely upon getting a finitely-failed execution as our means of recognizing this fact.

This problem is not a peculiarity either of logic programming or of the resolution method, but is rather a feature endemic to mathematical decision-making. It afflicts *almost all* activities relying upon the mechanization of mathematics. For instance, it determines that no computer-based tool can be built which always decides whether *or not* two programs in any formalism compute the same answers, or which always decides whether *or not* a program conforms to its specification, or which always decides whether *or not* a query can retrieve every correct answer from a database. It sets a limit upon what we can get out of computers, affecting logic programming to no lesser and no greater degree than it affects any other programming formalism. In conclusion, since we cannot do anything about this particular issue, it does not matter on this count whether we choose SLD as our formalism or not.

Exercises 39

1. The following logical implication holds:

$$(\forall X)(\forall Y)(A(X) \text{ or } A(Y)) \vDash (\exists W)(\exists Z)(A(W) \ \& \ A(Z))$$

(i)   prove that refutational resolution without factoring is incapable of confirming this;

(ii)   confirm the implication using resolution with factoring.

Note—you must first reformulate the problem in clausal form.

Theme 40

Herbrand interpretations and models

The theory of Herbrand interpretations and models (abbreviated respectively to 'H-interpretations' and 'H-models') provides a foundation for defining and analysing the **semantics** of logic programs. In particular, it provides information about the satisfiability of any logic program in the domain over which it computes. Some analyses of the logic programming formalism must of necessity consider non-Herbrand interpretations, but these lie beyond our present scope. Thus the only domain we shall consider here is the Herbrand domain. The first important fact to note is that the satisfiability properties of the program in this domain are the same as the satisfiability properties of its ground instantiation.

Let us look again at the simple clause-set **P** first discussed in Theme 24:

> likes(chris, X) if likes(X, logic)
> likes(bob, logic)

Taking **H** to be just {chris, bob, logic}, the ground instantiation **G(P)** is shown below. Alongside it is a highly abbreviated version written in propositional logic which we shall use for our subsequent analysis:

likes(chris, chris) if likes(chris, logic)	CC if CL
likes(chris, bob) if likes(bob, logic)	CB if BL
likes(chris, logic) if likes(logic, logic)	CL if LL
likes(bob, logic)	BL

We first define what is meant by an H-interpretation—it is just a free assignment of truth-values (**true** or **false**) to all the atoms in **B(P)**. Such an interpretation must therefore also assign either **true** or **false** to all the atoms in **G(P)**; the truth-values of these atoms then determine truth-values for all the clauses in **G(P)**.

Note that a compact way of referring to any **H**-interpretation is to refer simply to some subset **I** of **B(P)** on the understanding that, under this interpretation, any atom **q** occurring in **B(P)** is assigned **true** if q∈I but is otherwise assigned **false**.

Example—for the above clause-set, **B(P)** is the set of (abbreviated) ground atoms {CC, CL, CB, LC, LL, LB, BC, BL, BB}. The set {BL, CB} is a subset of **B(P)** and is thus an **H**-interpretation. **G(P)** is reproduced below with the associated truth values written in place of its atoms:

> false   if false
> true   if true
> false   if false
> true

With this assignment, all the clauses of $G(P)$ are **true**. This interpretation is therefore an **H-model** for $G(P)$ and hence an **H**-model for **P**.

When we first introduced the idea of an interpretation in Theme 11 we talked in terms of **associating** features of the given sentences with features of the given domain. This idea continues to apply in the case of an **H**-interpretation; specifically, it associates

> each constant with *itself*;
> each n-ary function symbol **f** with some *function* **F** from H^n to H
>   such that for any $t \in H^n$ we have $F(t)=f(t)$;
> each n-ary predicate symbol **p** with some *relation* R_p
>   such that $R_p \subseteq \{t \mid p(t) \in B(P)\}$.

These rather fussy formalities, however, are not really important: all you need to remember is that an **H**-interpretation freely assigns values **true** or **false** to the atoms of $G(P)$. More significantly, we have the following satisfiability property:

> a clause-set **P** has a model of some sort
>   if and only if **P** has an **H**-model
>   if and only if $G(P)$ has an **H**-model

Finally, note that everything stated above applies to *any* set **P** of arbitrary clauses. As we shall see presently, more specific properties of **P**'s models emerge when **P** is a set of *definite* clauses.

Exercises 40

Note—in Questions **2-5** assume that **P** is definite.

1. If $B(P)$ has n members, how many **H**-interpretations does **P** have?

2. Which subset of $B(P)$ is always an **H**-model for **P**?

3. What form must **P** take in order that $\emptyset$ shall be an **H**-model?

4. A ground atom is *relevant* to **P** if and only if it is a ground atom occurring in $G(P)$. An **H**-model is relevant if and only if it contains only relevant atoms. What form must **P** take so that it shall have exactly one relevant **H**-model?

Note—**B(P)** generally contains many atoms which are not relevant and which therefore contribute to models in which we have no interest.

5. What form must **P** take in order that every subset of **B(P)** shall be an **H**-model?

6. Assuming that **H**={A, B, C, D}, identify all the **H**-models of the following clause-set:

$$A \; \text{if} \; \neg B \, \& \, C$$
$$D \; \text{if} \; \neg C$$
$$\neg D$$

7. Identify the smallest **H**-model for the program

$$\text{list(nil)}$$
$$\text{list(a·X)} \; \text{if} \; \text{list(X)}$$

8. Taking **H** to be {**1, 2**}, identify all the **H**-interpretations for the clause

$$p(X) \; \text{if} \; \neg p(Y)$$

and say which, if any, are **H**-models for the clause.

Theme 41

Partial orders and lattices

Presently we shall want to examine the relationships between the various **H**-models of a definite program. The usual framework in which we investigate such matters is the theory of **lattices**, which are just particular kinds of partial order.

A (weak) **partial order** over a set **S** is any subset '$\leqslant$' of **S**×**S** having these properties:

> for all x∈**S**, x$\leqslant$x   **[reflexivity]**
> for all x∈**S** and y∈**S**, x=y if x$\leqslant$y & y$\leqslant$x   **[antisymmetry]**
> for all x∈**S**, y∈**S** and z∈**S**, x$\leqslant$z if x$\leqslant$y & y$\leqslant$z   **[transitivity]**

The structure [**S**, $\leqslant$] is called a **partially-ordered set** and will be denoted henceforth by the symbol **Γ**.

The relation $\leqslant$ is termed 'weak' owing to its reflexivity, in contrast to a 'strict' partial order '<' which has to be irreflexive, asymmetric and transitive. Clausal-form definitions of these basic properties of order relations can be found in the answers to Question **1** of Exercises 41.

The relation $\leqslant$ orders the members e_i of **S** into a collection of zero or more (directed) **paths**. We shall adopt the following convention about directedness:

$$\text{a path drawn as} \quad e_1 \rightarrow ... \rightarrow e_n \quad \text{satisfies} \quad e_n \leqslant ... \leqslant e_1$$

For example, the path shown on the left in Figure 41.1 signifies that b$\leqslant$a and c$\leqslant$b. Note that the notion of a path is distinct from that of a **chain** whose *every* pair of members x, y must satisfy either x$\leqslant$y or y$\leqslant$x, thus ensuring that an edge exists between them. A chain is shown on the right in the figure.

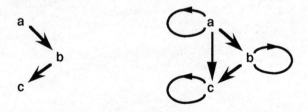

Figure 41.1. A path *(left)* and a chain *(right)* in a partially-ordered set.

The number, nature and interconnections of such paths all depend entirely upon the particular Γ being considered. Nevertheless there are certain potential properties of Γ, its subsets and its paths which are always of interest, as follows:

For any subset **s** of **S**,

an **upper bound** for **s** is any u∈**S** such that v≤u for all v∈**s**;
a **lower bound** for **s** is any u∈**S** such that u≤v for all v∈**s**;
a **greatest element** of **s** is any u∈**s** such that v≤u for all v∈**s**;
a **least element** of **s** is any u∈**s** such that u≤v for all v∈**s**;
a **least upper bound** for **s** is any u∈**S** which is the least element of
      the set of all upper bounds for **s**;
a **greatest lower bound** for **s** is any u∈**S** which is the greatest
      element of the set of all lower bounds for **s**;
a **minimal element** of **s** is any u∈**s** such that v≤u for no v∈**s**, v≠u;
a **maximal element** of **s** is any u∈**s** such that u≤v for no v∈**s**, v≠u.

Depending upon the precise nature of Γ and **s**, any of the above may or may not exist. Note the distinction between a least element and a minimal element. If a least element exists then it is both the unique least element and the unique minimal element; if a minimal element exists then it is neither necessarily uniquely minimal nor necessarily a least element. Analogous remarks apply to greatest elements and maximal elements. Observe also that least and greatest elements of **s** must belong to **s**, whereas lower and upper bounds for **s** need not.

Example—Figure 41.2 shows a partially-ordered set. In order to reduce clutter, the extra arrows that would be induced by the reflexivity and transitivity of ≤ have been omitted from the figure.

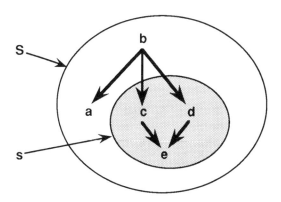

Figure 41.2. A partially-ordered set [**S**, ≤] with **s**⊆**S**.

For this example,

S has one **upper bound** b	s has one **upper bound** b
no **lower bound**	one **lower bound** e
one **greatest element** b	no **greatest element**
no **least element**	one **least element** e
one **least upper bound** b	one **least upper bound** b
no **greatest lower bound**	one **greatest lower bound** e
two **minimal elements** a and e	one **minimal** element e
one **maximal element** b	two **maximal** elements c and d

There are certain kinds of partially-ordered set which are of special interest to us. In particular, suppose that $\Gamma =[S, \leqslant]$ is such that every subset s of S has a least upper bound. In this case,

1. since S is itself a subset of S it follows that S has a least upper bound which, being a member of S, must be the (unique) greatest element of S;

2. since the empty set $\emptyset$ is a subset of S it follows that $\emptyset$ has a least upper bound and, because all the upper bounds of $\emptyset$ are exactly all the members of S, the least of them must be the (unique) least element of S.

The existence of least and greatest elements determines that every member of S must lie on some path in Γ which begins at the greatest element of S and ends at the least element of S. This gratifyingly tidy structure is called a **complete lattice**. Figure 41.3 gives an indication of what a complete lattice might look like (again omitting the arrows induced by reflexivity and transitivity).

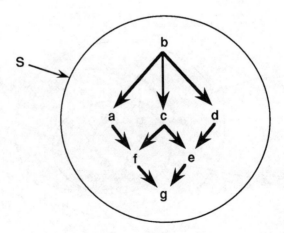

Figure 41.3. A complete lattice.

Here the elements of most interest are the greatest (unique maximal) element 'b' at the **top** of the lattice, and the least (unique minimal) element 'g' at the **bottom** of the lattice. Every other element lies on some path directed from the top element down to the bottom element.

Exercises 41

1. (i) Construct a clause-set which constrains a relation R to be a (weak) partial order, using just 'R' and '=' as predicate symbols.

   (ii) A **strict partial order** is a binary relation which is asymmetric and transitive. Using 'R' as the only predicate symbol, construct a clause set which constrains the relation named by 'R' to have these two properties. Then use resolution to prove that the relation must also be irreflexive.

   Hint—the transitivity property is not actually needed for the proof.

2. A partially-ordered set [S, ⩽] with a subset s⊆S is shown below.

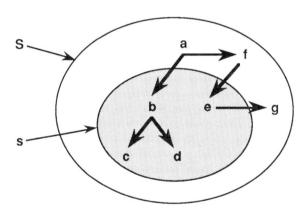

For both **S** and **s** identify

   (i)   the lower and upper bounds;
   (ii)   the least and greatest elements (if any);
   (iii)   the minimal and maximal elements.

3. Prove that a partially-ordered set [S, ⩽] is a complete lattice if every subset **s** of **S** has a greatest lower bound.

Theme 42

The lattice of models for a definite program

First, since we shall deal here only with (H-)models and (H-)interpretations, the prefix 'H-' will henceforth be omitted but assumed by default. We begin by recalling that a model is just a particular set of ground atoms deemed to be **true**. Our main interest is in the question of whether a given model makes more atoms **true** than it needs to in order to satisfy a given definite program—equivalently, whether that model *includes* any smaller models. Thus the primary relation of interest between models is that of **set-inclusion** ($\subseteq$).

Whenever we take the set $M(P) = \{M_1, M_2, ...\}$ of all models of a definite program P and choose $\subseteq$ as a partial order, the partially-ordered set $[M(P), \subseteq]$ necessarily forms a **complete lattice**; consequently there must always be a *unique* **minimal model** for P. There is insufficient space here to prove this important result, but an excellent account of it and related matters is given in the paper by Kowalski and Van Emden cited in Theme 4.

Consider again the ground instantiation $G(P)$ shown in Theme 40:

likes(chris, chris)	if likes(chris, logic)	CC	if CL
likes(chris, bob)	if likes(bob, logic)	CB	if BL
likes(chris, logic)	if likes(logic, logic)	CL	if LL
likes(bob, logic)		BL	

A fail-safe way of getting a model is to choose the entire Herbrand Base $B(P) = \{CC, CL, CB, LC, LL, LB, BC, BL, BB\}$, for then every atom in $G(P)$ is assigned **true** and this in turn makes all of its clauses **true**. This model is the (unique) **maximal model** for $G(P)$ and hence for P.

However, such a choice is clearly excessive—many of the atoms in $B(P)$ do not even occur in $G(P)$ and so their truth values are irrelevant. Stripping out those irrelevant atoms leaves a somewhat smaller model $\{CC, CL, CB, BL, LL\}$. Which of these atoms *must* appear in any model? Clearly BL must, in order to make the program's fourth clause **true**. Then, since BL must, so also must CB in order to make the second clause **true**. The first and third clauses employ only the remaining three atoms CC, CL and LL, and both those clauses can be made **true** by making those atoms **false**. In conclusion, only BL and CB *must* be **true**— thus the (unique) **minimal model** for $G(P)$, and hence for P, is $\{BL, CB\}$.

The **minimal model** of a definite program P will in future be denoted by $MM(P)$. For our example the unabbreviated expression of the minimal model is

$$MM(P) = \{likes(bob, logic), likes(chris, bob)\}$$

Some indication of the complete lattice of models for the program is shown in Figure 42.1 where, as usual, the reflexive and transitive arcs have been suppressed. Moreover, only a few of the models are shown—there are 64 models in the entire lattice. Note also that, in general, *most* subsets of **B(P)** will be **counter-models**—for our example there are 448 of these, of which the smallest is ∅.

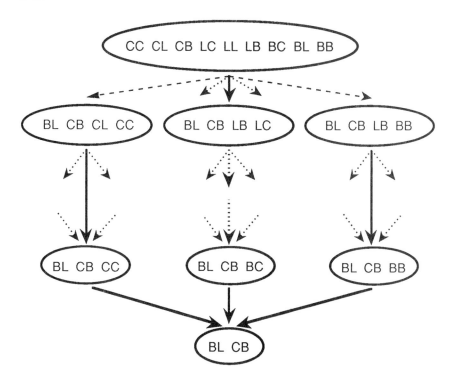

Figure 42.1. A complete lattice of Herbrand models.

The reason why the discussion above has focused solely upon *definite* programs is that, in general, an *indefinite* program does not yield a complete lattice and may therefore have multiple minimal models. The lack of a unique minimal model makes it harder to assign an *unambiguous* meaning to such a program.

Exercises 42

1. Using the example program **P** in the Theme,

    (i)   identify its minimal and maximal symmetric models;

    (ii)   identify the smallest symmetric model containing LL.

Note—a symmetric model **M** for this program is one satisfying

$$\text{for all } <X, Y> \in H^2, \ \text{likes}(Y, X) \in M \ \text{if} \ \text{likes}(X, Y) \in M.$$

2. Referring to the same program **P** used in the Theme, determine whether it has any

    (i)   reflexive models;

    (ii)   irreflexive models;

    (iii)   transitive models.

3. Referring to the same program **P** used in the Theme, determine its maximal counter-models.

4. Prove by a counter-example that the following does *not* generally hold for definite programs:

$$\textbf{MM(P1} \cup \textbf{P2)} \ = \ \textbf{MM(P1)} \cup \textbf{MM(P2)}$$

Theme 43

Minimal models and logical consequence

There is a simple but important connection between any definite program $\mathbf{P}$, its minimal model $\mathbf{MM(P)}$ and each of its ground atomic logical consequences $\mathbf{q}$, as follows:

$$\mathbf{P} \vDash \mathbf{q} \quad \text{if and only if} \quad \mathbf{q} \in \mathbf{MM(P)}$$

Thus $\mathbf{MM(P)}$ is exactly the set of all ground atoms which are implied by $\mathbf{P}$. We shall see later that this is just one of several ways of giving significance to a program's minimal model.

The proof of the above relationship makes use of the so-called **model intersection property**:

> if $\mathbf{M_1}, ..., \mathbf{M_n}$ are any $\mathbf{H}$-models for a definite program $\mathbf{P}$
> then their intersection is an $\mathbf{H}$-model of $\mathbf{P}$.

It is easy to show this by induction. For any k<n, let $\mathbf{I_k}$ denote $\mathbf{M_1} \cap ... \cap \mathbf{M_k}$. Now consider any clause $\mathbf{C}$ of $\mathbf{G(P)}$:

$$\mathbf{C} : \mathbf{A} \text{ if } \mathbf{B_1} \& ... \& \mathbf{B_m}$$

We shall prove that, for all k⩽n, $\mathbf{I_k}$ satisfies $\mathbf{C}$.

Base case (k=1): $\mathbf{I_1} = \mathbf{M_1}$ and therefore satisfies $\mathbf{C}$.

Induction step (1⩽k<n): assume that $\mathbf{M_k}$ satisfies $\mathbf{C}$;

if $\mathbf{I_k}$ satisfies $\mathbf{C}$ then	*either*	$\mathbf{B_i} \notin \mathbf{I_k}$ for some i
	or	$\mathbf{B_i} \in \mathbf{I_k}$ for all i, and $\mathbf{A} \in \mathbf{I_k}$
as $\mathbf{M_{k+1}}$ satisfies $\mathbf{C}$ then	*either*	$\mathbf{B_i} \notin \mathbf{M_{k+1}}$ for some i
	or	$\mathbf{B_i} \in \mathbf{M_{k+1}}$ for all i, and $\mathbf{A} \in \mathbf{M_{k+1}}$
it then follows that	*either*	$\mathbf{B_i} \notin \mathbf{I_k} \cap \mathbf{M_{k+1}}$ for some i
	or	$\mathbf{B_i} \in \mathbf{I_k} \cap \mathbf{M_{k+1}}$ for all i, and
		$\mathbf{A} \in \mathbf{I_k} \cap \mathbf{M_{k+1}}$
and hence that		$\mathbf{I_{k+1}}$ satisfies $\mathbf{C}$.

Thus for all k≤n, I_k satisfies **C** and—by a similar argument—every other clause in **G(P)**. Then I_k must also satisfy **P**.

Note—there is an even simpler, inductionless proof given in the answer to Question 1 of the Exercises.)

We next prove that the intersection **I*** of *all* the models of **P** is the minimal model **MM(P)**, as follows:

Assumption—**I*** is not the minimal model;

> then there must exist some model M_j such that $M_j \subset I^*$
> then there must exist some atom **q** such that $q \notin M_j$ and $q \in I^*$
> but $q \in I^*$ implies that $q \in M_i$ for all i, contradicting $q \in M_j$
> therefore the initial assumption is false.

Using this result it is now easy to prove the relationship between **MM(P)** and any atomic consequence **q** of **P**:

if **P ⊨ q**   then   **q** is **true** in every model of **P** on any domain
              then   **q** is **true** in every **H**-model of **P**
              then $q \in I^*$
              then $q \in MM(P)$;
if $q \in MM(P)$ then   **q** is in every **H**-model of **P**
              then   **G(P) ⊨ q**
              then   **P ⊨ q** since **P ⊨ G(P)**.

Other useful and interesting properties of **MM(P)** arise from the truth of the Skolem-Herbrand-Gödel Theorem which states that a clause-set **S** is unsatisfiable if and only if there exists some *finite* subset of **G(S)** which has no **H**-models. From this we can argue as follows, where **P** is any definite program:

$q \in MM(P)$ if and only if   **P ⊨ q**
           if and only if   **P** ∪ {¬**q**} is unsatisfiable
           if and only if   some finite subset of **G(P** ∪ {¬**q**})
                            has no **H**-models
           if and only if   some finite subset **g** of **G(P)** exists
                            such that **g** ∪ {¬**q**} has no **H**-models
           if and only if   some finite subset of **G(P)** implies **q**.

In short, even when **H**, **B(P)** and **G(P)** are infinite, every atom **q** in **MM(P)** can be sought as a consequence of some *finite* subset of **G(P)**. This fact is closely related to the refutation-completeness of resolution, which postulates that every solvable query ¬**q** can be refuted using **P** after some *finite* number of resolution steps, thus utilizing only some *finite* subset of **P**.

Exercises 43

1. Prove the model intersection property without using induction.

   Hint—consider whether some ground clause (**q** if **body**) can be made **false** in the intersection of its models.

Theme 44

Minimal models and derivability

We saw in the last Theme that the minimal model $\mathbf{MM(P)}$ of a definite program $\mathbf{P}$ comprises just the ground atomic logical consequences of $\mathbf{P}$:

$$\text{for all } \mathbf{q} \in \mathbf{B(P)}, \quad \mathbf{q} \in \mathbf{MM(P)} \text{ iff } \mathbf{P} \vDash \mathbf{q}$$

An immediate outcome of this is that $\mathbf{MM(P)}$ also characterizes the ground atomic queries $?\mathbf{q}$ which are *solvable* using SLD-resolution, since

$$
\begin{aligned}
\text{for all } \mathbf{q} \in \mathbf{B(P)}, \quad \mathbf{q} \in \mathbf{MM(P)} \text{ iff } &\mathbf{P} \vDash \mathbf{q} \\
\text{iff } &\mathbf{P} \cup \{\neg \mathbf{q}\} \text{ is unsatisfiable} \\
\text{iff } &\mathbf{P} \cup \{\neg \mathbf{q}\} \vdash_{\text{SLD}} \square
\end{aligned}
$$

The set of all ground atoms $\mathbf{q}$ for which $?\mathbf{q}$ succeeds from $\mathbf{P}$ using SLD-resolution is called the **success set** of $\mathbf{P}$ and is denoted by $\mathbf{SS(P)}$. Consequently we then have

$$\mathbf{SS(P)} = \mathbf{MM(P)}$$

which is owed to the soundness and completeness of SLD-resolution.

Moreover, $\mathbf{SS(P)}$ also delimits the computed answers to non-atomic and non-ground queries. Therefore consider a typical negative-clause query which takes the compound form

$$? \, \mathbf{q}_1 \, \& \, ... \, \& \, \mathbf{q}_n$$

in which each subquery $\mathbf{q}_i$ is atomic but not necessarily ground. Each successful computation yields some answer substitution θ which determines an associated computed answer

$$\forall((\mathbf{q}_1 \, \& \, ... \, \& \, \mathbf{q}_n)\theta)$$

and each such answer stands generically, over the Herbrand domain, for the ground instantiation $\mathbf{G}((\mathbf{q}_1 \, \& \, ... \, \& \, \mathbf{q}_n)\theta)$. It is then guaranteed that

$$\mathbf{G}(\mathbf{q}_i\theta) \subseteq \mathbf{SS(P)} \text{ for each } i \in \{1, ..., n\}$$

The collection of atoms in

$$G(q_1\theta) \cup ... \cup G(q_n\theta)$$

must also be a subset of **SS(P)**, comprising all those atoms computable by the query. In the special case where the query contains only *most-general* calls to *all* the relations named in **P**, that collection of atoms is exactly **SS(P)**—equivalently, exactly **MM(P)**.

Sometimes it is convenient to partition **SS(P)** into the form

$$SS(P) = SS(p_1) \cup ... \cup SS(p_m)$$

in which p_1, ... and p_m are the distinct predicate symbols occurring in **P**. Each subset **SS(p_i)** comprises the set of all the ground atomic answers computed by all ways of solving the most-general query

$$? \; p_i(X_1, ..., X_r)$$

in which r is the arity of p_i and X_1, ... and X_r are distinct variables. Figure 44.1 indicates the structure of the success set for a program referring to just three relations p1, p2, and p3.

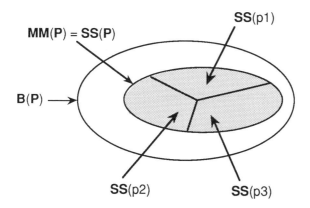

Figure 44.1. Success set for a program using three relations.

Example—consider this definite program **P** where **H**={dov, chris}:

kind(X) if helps(X, Y)
helps(dov, Z)

The most-general query ? kind(X) yields the answer set

$$G(kind(X)\{X/dov\}) = \{kind(dov)\} = SS(kind)$$

whilst the most-general query ? helps(X, Y) yields the answer set

$$G(helps(X, Y)\{X/dov\}) = \{helps(dov, dov), helps(dov, chris)\}$$
$$= SS(helps)$$

Hence $SS(P) = \{kind(dov), helps(dov, dov), helps(dov, chris)\} = MM(P)$.

Exercises 44

1. SLD-execution of the query ? append(nil, X, Y) yields just the output substitution {Y/X} and terminates. Assuming that the Herbrand domain **H** is {nil, a•nil, a•a•nil, ...}, which part of the program's minimal model is computed by the query?

2. SLD-execution of the query ? arc(a, X) & path(X, Y) yields just the two output substitutions {X/b, Y/d} and {X/c, Y/d} and terminates. Which part of the program's minimal model is computed by the query?

3. SLD-execution of the query ? p(X, Z) yields just the two output substitutions {X/0} and {X/U, Z/s(U)} and terminates. Assuming that the Herbrand domain **H** is {0, s(0), s(s(0)), ...} and that the only predicate symbol in the program is 'p', what is the program's minimal model?

4. Show, by constructing their minimal models, that the following two programs give identical answers to any query:

even(0)	even(0)
even(s(s(X))) if even(X)	even(s(X)) if odd(X)
odd(s(0))	odd(s(X)) if even(X)
odd(X) if even(s(X))	

Theme 45

Incremental construction of the minimal model

There is a simple incremental method for constructing the minimal model of any definite program **P**. This method is not strictly an *algorithm* since, in the case where **MM(P)** is infinite, it may not complete the construction in a finite number of steps; however, the more steps we perform, the better the approximation.

The method starts by choosing some interpretation $I_1 \subseteq B(P)$. Later on we shall see that there is a preferred choice of I_1 and that not all choices are adequate. Choosing I_1 can be viewed as guessing which atoms have to be **true** in any model of **P**. Now consider any clause in **G(P)**

$$q \text{ if } body$$

If our guess assigns **true** to all the atoms in this **body** then an *immediate consequence* of that guess is that **q** should also be made **true**, for otherwise the clause as a whole would be made **false**. Our next iterate I_2 comprises just those heading atoms **q** made **true** by this argument. This new iterate will not necessarily contain all those body atoms which justified the introduction of the new atoms **q**; this does not matter—successive iterates will eventually introduce *and retain* all of those atoms which *must* be **true** in any model of the program.

Consider this example of a program **P** on the domain **H**={dov, chris}:

$$kind(X) \text{ if } nice(X)$$
$$nice(dov)$$

whose ground instantiation **G(P)** in highly abbreviated form is

$$KD \text{ if } ND$$
$$KC \text{ if } NC$$
$$ND$$

(where K=kind, N=nice, D=dov and C=chris)

and suppose we choose I_1={KD, NC}. Applying the above method yields I_2={ND, KC} and then I_3={ND, KD}. All further iterates merely replicate I_3, which is accordingly referred to as a *fixpoint*. We have, in fact, converged upon the minimal model **MM(P)**.

Figure 45.1 shows the result of imposing the partial order $\subseteq$ upon the **powerset** (the set of all subsets) of **B(P)**. Each member of that powerset is some

interpretation, and there are $2^4 = 16$ of these because **B(P)** contains just four
atoms. Only the three shaded interpretations are models. This partially-ordered set
of interpretations forms a complete lattice, as is *always* the case when ⊆ is
imposed upon a powerset; and the models themselves are also ordered by ⊆ into a
complete lattice, as we have noted previously. As usual, reflexive and transitive
arcs have been omitted from the figure.

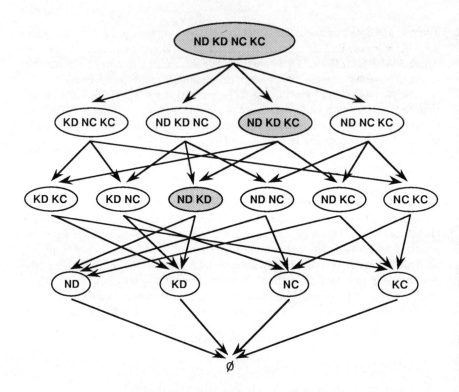

Figure 45.1. A complete lattice of interpretations.

Our construction method traces out a trajectory through the lattice which we
would like to converge upon the minimal model. In general, when we begin with
an interpretation which is a *not* a model then the trajectory does not necessarily
converge upon **MM(P)**, although it may do so in some cases; in fact it is not
bound, in general, either to converge, or to follow a path through the lattice or
even to encounter any models at all.

By contrast, when we either begin or arrive at an interpretation that *is* a
model, the trajectory thereafter follows some path *exclusively within the model
sub-lattice* and must converge upon some model, though not necessarily upon
MM(P).

In the situations just described, the precondition for failing to converge upon **MM(P)** is that **G(P)** shall define some ground atom **q** in terms of itself. As a simple example, consider the case where **G(P)** is{(q if r), (r if q)}. If we begin with {q} then the iteration never converges but merely alternates indefinitely between {q} and {r}, neither of which are models. If we begin with {q, r} instead then we immediately have a fixpoint which—despite being a model—is not **MM(P)**.

Finally, in the absence of any information about **MM(P)**, it is often—though not always—most economical to begin with the empty interpretation ∅; irrespective of whether this is a model or not, it has the special virtue that the subsequent trajectory will *always* converge upon **MM(P)**.

Exercises 45

1. For each of these initial guesses

   (i) $I_1 = B(P)$
   (ii) $I_1 = \{$likes(bob, bob}, likes(logic, logic)$\}$
   (iii) $I_1 = \emptyset$

   use the iterative method to determine the minimal model of this program **P**

   > likes(chris, X) if likes(X, logic)
   > likes(bob, logic)

   Assume that **H** is {chris, bob, logic}.

2. Determine the minimal model for each of the programs below. In each case assume that the domain **H** is {0, s(0), s(s(0)) ...} and begin the construction with $I_1 = \emptyset$.

   (i)   even(s(s(X))) if even(X)

   (ii)   even(0)
           even(s(s(X))) if odd(s(X))

   (iii)   even(0)
           even(s(s(X))) if odd(s(X))
           odd(s(0))

   (iv)   even(0)
           even(s(s(X))) if even(X)

3. Repeat the above exercise but in each case begin with $I_1=B(P)$.

4. Application of the method to some ground definite program P containing just one clause C yields $I_1=\{p(a)\}=I_k$ for all $k>1$. There are infinitely many possible choices of C which would yield this outcome. What are they?

Use your answer to demonstrate that, in general, if the method begins with a non-minimal model and converges then the model which it converges upon is not necessarily the minimal model.

5. Determine the simplest possible ground definite program for which application of the method yields

$$I_1=\{p(a)\}$$
$$I_2=\{p(b)\}$$
$$I_3=\{p(b), p(c)\}=I_k \text{ for all } k>3.$$

Theme 46

Fixpoint interpretation of the minimal model

The process by which the method in Theme 45 generates each interpretation I_{k+1} from its predecessor I_k can be cast as the application of a function T_P:

$$T_P(I_k) = I_{k+1}$$

This function, which is a total mapping from the powerset of $B(P)$ to itself, is specific to the given program P (hence the subscript P in its name) and is defined as follows:

$$T_P(I) = \{q \mid (q \text{ if } \textbf{body}) \in G(P) \text{ } and \text{ } \textbf{body} \text{ is } \textbf{true} \text{ in } I\}$$

Clearly this definition just formalizes our earlier informal account of how one interpretation is obtained from another.

Given any function f defined on a partially-ordered set $[S, \leqslant]$, it is of primary interest to know whether or not that function is monotonic and/or continuous. It is **monotonic** if and only if

$$\text{for all } u \in S \text{ and } v \in S, f(u) \leqslant f(v) \text{ whenever } u \leqslant v$$

and it is **continuous** if and only if

$$\text{for all directed subsets } \textbf{s} \text{ of } S, f(\text{lub } \textbf{s}) = \text{lub}\{f(u) \mid u \in \textbf{s}\}$$

where 'lub' stands for 'the least upper bound of' and $\textbf{s}$ is **directed** if and only if

$$\text{for all } u \in \textbf{s} \text{ and } v \in \textbf{s}, \text{ there exists } w \in \textbf{s} \text{ such that } u \leqslant w \text{ and } v \leqslant w$$

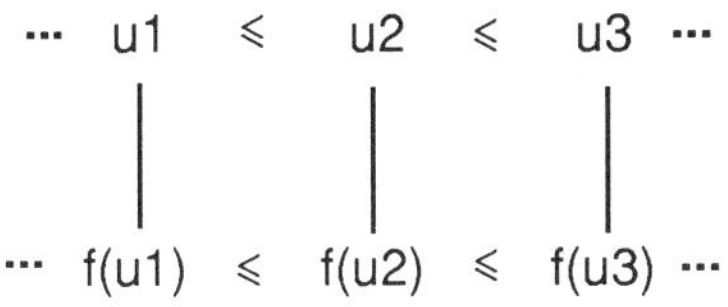

$$\cdots \quad u1 \quad \leqslant \quad u2 \quad \leqslant \quad u3 \quad \cdots$$

$$\cdots \quad f(u1) \quad \leqslant \quad f(u2) \quad \leqslant \quad f(u3) \quad \cdots$$

Figure 46.1. Structure-preservation under monotonicity.

Monotonicity can be regarded as a structure-preserving property as indicated in Figure 46.1: the structure of a partially-ordered set is preserved in the set obtained by applying a given monotonic function to its members.

By contrast, continuity can be viewed as a limit-preserving property as shown in Figure 46.2: if a directed subset **s** has a least upper bound lub **s**, then the set obtained by applying a continuous function **f** to the members of **s** has **f**(lub **s**) as its least upper bound.

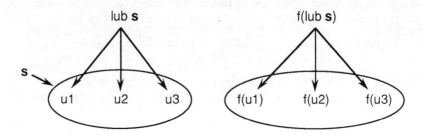

Figure 46.2. Limit-preservation under continuity.

The T_P function is continuous and, like any such function on a complete lattice, is then necessarily monotonic.

The significance of these properties lies in the guarantees they afford regarding the existence of fixpoints; for a function **f** on [**S**, ⩽], an element u∈**S** is a **fixpoint** of **f** if and only if

$$f(u) = u$$

It is useful also to have the notion of a pre-fixpoint; for a function **f** on [**S**, ⩽], an element u∈**S** is a **pre-fixpoint** of **f** if and only if

$$f(u) \leqslant u$$

We can now state—or rather paraphrase—two very important theorems, adapted here for the case of complete lattices.

Knaster-Tarski Theorem

> Every monotonic function **f** on a complete lattice [**S**, ⩽] has a least fixpoint in **S** which is also the least pre-fixpoint in **S**.

This theorem tells us about the existence of a least fixpoint but does not offer any clue as to how to construct it. The next theorem provides a constructive definition of the least fixpoint.

Kleene's First Recursion Theorem

Let N denote the set of natural numbers $\{0, 1, 2, ...\}$ and let ω denote its cardinality (that is, the first limit ordinal). Then every continuous function f on a complete lattice $[S, \leqslant]$ whose bottom (least) element is $\bot$ has a least fixpoint in S which is

$$f \uparrow \omega = \text{lub}\{f^k(\bot) \mid k \in N\}$$

Moreover, when $\leqslant$ is the partial order $\subseteq$ with bottom element $\emptyset$ we then have

$$f \uparrow \omega = \text{lub}\{f^k(\emptyset) \mid k \in N\} = \bigcup_{k \in N} f^k(\emptyset)$$

The expression $f \uparrow \omega$ (pronounced "f up omega") assumes particular importance when f is the function T_P on the lattice of interpretations for a definite program P—it turns out to be exactly the minimal model of P.

Our earlier method for constructing $MM(P)$ is directly reflected in the second theorem: we just construct, incrementally, the set $\{\emptyset, T_P^1(\emptyset), T_P^2(\emptyset), ...\}$ and seek its least upper bound, which is $MM(P)$. In the case where $MM(P)$ is finite we shall generate a least $k \in N$ for which $T_P^k(\emptyset) = T_P^{k+1}(\emptyset) = MM(P)$. In the case where $MM(P)$ is infinite there may or may not be such a least $k \in N$, depending upon the nature of P; whichever is the case, however, the least upper bound will exist even if it cannot be fully constructed in a finite number of steps.

The fact that $MM(P)$ *is* the least fixpoint of T_P can be proved as follows. The definition of T_P requires that

for all $I \subseteq B(P)$ and for all q,
$\quad q \in T_P(I)$ iff $(\exists \text{body})[(q \text{ if body}) \in G(P)$ and **body** is **true** in $I]$

whilst the definition of a model requires that

for all $I \subseteq B(P)$,
I is a model for $G(P)$ iff for all q,
$\quad q \in I$ if $(\exists \text{body})[(q \text{ if body}) \in G(P)$ and **body** is **true** in $I]$

These two sentences jointly imply

for all $I \subseteq B(P)$,
I is a model for $G(P)$ iff for all q, $q \in I$ if $q \in T_P(I)$
$\qquad\qquad\qquad\qquad$ iff $T_P(I) \subseteq I$
$\qquad\qquad\qquad\qquad$ iff I is a pre-fixpoint of T_P

Hence, since the models are exactly the pre-fixpoints, the least model **MM(P)** must be the least pre-fixpoint. Finally, by the Knaster-Tarski theorem, **MM(P)** must also be the least fixpoint.

So we now have several equivalent characterizations of the minimal model, including the new one posed in terms of the least fixpoint of T_P, denoted **LFP(T_P)**:

$$\mathbf{MM(P)} = \mathbf{SS(P)} = \mathbf{LFP(T_P)} = T_P{\uparrow}\omega$$

The next Theme considers their association with various kinds of semantics.

Exercises 46

1. For each program below, generate $T_P{}^k(\emptyset)$ for $k = 0, 1, \ldots$ etc. until you either reach or can infer the fixpoint, and hence identify the minimal model. **Note**—in each case assume that **H**={0, s(0), s(s(0)), ...}.

   (i)   p(s(X)) if p(X)

   (ii)   p(0)
            p(s(X)) if p(X)

   (ii)   p(X)
            p(s(X)) if p(X)

2. Take the same approach in order to identify the minimal model of the following program, assuming that **H**={a, b, c}:

   permute(X, Y, Z) if X<Y & Y<Z
   permute(X, Y, Z) if Y<X & permute(Y, X, Z)
   permute(X, Y, Z) if Z<Y & permute(X, Z, Y)
   a<b
   b<c
   a<c

3. Prove that if T_P is continuous then it must also be monotonic.

   Hint—use the fact that T_P is continuous over *any* complete lattice.

4. Using the fact that **I** is a model if and only if $T_P(I){\subseteq}I$, prove that if **I** is a model then so is $T_P(I)$

   (i)   by assuming that T_P is monotonic;
   (ii)   by exploiting the definition of T_P.

Denotational semantics for definite programs

The general aim of a **denotational semantics** in the logic programming context is to attribute to each *predicate symbol* **p** in a program **P** some well-defined *relation* **r**. The chosen relation then represents the *meaning* of **p** in **P**—it is what **p** is considered to *denote* in this program.

Ideally we want to define **r** for **p** in the least redundant way, that is, to define the *minimal* **r** sufficient for the task. Moreover, we prefer this smallest **r** to be *uniquely* minimal, so that the meaning given to **p** shall be unambiguous. For the case where **P** is definite these requirements are met by the minimal model **MM(P)** which, for all n, attributes to the n-ary predicate symbols in **P** the *smallest* respective n-ary relations in H^n which jointly determine a model. Every other model would redundantly enlarge the relations' extensions, thereby rendering them 'more defined' than necessary.

The different ways we have seen of characterizing the minimal model correspond to different semantic notions.

A **consequence-based semantics** expresses the denotation of any **p** in **P** in terms of *logical consequence* as the relation

$$\{t \mid P \vDash p(t)\}$$

An **operational semantics** presupposes some abstract computational mechanism from whose *behaviour* we can determine which denotation is given to the various predicate symbols. When we choose SLD-resolution as that computational mechanism the denotation of any **p** in **P** is expressed in terms of *derivability* as the relation

$$\{t \mid P \cup \{?p(t)\} \vdash_{SLD} \square\} = \{t \mid p(t) \in SS(P)\}$$

A **fixpoint semantics** expresses the denotation of any **p** in **P** as the least-defined relation which is closed under application of a continuous function T_P, namely

$$\{t \mid p(t) \in LFP(T_P)\} = \{t \mid p(t) \in T_P \uparrow \omega\}$$

For each kind of semantics considered above, the denotation of any **p** in **P** turns out to be simply $\{t \mid p(t) \in MM(P)\}$. Thus the minimal model plays a pivotal role in the semantic properties of any definite program. An indefinite program, by contrast, may have multiple minimal models. Depending upon how that program is executed, it may not be obvious which of these (or other) models is an appropriate basis on which to define the program's semantics.

Exercises 47

1. Another way of computing answers from definite programs is to employ just the **hyper-resolution** inference rule $\vdash_{HYP}$:

   from any clause-set q if b_1 & b_2 & ... & b_m
                          B_1
                          B_2
                            :
                          B_m

   such that θ exists satisfying $b_i\theta = B_i\theta$ for i = 1, 2, ... m, infer the **hyper-resolvent** $q\theta$.

   The set of (ground) answers computed from this inference step is $G(q\theta)$.

   (i)   Recalling the affirmation-completeness results of resolution (see Theme 39), show that the operational semantics of both this new mechanism and the SLD mechanism determine identical denotations for a program's predicate symbols.

   (ii)   Relate the new mechanism to the standard fixpoint semantics.

Theme 48

Partial evaluation of programs

In general, a program caters for a multitude of cases; we know that the execution of a most-general query to a relation will extract from the program all the possible cases covered by that relation. Sometimes, however, we are interested only in particular queries—or in particular classes of query—which make more specialized uses of the program. Under this assumption it is generally more efficient *to specialize the program itself* before executing the queries, so that it will not waste time considering cases that can no longer arise. The standard technique for specializing a program in this way is **partial evaluation**.

As an example, consider this simple program for testing whether a list L is (strictly) ordered:

> ord(L) if L=nil
> ord(L) if L=U•nil
> ord(L) if L=U•V•W & U<V & ord(V•W)

This program is sufficiently general to deal correctly with *all* queries to the 'ord' relation. Now suppose that we were interested only in testing the orderedness of lists having just two members. A simple way of specializing the program for this purpose is to *evaluate* a query which characterizes just the class of interest, namely

> ? ord(X•Y•nil)

Moreover, we are under no obligation to make this evaluation *total*. That is, rather than attempting to *solve* the query, we may instead seek only to *reduce* it to a certain extent, in which case our evaluation is only *partial*. In effect, we arbitrarily truncate certain derivations at convenient points. From each of these truncated derivations we then recover a new program clause. The totality of these new clauses will constitute a new, specialized program dealing with just the queries of interest.

Figure 48.1 shows one possible partial evaluation for our example. Observe that all the derivations except for one have been reduced sufficiently far to reach (unsuccessful) termination. The remaining one has been truncated (shown marked by the triple line).

In order to recover a new program from such a tree we first identify each derivation which has either terminated successfully or been truncated. Suppose that, for any such derivation, the composition of its output substitutions is θ and that the residual calls, if any, at its leaf node are denoted by **calls**. The root node of the derivation will be some initial query ?**q**. Then the clause recovered from this derivation is

$$\forall((\mathbf{q} \ \ \text{if} \ \ \mathbf{calls})\theta\,)$$

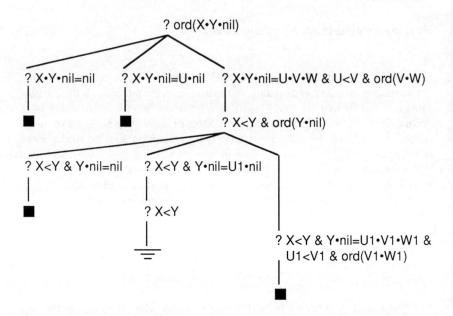

Figure 48.1. Partial evaluation of a query to 'ord'.

The new program is the set of all such clauses, which in our example will comprise just the single clause

$$\text{ord}(X \cdot Y \cdot \text{nil}) \ \ \text{if} \ \ X < Y$$

There is no great surprise to be had in this particular outcome, which might otherwise have been recovered by no more than an intuitive inspection of the original program. In general, however, the recovery of a specialized program may be much too difficult and error-prone to be left to mere intuition. In particular, recursive derivations may have to be pursued through many steps in order either to fail them, or to succeed them or to truncate them at some appropriate level. Moreover, there are many options open to choice, since we have taken a liberal attitude to the matters of call-selection and the depth of the search; different choices correspond to alternative specialized programs, not all of which can be discovered without proper exploration.

Finally, note that the specialized program *is* more efficient for the queries of interest, since queries posing lists of length other than 2 fail immediately, whilst those of length equal to 2 are processed without requiring any recursive steps.

Partial evaluation is the foundation of most technologies employed for analysing and transforming programs (in various formalisms) and has been implemented in a wide range of tools supporting logic program development. Usually it can be implemented simply by modifying the control strategies of standard program interpreters.

Exercises 48

1. Use partial evaluation to obtain a specialized append program for queries of the form ? append(U•nil, Y, Z) starting with the program

> append(nil, Z, Z)
> append(U•X, Y, U•Z) if append(X, Y, Z)

2. Use partial evaluation to obtain a specialized append program for queries of the form ? append(X, Y, X) starting with the same program as above. Construct an argument to show that your result could be specialized further to just the clause

> append(X, nil, X)

provided that X is a list.

3. Given the program

> num(0)
> num(s(U)) if num(U)
> twice(0, 0)
> twice(s(U), s(s(Z))) if twice(U, Z)
> even(Y) if num(X) & twice(X, Y)

use partial evaluation to derive the clause

> even(s(s(Z))) if num(U) & twice(U, Z)

Theme 49

Unfolding programs

We now introduce a very useful form of partial evaluation called **unfolding**, which is one of the key techniques employed for performing program transformation. This technique operates wholly upon the program clauses without regard to any particular query, and its effect is indicated by Figure 49.1.

program before unfolding   program after unfolding

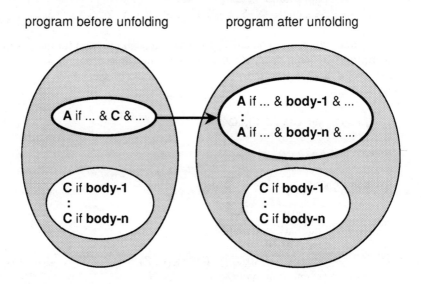

Figure 49.1. The unfolding operation.

To perform an **elementary unfolding operation** (henceforth an 'EUO') we first select some clause in the program, say

$$A \text{ if } ... \& C \& ...$$

and then select one of this clause's calls, say **C**. Next we select one of the program's clauses for **C**, say

$$C \text{ if } \textbf{body-i}$$

The operation infers from these two clauses their resolvent

$$A \text{ if } ... \& \textbf{body-}i \& ...$$

This propositional description generalizes to the predicate-logic context by simply requiring that the relevant m.g.u. be applied, in the usual way, to the resolvent.

Two points should be noted straightaway: the operation is *sound*—since it is only doing resolution—and is in effect a *partial evaluation* of the first clause's sub-query ?C, the various results of which become encoded as various alternative expansions of that clause.

To perform a **complete one-step unfolding** of the first clause upon its call **C** we just perform an **EUO** using each clause for **C** and thus obtain a corresponding set **A*** of new clauses for **A**.

To perform a **complete two-step unfolding** of that same first clause we take each of **A***'s clauses in turn and perform a complete one-step unfolding on any one of *its* calls. The generalization of this idea to a **complete m-step unfolding** of the original clause should be obvious. The result at each stage is always some set of new clauses for **A** which just represents a particular expansion of the original clause using the resources of the program as a whole.

The correctness properties for unfolding are straightforward. Let **CL** denote any clause in our program **P** and let **U(CL)** denote the set of new clauses obtained by performing any complete one-step unfolding of **CL**. Then unfolding is *sound* in that we always have

$$\textbf{P} \vDash \textbf{U(CL)}$$

A slightly less obvious point is indicated in our figure above—**U(CL)** can *replace* **CL** in the program without altering the program's ground atomic consequences. This is a kind of *computational equivalence* property for unfolding which may be summarized as follows:

$$\text{for all } \textbf{q} \in \textbf{B(P)}, \quad \textbf{P} \cup \textbf{U(CL)} - \{\textbf{CL}\} \vDash \textbf{q} \quad \text{iff} \quad \textbf{P} \vDash \textbf{q}$$

The replacement of **CL** by **U(CL)** is not part of the unfolding process, but is a natural concomitant of it—clearly, no computational advantage flows from merely *adding* to the existing clauses any new clauses which they imply—in fact, that would inevitably *degrade* the program's performance (why?). However, significant computational advantage may flow from the act of replacement, as we shall see presently.

It is now certainly time to present an example. Here is a program **P** which, given a query of the form ? cp(**el**, **e2**, **list**), decides whether **list** is a list containing the consecutive pair <**el**, **e2**>:

$$P1 : cp(U, V, U \bullet V \bullet X)$$
$$P2 : cp(U, V, W \bullet Y) \text{ if } cp(U, V, Y)$$

The complete one-step unfolding of the call in clause P2 yields the following clause-set **U**(P2):

C1 : cp(U, V, W•U•V•X)
C2 : cp(U, V, W1•W2•Y) if cp(U, V, Y)

C1 is obtained by invoking P1 in response to the selected call, and C2 by invoking P2. These new clauses can then *replace* P2 to give a new program such that

for all tuples **t**, {P1, C1, C2} ⊨ cp(**t**) iff {P1, P2} ⊨ cp(**t**)

If we wished, we could now perform a further unfolding operation pivoted on the call in C2. However, there is no need to do this in order to demonstrate here the computational significance of unfolding. This is because, in general, *any* individual step of unfolding and replacement potentially improves execution efficiency.

Figure 49.2 demonstrates this improvement by comparing the SLD-tree for the query ? cp(3, 4, 1•2•3•4•5•nil) using the original program **P** with that using the new program {P1, C1, C2}.

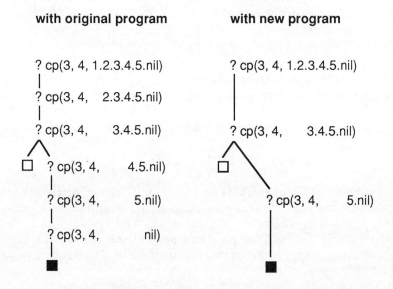

Figure 49.2. The computational effect of unfolding.

The efficiency gain lies in the fact that certain computation steps in the first tree are absent from the second one. Loosely speaking, unfolding can be regarded as operation which, prior to execution, probes some way ahead through the program in order to seek *and compound together* viable computation steps. These compounded steps become encoded in the term-structure of the new program, from whence they function as *single* steps during execution; the original program, however, has to explore all those steps individually. Thus, whereas the derived query ? cp(3, 4, 5•nil) using program **P** invokes clause P2 and thereby extends the computation one stage further, the same derived query fails immediately from the new program since it can invoke no clause.

It is important to be quite clear about the way unfolding and replacement influences execution efficiency—its effect is to reduce the lengths of one or more computations. Surprisingly, however, this does not necessarily result in an overall improvement in efficiency. To see why, consider the two programs shown below: the program on the right is obtained by unfolding the first clause of the program on the left (on the C call):

original program	after unfolding
A if B & C	A if B & D
	A if B & E
C if D	C if D
C if E	C if E
D	D
E	E

Given the query ?A, the original program evaluates B just once, but the new program evaluates it twice. In general, it is possible that the extra evaluation of B will far outweigh the benefit of reducing the lengths of the computations. The problem here is that the ,tandard interpreter is not intelligent enough to solve the second evaluation of B directly by saving and reusing the solutions from the first evaluation. In fact it is an irony that a typical compiler-optimizer presented with the new program would convert it to the original program in order to eliminate the efficiency of evaluating B twice!

Thus, in summary, the most we can say is that unfolding reduces computation length: but whether this in turn leads to an overall gain in performance depends very much upon the intelligence of the interpreter. Moreover, even in the cases where we do gain some overall speed advantage, the new program is bound to be *textually longer*, thereby increasing the run-time memory requirement.

Whatever its effect upon performance may be, we shall see later on (in Theme 53) that the purpose of unfolding (and of partial evaluation in general) is not necessarily to secure improved efficiency by *executing* the unfolded program: more often the aim is to derive a preliminary clause-set upon which to perform *further transformation* through the application of other, more sophisticated techniques. But in order to explain the logical justification of these techniques we shall first have to deal with the distinction between open and closed theories, as discussed in the next three Themes.

Exercises 49

1. (i)   Starting with the program

                 even(0)
                 odd(s(0))
                 even(s(X)) if odd(X)
                 odd(s(X)) if even(X)

       use unfolding to show that this is computationally equivalent to the
       program

                 even(0)
                 even(s(s(0)))
                 even(s(s(X))) if even(X)
                 odd(s(0))
                 odd(s(s(X))) if odd(X)

   (ii)   By partially evaluating the query ? even(X) show that the second
           clause of this new program is redundant.

2. (i)   Unfold 'one-and-zero' through two steps using the program

                 one-and-zero(X) if ones(X) & zeros(X)
                 ones(nil)
                 ones(1•V•Y) if ones(Y)
                 zeros(nil)
                 zeros(U•0•Y) if zeros(Y)

   (ii)   Hence construct an argument to show that, for querying the predicate
           'one-and-zero', this program is computationally equivalent to the
           program

                 one-and-zero(nil)
                 one-and-zero(1•0•Y) if one-and-zero(Y)

3. Figure 49.2 in the Theme shows how the SLD tree becomes simplified after a
   complete *one*-step unfolding. What would the tree look like after a complete
   two-step unfolding?

Theme 50

The closed-world assumption

Given any sentence-set **P**, the **closed-world assumption** is the assumption that **P** determines all the knowledge there is to be had about the relations named in our language. Thus, if we consider any proposition **q** about such a relation then **q** is taken to be **true** exactly when **P** implies **q**, but is otherwise taken to be **false**.

Consider an example from daily life. Whenever I walk to my local sweet-shop I assume that I will not be waylaid by a tiger, since if tigers roamed my neighbourhood then I would surely be already aware of it. The proposition that tigers lie in wait for me is not implied by anything I know about my local world and so I take it to be **false**, thereby permitting me to visit the sweet-shop without trepidation. It is not, of course, always appropriate to apply the closed-world assumption. For example, I know that I might well be waylaid on the way to the sweet-shop by my children demanding their pocket money. It would be unreasonable for me to tell them that I had brought no small change with me owing to an assumption that they would never ask me for any. In deciding to take some small change with me I apply the **open-world assumption**, according to which the proposition that my children will be lying in wait for me when I set out to the shop is not necessarily **false**.

The closed-world assumption underlies the mode of reasoning known as **default inference**. There are many situations, both in ordinary daily life and in specific technical computing matters, when default inference is a necessary supplement to deductive inference. We shall meet such situations presently when we come to examine certain methods of program transformation, and we shall also need them later on to explain the theory of finite failure and the relationship which it bears to reasoning with negative information.

In the logic programming context the propositions in which we are primarily interested are the atoms of the Herbrand base. Consider this simple example of a single-clause program **P**

$$A \text{ if } B$$

and suppose also that **B(P)** is just $\{A, B\}$. Under the closed-world assumption we may infer ¬**q** for any ground atom **q**∈**B(P)** that is *not* implied by **P**. This is a constrained application of the general rule of default inference:

$$\text{infer } \neg\mathbf{q} \text{ in default of } \mathbf{P} \text{ implying } \mathbf{q}$$

It is constrained in two respects: first, we assume that **P** is consistent, otherwise **P** would necessarily imply both **q** *and* ¬**q**; secondly, we consider only the case where **q** is atomic—otherwise if **P** implied, say, neither **r** nor ¬**r** then the default rule would infer both ¬**r** *and* ¬¬**r**, which would again be inconsistent.

Returning to our example, since **P** is definite it must be consistent, and since it implies neither A nor B we may infer, by the closed-world assumption, both ¬A and ¬B. More generally, the combination of **P** with the default conclusions inferred from it is denoted by **CWA(P)** and is defined by

$$\mathbf{CWA(P)} = \mathbf{P} \cup \{\neg q \mid q \in \mathbf{B(P)} \text{ and } \textit{not } \mathbf{P} \vDash q\}$$

So for our example we shall have

$$\mathbf{CWA(P)} = \{A \text{ if } B, \neg A, \neg B\}$$

Figure 50.1 indicates how, in general, **CWA(P)** is constituted from the components of **P** and **B(P)**.

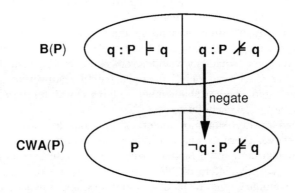

Figure 50.1. Applying the closed-world assumption.

Our main motivation in all this is the desire to draw sound conclusions about *negative* information. Arguably, this is a perfectly natural requirement in many problem-solving contexts. Consider, for example, the desire to create and query a database **P** containing entries for all the children of 'chris' *that we know about*— 'brendon' and 'emlyn'. The most economical way of recording these facts is

child(brendon, chris)
child(emlyn, chris)

Under the open-world assumption there is no basis for concluding that, say, 'amelia' is not also a child of 'chris'—nothing has been said which excludes such a possibility. But under the closed-world assumption the database wholly determines who is a child of whom, and so we would infer ¬child(amelia, chris).

The question now arises as to how we should formalize, *in terms of logical consequence*, the notion of *soundness* for this sort of inference. We have already seen, in Theme 21, how to formalize soundness for the deduction of *positive* conclusions under the open-world assumption:

$$\text{for all } q{\in}B(P), \ P \vDash q \ \text{ if } \ P \vdash_{\text{OWA}} q$$

Here the soundness of ⊢ OWA has been *referred* to (the logical consequences of) the program **P**. To what logical construction should we refer soundness for the default inferral of *negative* conclusions under the closed-world assumption? One potential candidate is **CWA(P)**, so that we might write

$$\text{for all } q{\in}B(P), \ \mathbf{CWA(P)} \vDash \neg q \ \text{ if } \ P \vdash_{\text{CWA}} \neg q$$

This is adequate in some respects but not in others. One practical problem is that, given **P**, we have no immediate way of writing down **CWA(P)**, for we cannot directly discern which particular negative facts ¬q to include in it—we would have to infer them all first. A more serious defect is that, whilst **CWA(P)** is always consistent when **P** is definite, it is likely to be inconsistent otherwise. For example, if **P** comprises just the clause

A or B

then **CWA(P)** = {A or B, ¬A, ¬B} which is inconsistent. Later on we shall be considering default inference applied to indefinite programs: we shall then want to refer the soundness criterion for such inference to some directly-discernible logical construction that can usually be relied upon to be consistent. One such construction is the so-called **completion** of P, also known as the **completed database** of **P**. This is the subject of the next Theme.

Exercises 50

1. Construct **CWA(P)** for each of the following clause-sets **P** and say whether or not it is consistent.

   Note—assume in each case that H={dov, chris}.

   (i)   likes(chris, X) if likes(dov, X)

   (ii)   likes(chris, X) if ¬likes(X, chris)

(iii) likes(dov, X) or likes(X, chris)

(iv) likes(dov, X)
      likes(X, chris)

(v) ¬likes(dov, dov)
     likes(X, dov) if likes(chris, X)
     likes(chris, X)

2. Assume that **H**={chris, dov}. If we then have, for definite **P**,

$$\mathbf{CWA(P)} = \mathbf{P} \cup \{\neg likes(chris, dov), \neg likes(chris, chris)\}$$

identify the simplest possible **P** which consists of

(i)   two clauses;
(ii) one clause.

3. How many **H**-models does **CWA(P)** have when **P** is definite?

4. Show that, for any definite program **P**,

$$\mathbf{CWA(P)=P} \ \ if \ \ \mathbf{MM(P)=B(P)}$$

Theme 51

Program completion in propositional logic

The **completion** of a program **P** is a particular set of sentences which we denote by **Comp(P)**. In some texts you will find it called instead the **completed database** of **P** and denoted there by **CDB(P)**.

Like the construction **CWA(P)**, the completion provides a consequence-oriented meaning for default inference under the closed-world assumption. Unlike **CWA(P)**, however, it can be written down more-or-less directly and is consistent for all well-structured programs. In general it is also a more economical construction in that it implies, *but does not necessarily declare*, various negative propositions which **CWA(P)** would have to declare explicitly. In the case of propositional logic the construction is particularly simple:

1. assume that **P** is any set of clauses of the form (**q** if **body**);

2. for each **q** mentioned in **P** but not defined in **P**, construct ¬**q**;

3. for each **q** having a definition in **P** of the form

$$q \text{ if } \textbf{body-1}$$
$$\vdots$$
$$q \text{ if } \textbf{body-n}$$

construct the sentence **q** iff (**body-1** or ... or **body-n**);

Note—the body of any assertion in **P** is treated as the atom *True*;

4. a sentence obtained by either of the previous two steps is called a **completed definition** for the **q** relation; then **Comp(P)** comprises exactly the completed definitions for all relations mentioned in **P**.

Example—let **P** be the program

$$A \text{ if } B$$

Then **Comp(P)** comprises the sentences

$$¬B$$
$$A \text{ iff } B$$

This program **P** neither implies A nor implies B. Accordingly we find that
Comp(P) implies both ¬A and ¬B, which is exactly the same outcome as we
would obtain using **CWA(P)** instead. Observe, however, that **CWA(P)** declares
¬A explicitly whereas **Comp(P)** does not.

In certain cases there are subtle differences between what the two
constructions imply, as we show next.

Example—let **P** be the program

$$A \text{ if } A$$

Then **CWA(P)** implies ¬A whereas **Comp(P)** does not.

Example—let **P** be the program

$$A \text{ if } \neg B$$

Then **CWA(P)** implies both ¬A and ¬B and is inconsistent, whereas **Comp(P)**
is consistent and implies ¬B but does not imply ¬A.

In both these examples the completion is more conservative than the closed-world
assumption in the negative facts that it implies. In some cases, however, the
completion is less conservative, as shown by the next example.

Example—let **P** be the program

$$A \text{ if } \neg A$$

Then **CWA(P)** is consistent and implies no negative facts, whilst **Comp(P)** is
inconsistent and so implies everything.

We shall be able to make more sense of all these examples when we consider,
later on in Theme 57, the **finite-failure interpretation** of ¬.

In order to clarify the rationale of program completion it is useful to view
Comp(P) as the result of simplifying **P** ∪ **only-if(P)** where **only-if(P)**
comprises both

> (a)   every completed definition of the form ¬**q**, and

> (b)   the sentence (**q** only-if **W**) for every completed definition of
>   the form (**q** iff **W**).

Let us see how this view applies to another example, where we take **P** to be the
program

$$
\begin{array}{ll}
\text{A if B} & \\
\text{B if C} & \\
\text{B if D} & \\
\text{C} & (\equiv \text{C if } \textit{True})
\end{array}
$$

We see that A holds only if B does, and that B holds only if either C does or D does. C always holds, whilst D never does. This is exactly what is expressed in **only-if(P)**:

$$
\begin{array}{ll}
\text{A only-if B} & \\
\text{B only-if (C or D)} & \\
\text{C only-if } \textit{True} & (\equiv \textit{True}) \\
\neg\text{D} &
\end{array}
$$

The completion is

$$
\begin{array}{ll}
\text{A iff B} & \\
\text{B iff (C or D)} & \\
\text{C} & (\equiv \text{C iff } \textit{True}) \\
\neg\text{D} &
\end{array}
$$

in which each completed definition (**q** iff **W**) is clearly the result of

(a) taking the definition of **q** from **P**;
(b) taking (**q** only-if **W**) from **only-if(P)**;
(c) conjoining the above material and simplifying the result.

Arguably, the completed definitions capture the programmer's *intentions* more fully than do the uncompleted definitions in the original program. The argument goes as follows: since the programmer has arranged that, say, A holds only when B does, he must really be assuming (A iff B)—for had he wanted A to hold by any other means then his program would have said so, which it does not. For computational purposes, however, the program alone happens to be sufficient for deducing all the intended answers.

For the example just considered, the positive atomic consequences of **Comp(P)** are A, B and C, whilst its only negated atomic consequence is ¬D. The former consequences arise *solely* from the contribution of **P** to **Comp(P)**, whilst the latter consequence follows *solely* from the contribution of **only-if(P)** to **Comp(P)**. This phenomenon is observed whenever **P** is definite.

In cases where **P** is indefinite the elementary consequences of **Comp(P)** may arise from the *joint* contributions of **P** and **only-if(P)**, as in this example:

$$
\begin{array}{l}
\text{A if } \neg\text{B \& } \neg\text{C} \\
\text{C if B} \\
\text{B if D}
\end{array}
$$

Here, the negated atomic consequences of **Comp(P)** are ¬B, ¬C and ¬D, which all arise solely from **only-if(P)**. The only positive atomic consequence of **Comp(P)** is A, but assumptions from *both* **P** *and* **only-if(P)** are needed in order to infer it.

Observe also that there is a syntactic bias built into the process of program completion. The simplest illustration uses the two programs

$$A \text{ if } \neg B \qquad \text{and} \qquad B \text{ if } \neg A$$

whose respective completions are

$$\{A \text{ iff } \neg B, \neg B\} \quad \text{and} \quad \{B \text{ iff } \neg A, \neg A\}$$

These completions are not logically equivalent despite the fact that the programs are. In fact the two programs are just alternative ways of presenting the same clause (A or B). The difference between their completions deliberately reflects the difference between the procedural intentions suggested by the programs' syntaxes: the first program anticipates queries of the form ?A whilst the second anticipates queries of the form ?B.

The next Theme generalizes all these ideas in order that they shall apply also to predicate-logic programs.

Exercises 51

Note—all questions here assume that **P** is propositional.

1. Construct **Comp(P)** for each of the following programs **P**:

    (i)   A if B
             A if ¬C
             B

    (ii)   A if ¬B & C
             B if C
             C

    (iii) A if A & C
             A if B
             C if ¬B

2. (i)   Demonstrate by an example that for some cases where **P** is indefinite **Comp(P)** has a unique minimal **H**-model.

    (ii) Demonstrate by another example that for some cases where **P** is indefinite **Comp(P)** does *not* have a unique minimal **H**-model.

3. Every program completion **Comp(P)** can be partitioned into two sentence-sets **Comp1(P)** and **Comp2(P)**. **Comp1(P)** comprises only completed definitions of the form

q iff **body**-1 or ... or **body**-n

where for each i there is some clause (**q** if **body**-i) in **P**. **Comp2(P)** comprises only completed definitions having the form (**r** iff *False*) (equivalently, of the form ¬**r**) where **r** is mentioned in **P** but not defined in **P** (that is, **r** appears in no clause heading). Assuming that **P** is definite, prove that **MM(P)** is a model both for **Comp1(P)** and for **Comp2(P)**, and hence for **Comp(P)**. Is it necessarily the *unique* **H**-model of **Comp(P)**?

Theme 52

Program completion in predicate logic

The construction of the completion **Comp(P)** when **P** is a predicate-logic program is slightly more complicated than in the propositional case. Consider first the simplest example in which **P** comprises just a single ground assertion

$$q(a)$$

The completion must express that 'q' holds for 'a' *and for that term only*—that is, $(\forall X)(q(X)$ iff $X=a)$. The 'if' component of the latter sentence is obtained by **generalizing** the given clause for 'q', so that in place of q(a) we write

$$q(X) \text{ if } X=a$$

Then the completed definition merely strengthens the 'if' to 'iff'.

This example illustrates a standard policy which we apply to any clause of **P** whose heading is not already most-general—we *make* that heading most-general and then add suitable compensating '=' calls to the clause body. For instance,

$$q(X, X, a, f(U)) \text{ if } \textbf{calls}$$

would first be transformed to

$$q(X, Y, Z, W) \text{ if } Y=X \text{ \& } Z=a \text{ \& } W=f(U) \text{ \& } \textbf{calls}$$

After performing all necessary generalizations upon the clauses of **P** we construct **Comp(P)** exactly as we did for the propositional case, apart from two special provisions:

(a)   in each generalized clause we must first quantify existentially every variable which is *local* to the clause's body;

(b)   we must express, as an integral part of the completion, exactly what we mean by '='.

In order to see why provision (a) is necessary, consider the following generalized clause in which Y is local to the body:

$$parent(X) \text{ if } child(Y, X)$$

This says that, for all X and Y, X is a parent if Y is a child of X. If we naively took the only-if component to be

$$\text{parent}(X) \ \text{only-if} \ \text{child}(Y, X)$$

then this would be contrary to our intentions, for it is equivalent to the following clause

$$\text{child}(Y, X) \ \text{if} \ \text{parent}(X)$$

which says that, for all X and Y, Y is a child of X if X is a parent. Certainly, no-one is the parent of *everyone*! The original clause, however, can be written equivalently as

$$\text{parent}(X) \ \text{if} \ (\exists Y)\text{child}(Y, X)$$

When constructing **Comp(P)** it is our obligation first to insert, after the 'if', an explicit existential quantifier for each such local variable. Only after this do we construct the only-if component

$$\text{parent}(X) \ \text{only-if} \ (\exists Y)\text{child}(Y, X)$$

and hence the completed definition

$$\text{parent}(X) \ \text{iff} \ (\exists Y)\text{child}(Y, X)$$

Example—in which the relation 'perfect' appears in **B(P)** but not in the heading of any clause:

    from   kind(X) if helps(X, Y)
                    helps(dov, Z)

    construct   kind(X) iff ($\exists$Y)helps(X, Y)
                    helps(X, Z) iff X=dov
                    ¬perfect(X)

Informally, kind persons are exactly those who help someone, the only person who helps everyone is dov and no-one is perfect.

Continuing with this example, suppose that **H**={dov, chris}. Then we shall expect to obtain such negative consequences as

               ¬perfect(dov)
               ¬perfect(chris)
    and   ¬kind(chris) among others.

However, we shall not obtain all such consequences unless we add a correct definition of the '=' relation. What should this be? Let us return for a moment to the first example using the clause q(a) and consider any query of the form ?q(t). Then this succeeds if and only if **t** unifies with 'a'. Now consider the generalized version of the query, namely

$$?q(V) \ \& \ V=t$$

and the generalized version of the clause, namely

$$q(V) \ \text{if} \ V=a$$

From these we can derive, without performing unification, the query ?V=t & V=a which amounts to solving ?t=a. This suggests that whatever definition we provide for '=' it should be such as to imply, for any terms **t1** and **t2**, that **t1**=**t2** if and only if **t1** and **t2** unify. Suppose we had a finite domain **H**={a, b}. Then a sufficient definition of '=' would be this finite set of clauses:

¬a=b	X=X
¬b=a	X=Y if Y=X
q(X) if q(Y) & X=Y	X=Z if X=Y & Y=Z

In many cases, however, **H** is infinite and hence so also would be the corresponding definition of '=' if presented in this itemized ('extensional') style. We prefer to have a finite definition. Thus the following intensional and finite definition of '=', essentially in clausal form, is the one customarily used:

¬t1=t2	for each pair <t1, t2> of distinct constants	(1)
¬f1(X1, ..., Xm)=f2(Y1, ..., Yn)	for each pair <f1, f2> of distinct function symbols	(2)
¬f(X1, ..., Xm)=t	for each function symbol **f** and each constant **t**	(3)
for all i from 1 to m, ¬f(X1, ..., Xm)=f(Y1, ..., Ym) if ¬Xi=Yi	for each function symbol **f**	(4)
¬f(... X ...)=X	for each functional term f(... X ...) containing X	(5)
X=X		(6)
X=Y if Y=X		(7)
X=Z if X=Y & Y=Z		(8)
f(X1, ..., Xm)=f(Y1, ..., Ym) if X1=Y1 & ... & Xm=Ym	for each function symbol **f**	(9)
p(X1, ..., Xm) if p(Y1, ..., Ym) & X1=Y1 & ... & Xm=Ym	for each predicate symbol **p**	(10)

You should be able to recognize that these sentences characterize the rationale of the unification algorithm (if necessary, refer back to Theme 33). For instance, sentences **1-3** deal with non-unifiability due to mismatches between constants and function symbols; sentence **4** corresponds to non-unifiability of terms due to some pair of their corresponding components being non-unifiable; sentence **5** corresponds to non-unifiability due to occur-check failure; and sentences **6-10** are the standard axioms of equality, these corresponding to the conditions under which terms *are* unifiable. The sentences as stated above are slightly redundant, in that **7** and **8** can be dropped if **10** includes the case where **p** itself is '='.

Sentences **1-10** establish an **equality theory** over a given Herbrand domain **H** and clause-set **S**. Accordingly we shall denote it by **Eq(H, S)**. The completion of a program **P** in predicate logic is then defined as the union of its completed definitions and its associated equality theory **Eq(H, P)**. As in the propositional case we can decompose the completion to make its **only-if** component explicit:

$$\textbf{Comp(P)} \equiv \textbf{P} \cup \textbf{only-if(P)} \cup \textbf{Eq(H, P)}$$

As intended, this construction implies negative atomic consequences besides positive ones. When **P** is definite, **P** and **only-if(P)** separately determine, respectively, the positive and negative atomic consequences—see Figure 52.1.

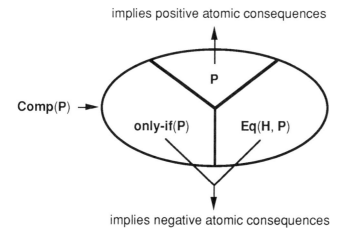

Figure 52.1. Origins of **Comp(P)**'s consequences for definite **P**.

Perhaps more importantly, the completion also implies *new programs* which cannot be derived (e.g. by unfolding) from **P** alone. So we shall have cause to invoke the completion in several later Themes variously dealing with negation and program transformation.

A little more needs to be said about the connection between unification and equality. This connection was hinted at earlier on by rewriting clauses so as to generalize their predicate arguments by the introduction of '=' calls. It is useful to establish the logical status of such rewritings. Suppose our clause-set **P** contains some clause

C : heading if **body**

Note that this covers the case where **C** is a query, in which case the **heading** is simply *False*. Let $\eta[t]$ denote any occurrence of any term **t** in **C** and let **V** be a variable not already occurring in **C**. Then the **generalization** of **C** with respect to $\eta[t]$ is defined to be the new clause obtained by replacing $\eta[t]$ by **V** and adding the call **V=t** to the **body**. We denote this new clause by **Gen(C, $\eta[t]$)**. Here are a couple of examples, in which the selected occurrence $\eta[t]$ is marked in bold face:

C :	p(a, **f(X)**, Y) if q(X, Y, g(Y))
Gen(C, $\eta[f(X)]$) :	p(a, V, Y) if q(X, Y, g(Y)) & V=f(X)

C :	? p(a, f(X), Y) & q(X, **Y**, g(**Y**))
Gen(C, $\eta[Y]$) :	? p(a, f(X), Y) & q(X, Y, g(V)) & V=Y

The logical status of any such generalization is then as follows:

for all **q∈B(P)** and **C∈P**,
$$P \vDash q \quad \text{iff} \quad P \cup \text{Gen}(C, \eta[t]) \cup Eq(H, P) - \{C\} \vDash q$$

This establishes that, provided we add the equality theory, any generalization of any clause preserves the atomic consequences of **P**. So suppose that we can resolve two clauses of **P** upon particular literals, making full use of unification. We can reformulate this inference step by first generalizing the clauses so as to make the atomic parts of those literals both identical and most-general, then performing resolution without unification and finally using **Eq(H, P)** to eliminate all the newly-introduced '=' calls. According to the property stated above, this reformulation is bound to preserve the atomic consequences. Thus unification and reasoning with equality are logically interchangeable.

Exercises 52

1. Rewrite the following clauses to make their headings most general:

(i)   is(love_of_money, source_of(X)) if evil(X)
(ii)   relies_upon(X, X) if self_sufficient(X)
(iii)   append(U•X, Y, U•Z) if append(X, Y, Z)

2. Construct the completions of the following clause-sets (omit their equality theories):

    (i)   num(0)
            num(s(X)) if num(X)

    (ii)   dup(U•X) if U∈X
            dup(V•X) if dup(X)

    (iii)   knows(frank, Y) if computer(X) & aspect_of(X, Y)
            knows(chris, Y) if tells(frank, Y, chris)

3. Show that the process of resolving the clauses

$$r(X) \text{ if } p(a, f(X))$$
$$p(Y, f(b)) \text{ if } q(Y)$$

using unification can be reformulated as a process of reasoning with the equality theory without using unification.

Hint—first make the clauses' 'p' literals most general.

Theme 53

Folding programs

Folding is a program transformation technique which is essentially the inverse of unfolding. The effect of any single folding step is to derive one new clause from some existing clause; the new clause can then replace the old one to yield a new program. Figure 53.1 gives an indication of what is involved.

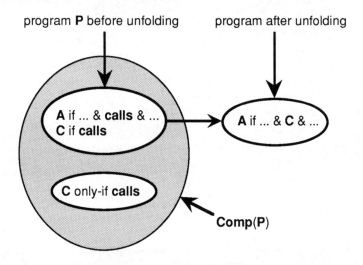

Figure 53.1. The folding operation.

Taking the propositional case first, the preconditions for performing a **folding operation** are as follows. We select any two clauses in **P** of the form

$$\text{CL}: \quad \text{A if ... & calls & ...}$$
$$\text{C if calls}$$

the second of which must be the *only* clause for **C** in **P**—equivalently, the sentence (**C** only-if **calls**) must be implied by **Comp(P)**. Then we derive a new clause **F(CL)** called the 'folding' of **CL**:

$$\text{F(CL)}: \quad \text{A if ... & C & ...}$$

The derived clause $F(CL)$ is not a logical consequence of **P** but is nevertheless a logical consequence of **Comp(P)**. The operation's rationale is that, since **calls** is the *only* condition upon which **C** holds (by the closed-world assumption), solving **calls** is equivalent to solving **C**.

Observe that the step can also be viewed as the composition of one or more elementary *unfolding* operations performed using **Comp(P)** as the assumption set. For suppose that **calls** has the form

$$B_1 \ \& \ ... \ \& \ B_n$$

where each B_i is atomic. Then **Comp(P)**'s sentence (**C** only-if **calls**) is equivalent to the clause-set

$$B_1 \ \text{if} \ C$$
$$\vdots$$
$$B_n \ \text{if} \ C$$

If we now use these to unfold the original clause

$$CL : \quad A \ \text{if} \ ... \ \& \ B_1 \ \& \ ... \ \& \ B_n \ \& \ ...$$

by doing an **EUO** upon each of its B_i calls, the result is

$$A \ \text{if} \ ... \ \& \ C \ \& \ ... \ \& \ C \ \& \ ...$$

which, after factoring (merging the identical **C** calls), is our new clause

$$F(CL) : \quad A \ \text{if} \ ... \ \& \ C \ \& \ ...$$

Thus, since we know that unfolding is always sound relative to the assumption-set—in this case **Comp(P)**—so also is folding.

Observe also that if we take $F(CL)$ and perform a complete one-step unfolding upon its **C** call then the result is our original clause **CL**—in fact, this property is generally given as the *criterion* for a correct fold-and-replace operation: the replacement of **CL** by $F(CL)$ is then guaranteed to preserve all the computable answers—that is, the new program has the same minimal model as the original one. This invertibility property provides an important safeguard when we have to deal with predicate-logic clauses whose bodies may contain local variables, as we show next.

Suppose our program **P** is the following:

$$A(Y) \ \text{if} \ B(X, X, Y)$$
$$C \ \text{if} \ B(U, 2, 3)$$
$$B(1, 2, 3)$$

Note that the first two clauses both contain local variables. It is tempting, but incorrect, to fold upon the first clause's B call subject to first applying the m.g.u. $\theta = \{X/2, U/2, Y/3\}$ which unifies that call with the B call of the second clause; for then we would obtain the clause instances

$$A(3) \ \text{if} \ B(2, 2, 3)$$
$$C \ \text{if} \ B(2, 2, 3)$$

from which the result of folding and replacing would apparently be the new program

$$A(3) \ \text{if} \ C$$
$$C \ \text{if} \ B(U, 2, 3)$$
$$B(1, 2, 3)$$

However, this new program implies A(3) whereas the original program does not, and so we have not preserved the minimal model. We become warned of this if we unfold the new program upon its C call, which yields a clause

$$A \ \text{if} \ B(U, 2, 3)$$

that is different from the original clause for A. Alternatively, we become warned of it by finding that the clause generated by (incorrectly) folding, namely

$$A(3) \ \text{if} \ C$$

is *not* a logical consequence of **Comp(P)**.

We shall state the formal conditions for folding in predicate logic after looking at a simple example and dealing with it intuitively.

Example—a transformation exploiting both unfolding and folding. We begin with the following program **P** which seeks pairs <U, V> satisfying p(U, V) from the members of a list X, where the definition of 'p' can be supplied as independent input data:

$$P1: \quad \text{pair}(U, V, X) \ \text{if} \ \textbf{m(U, X)} \ \& \ m(V, X) \ \& \ p(U, V)$$
$$P2: \quad m(U, U \cdot X)$$
$$P3: \quad m(U, V \cdot X) \ \text{if} \ m(U, X)$$

In the absence of any other information about either the given list or the 'p' relation, this program serves well enough for computational purposes. If, however, we have special knowledge about the 'p' relation then the program can be usefully modified by unfolding, folding and replacement, as we now show.

First we do a complete one-step unfolding of clause P1 upon the call shown in bold face to obtain

P4 :   pair(U, V, U•X) if **m(V, U•X)** & p(U, V)
P5 :   pair(U, V, W•X) if m(U, X) & **m(V, W•X)** & p(U, V)

We know that these can replace P1 without affecting the minimal model. Next, we similarly unfold each of the clauses P4 and P5 on their boldface calls to obtain

P6 :   pair(U, U, U•X) if p(U, U)
P7 :   pair(U, V, U•X) if m(V, X) & p(U, V)
P8 :   pair(U, V, V•X) if m(U, X) & p(U, V)
P9 :   pair(U, V, W•X) if m(U, X) & m(V, X) & p(U, V)

Again, we know that these can replace **U(P1)**—and hence P1—without affecting the minimal model. Finally, noting that

Comp(P) ⊨ pair(U, V, X) only-if m(U, X) & m(V, X) & p(U, V)

we can **fold** clause P9 to obtain the recursive clause

P10 : pair(U, V, W•X) if pair(U, V, X)

which we know can replace P9 without affecting the minimal model. The end result of making all the suggested replacements is the new program

P6   : pair(U, U, U•X) if p(U, U)
P7   : pair(U, V, U•X) if m(V, X) & p(U, V)
P8   : pair(U, V, V•X) if m(U, X) & p(U, V)
P10 : pair(U, V, W•X) if pair(U, V, X)
P2   : m(U, U•X)
P3   : m(U, V•X) if m(U, X)

What have we achieved by all this effort? The answer is, a program which is slightly more efficient to execute and significantly more easy to specialize than the original one. For instance, if we know that 'p' is irreflexive then P6 can be safely deleted. If we know that 'p' is symmetric then one of either P7 or P8 can be safely deleted and we can simply add to the answers their symmetric counterparts. The run-time gains procured by these adaptations are not achievable by any comparable modification of the original program—instead, we would have to impose problem-specific restrictions upon the execution strategy, this being a non-trivial task.

We now return to the question of how to formalize the general folding step for predicate logic in order that it shall deal correctly with all cases, including those which involve clauses having local variables. The initial conditions are that **P** shall contain a clause

CL : A if ... & **calls** & ...

and a second clause

C only-if **calls***

The fold operation yields the following new clause which may correctly replace
CL

$F(CL) : A$ if ... & $C\theta$ & ...

provided that the substitution θ satisfies each of the following conditions:

(a) **calls=calls***θ ; [Note that **calls**θ=**calls***θ is not good enough.]
(b) for every local variable **x** in **CL**, **x**θ must be a variable which occurs in
     calls but nowhere else in **CL**, and also does not occur in $C\theta$;
(c) for any distinct local variables **x** and **y** in **CL**, **x**θ ≠ **y**θ ;
(d) the second clause is the only clause in **P** whose heading unifies with $C\theta$.

These conditions are rather tedious to explain, but their net effect is to ensure
satisfaction of the invertibility criterion and hence ensure that the fold-and-replace
operation is correct relative to **Comp(P)**.

    As a more general comment, the transformation paradigm which comprises
just folding and unfolding enables one to derive, from a given program **P**, many
alternative programs which are logical consequences of **Comp(P)**. Some of these
may be much more useful computationally than **P**, whilst others may be much
less useful. We do not yet possess any universal strategy for controlling the
selection of transformation steps in such a way as to improve computational utility
—in the main, we just have to rely upon intuition.

    There is another, potentially more serious, weakness of this particular
paradigm. In general there will exist many programs in the language of **B(P)**
which—though computationally equivalent to **P** in the sense of delivering the
same minimal model—are not derivable from **P** using just folding and unfolding;
yet some of these may be highly desirable in terms of efficiency. For instance, the
program **P1** below (on the left) is much better for computing even numbers than
is program **P2** (on the right), yet not all of its clauses can be derived from **P2**
using just folding and unfolding:

E1 : even(0)	E1 : even(0)
E2 : even(s(s(X))) if even(X)	E3 : even(s(X)) if odd(X)
O1 : odd(s(0))	O3 : odd(s(X)) if even(X)
O2 : odd(X) if even(s(X))	

Likewise, **P2**—which is slightly better than **P1** for computing odd numbers—
cannot be derived from **P1** using just folding and unfolding. Fundamentally,
what we lack in both cases is the power of **induction**.

The computational equivalence of the two programs just shown can, in fact, be established easily by supplementing them with the following induction schema:

> for any property **R**,
> $(\forall X \in \mathbf{N})(\mathbf{R}(X)$ iff $\mathbf{R}(0)$ & $(\forall Y \in \mathbf{N})(\mathbf{R}(s(Y))$ if $\mathbf{R}(Y)))$
>
> where **N** denotes $\{0, s(0), s(s(0)), ...\}$.

Exercises 53

1. Prove that folding-and-replacement preserves the minimal model of a propositional, definite program **P**.

2. Taking the A-B-C example in the Theme, show that **Comp(P)** does not imply the clause (A(3) if C).

   Hint—show that **Comp(P)** has models in which C is **true** but A(3) is not.

3. Use fold-unfold to derive each of these two clauses

   > A if B
   > A if E

   from these

   > A if B & C
   > C if D1
   > C if D2
   > E if B & D2
   > D1
   > D2

   Note—we are not interested here in the correctness or otherwise of *replacing* the given clauses by the derived ones.

4. Use fold-unfold to derive this program

   > last(U•nil, U)
   > last(V•Z, U) if last(Z, U)

   from this one

   > C :   last(L, U) if append(W, U•nil, L)
   > A1 :   append(nil, Z, Z)
   > A2 :   append(V•X, Y, V•Z) if append(X, Y, Z)

5. Use fold-unfold to derive this program

$$sub(X, Y) \text{ if } pre(X, Y)$$
$$sub(X, U \cdot W) \text{ if } sub(X, W)$$
$$pre(nil, Y)$$
$$pre(U \cdot X, U \cdot Y) \text{ if } pre(X, Y)$$

from this one

C : sub(X, Y) if append(Y1, X, Y2) & append(Y2, Y3, Y)
D : pre(X, Y) if append(X, L, Y)
A1 : append(nil, Z, Z)
A2 : append(V·X, Y, V·Z) if append(X, Y, Z)

6. Consider the programs **P1** (on the left) and **P2** (on the right):

N1 :	num(0)	N1 :	num(0)
N2 :	num(s(X)) if num(X)	N3 :	num(s(s(X))) if num(X)
		N4 :	num(X) if num(s(X))

See how many clauses of each program you can derive from the other program using fold-unfold.

7. This question refers to the programs **P1** and **P2** for 'even' and 'odd' shown at the end of the Theme.

(i)   See how many clauses of each program you can derive from the other program using fold-unfold.

(ii)   Show, informally, that **MM(P1)=MM(P2)**.
        Hint—compare, for instance, their fixpoint constructions.

(iii)   **P2** does not imply **P1** because it does not imply **P1**'s fourth clause (call this clause 'C'). Prove the latter to be so by

        (a)   exhibiting a Herbrand counter-model;
        (b)   showing that no refutation can be obtained from the clausal-form translation of **P2** ∪ {¬C}.

(iv)   Does **Comp(P2)** logically imply C?
        Hint—investigate this by seeking a refutation from the clausal-form translation of **Comp(P2)** ∪ {¬C}. You will need to use several axioms from the equality theory.

Theme 54

Extending SLD with finite failure

Although the SLD paradigm is theoretically adequate for all computational purposes, the pure Horn-clause language on which it is based is unlikely to become the dominant logic-programming language of the future. In fact it never *has* been the mainstream logic-programming language, as every Prolog programmer will testify—writing a logic program for a real-world application nearly always seems to require the expression of some intention or other for which there is apparently no *practical* representation in pure Horn-clause logic. It is futile to resist this fact of computational life; in the end, the cumulative and collective experience of serious practitioners has to be respected.

The designers of Prolog anticipated this and consequently felt obliged to add many non-logical extensions to the Horn-clause kernel. In doing so they placed greater weight upon the concrete needs of the practitioners than upon the more abstract desires of the theoreticians. A lot of research effort has since been devoted to the problem of rendering those extensions either semantically intelligible or methodologically redundant. A substantial part of that effort has concentrated upon one particular issue—the **finite failure extension**.

The finite failure extension enables one to express, via a call *fail* q, the condition that a call q shall finitely fail. (In Prolog the *fail* operator is denoted by 'not' and is referred to as 'negation by failure', as explained in Theme 57.) The operational meaning of *fail* is summed up by the **finite failure rule**:

a call *fail* q succeeds   iff   its subcall q finitely fails

This rule can be incorporated directly into the execution strategy for virtually no cost in terms of implementation overheads—to evaluate a call *fail* q the interpreter merely evaluates q in the standard way and then responds to the outcome as just prescribed.

Note carefully what is meant in the definition above by the phrase 'q finitely fails': it means that the execution tree generated by the evaluation of q must be a finitely-failed tree exactly as first defined in Theme 30—that is, it must have *finite depth, finite breadth* and *all* the computations contained within it must *terminate with failure*. By contrast, should one or more of those computations terminate with success then the call *fail* q is itself deemed to have finitely failed. Finally, if the evaluation of q neither succeeds nor finitely fails then the same holds for the evaluation of *fail* q.

In order to see why *fail* is a useful facility, consider the simple task of querying this ground atomic database:

> person(chris)
> person(brendon)
> person(emlyn)
>
> child(brendon, chris)
> child(emlyn, chris)

We know that SLD alone is able to deal soundly and completely with all positive atomic queries ?**q** posed to this database. But with the finite failure facility we can now also ask directly, in our extended language, whether some atom is *not* in the database, for instance:

> ? person(X) & *fail* child(X, chris)

Executing this in the usual way we first compute the first solution X/chris of the 'person' call. This reduces the query to

> ? *fail* child(chris, chris)

The finite failure rule now comes into play: the subcall child(chris, chris) finitely fails and so the *fail* call succeeds. This first computation therefore terminates with success. After backtracking we get a second solution X/brendon from the 'person' call and the query reduces to

> ? *fail* child(brendon, chris)

The subcall child(brendon, chris) succeeds and so the *fail* call finitely fails. This second computation therefore terminates with failure, as does the third computation. Figure 54.1 shows how we represent the execution as a whole:

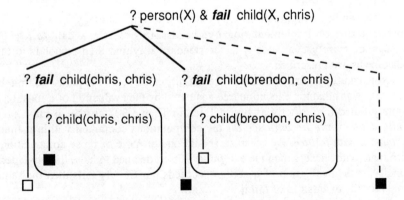

Figure 54.1. Execution using the finite failure extension.

We were careful in this first example to ensure that the *fail* call had become *ground* by the time it was selected for execution. In general, ground *fail* calls present no difficulties for the finite failure rule. The execution of a non-ground *fail* call, however, is more problematic. Suppose we begin execution with the following non-ground query:

$$Q : \ ? \textit{fail} \ \text{child}(X, \text{chris})$$

It is important to be clear as to what this query is asking. If we follow the standard convention regarding the quantification of query variables then this query questions whether some X exists such that child(X, chris) finitely fails. The finite failure rule effectively poses the subquery

$$Q' : \ ? \ \text{child}(X, \text{chris})$$

which questions whether some X exists such that child(X, chris) holds. Unfortunately, that same rule then incorrectly relates the answers to these two questions. Q' will succeed (in two ways), so that Q will finitely fail and the execution as a whole must terminate without computing any answers: nonetheless, there *does* exist an X such that child(X, chris) finitely fails— namely, X=chris. So we have the strange situation whereby Q finitely fails despite that fact that an *instance* of it—namely Q{X/chris}—succeeds. The finite failure rule is thus *incomplete* when applied to activated non-ground *fail* calls. Its incompleteness is exacerbated if we permit *fail* calls also to appear in clause bodies.

But there are worse problems than this incompleteness. Suppose we add to our database these definitions of 'parent' and 'childless'

$$\text{parent}(Y) \quad \text{if } \textit{fail} \ \text{childless}(Y)$$
$$\text{childless}(Y) \ \text{if } \textit{fail} \ \text{child}(X, Y)$$

and then pose the query ? parent(Y). Executed using the finite failure rule this query succeeds, suggesting that a parent exists—though without binding Y to say who this parent is (since bindings are not returned from solved *fail* calls). Yet the new definitions together with the closed-world assumption imply, when they are read declaratively with the usual convention governing the assumed quantification of clause variables, that parent(Y) holds if and only if there exists no X such that child(X, Y) does not hold. But since such an X (namely X=chris) does exist, it follows that parent(Y) should *not* hold for any Y. Relative to this declarative reading of the definitions, the computed answer is wrong and the finite failure rule is *unsound*.

One could, of course, take the alternative view that it is not the answer that is wrong but the declarative reading whose convention is always to treat clause variables as being subject to outermost universal quantifiers—but to maintain such a view one would then have to operate a different, and rather unsatisfactory, context-dependent quantification policy according to which, for instance,

(i)   p(X) if *fail* q(X)   is read as $(\forall X)(p(X)$ if *fail* q(X)$)$
(ii)   p(X) if *fail* q(Y)   is read as $(\forall X)(p(X)$ if *fail* $(\exists Y)q(Y))$

The standard convention reads (ii) as $(\forall Y)(\forall X)(p(X)$ if *fail* q(Y)$)$

$$\equiv (\forall X)(p(X)$ if $(\exists Y)\textit{fail}\ q(Y))$$

and thus, when applied to our example above, fails to give 'childless', and hence 'parent', their intuitive meanings.

Unsoundness is less tolerable than incompleteness. What should we do about it ? The most well-known solution is to *restrict the computation rule* by insisting that, whatever else it might do, it shall (i) never be allowed to select a non-ground *fail* call and (ii) always evaluate any selected ground *fail* call completely before attempting to select any of the remaining calls in the query. Such a selection policy is called a **safe computation rule** and ensures that the finite failure rule behaves soundly.

Let's see what happens when we evaluate the query

? *fail* child(X, chris) & person(X)

using a safe computation rule. Only the second call is eligible for selection. Selecting it and solving it for the case X/chris results in a successful computation which, moreover, *returns as output* the correct and unique answer X/chris; backtracking then yields two further computations both of which (correctly) finitely fail. By contrast, had we used the unsafe standard computation rule (which insists upon selecting the first call, whatever it may be), execution would have generated just one, unsuccessful computation and hence no answers at all.

Now consider again the query ? parent(Y) but this time using a safe computation rule. Execution generates the non-ground query ? *fail* childless(Y) from which *no call is selectable*. In this circumstance we say that the computation has **floundered**—the computation must then be aborted with no conclusion reached as to whether there is an answer or not. Nevertheless, this outcome has at least protected us from computing an *unsound* answer.

The incorporation of the finite failure rule into our formalism under the presumption of a safe computation rule yields the so-called **SLDNF inference system** ("SLD plus negation by failure") and is sound. It is clearly incomplete because of the possibility of floundering. In effect, its incompleteness is the price we must pay for its soundness.

Safe computation rules are somewhat expensive to implement because they have to monitor the binding environments of candidate calls to see whether they are eligible for selection. Very few Prolog systems implement the safety condition, leaving it instead to the programmer to arrange calls in a suitable order for selection by the standard computation rule.

There are other complications attending SLDNF which we shall have to address in due course—primarily to do with the provision of a suitable semantics. Before we plunge into these matters it is worth considering why we should bother at all to support the finite failure rule—after all, kindred formalisms such as functional programming seem to get on very well without it. Even conventional programming languages, which seem happy to support just about anything under the sun, stop short of explicit failure analysis.

The chief motivation, arguably, is to implement default reasoning, which is in turn an important element in common-sense reasoning. The sort of application areas upon which much of logic programming practice is targeted are typically ones requiring the formalization of everyday human thought processes. This is an ambition apparently not shared by, say, the functional programmers.

There are other important spin-offs as well. We shall see later on, in Theme 58, that there is a close analogy between applying the finite failure rule to definite-clause logic augmented by *fail* and applying classical inference to general first-order logic. Computing classically with full first-order logic is not easy to implement in a practical way, partly because we do not possess a good procedural interpretation for it. SLDNF inference provides a highly effective alternative, despite its limitations.

Another benefit arises from the capacity of finite failure to support various kinds of consistency-checking tasks. The provision of the *fail* facility makes it easy to formulate, for instance, procedures for checking whether database updates respect integrity constraints, or procedures for determining whether programs are computationally equivalent. There are many other important exemplars amongst this category of applications.

In summary, it is due to the wide-ranging ambitions of logic programming that we tolerate the complexities entailed in extensions such as finite failure.

Exercises 54

1. Using the atomic database shown in the Theme, sketch the SLDNF-trees for the following queries under a safe computation rule which always selects the left-most selectable call:

   (i)   ? *fail* child(X, Y) & person(Y)
   (ii)   ? person(Y) & *fail* child(Y)
   (iii) ? person(Y) & *fail* person(Y)
   (iv)   ? *fail* child(X, X)

2. Using any clause of the form

   p if *fail* q(X) & **others**

   where X is local to the *fail* call, is bound to cause floundering under any safe computation rule. This floundering can be eliminated by replacing the clause by a simple transform consisting of two clauses:

(i)   what are they?
(ii)   using the atomic database of the Theme, compare the executions of the
        queries

> ? childless(brendon)
> ? childless(chris)

(a) using the clause

> childless(Y) if *fail* child(X, Y)

(b) using its transform instead.

(iii)   How does the transform behave for the query

> ? childless(Y)

and is there any simple remedy?

Theme 55

The SLD finite failure set

In this Theme we introduce the notion of a finite failure set. Relative to a given program **P** and a given inference system, this set comprises exactly those ground atoms **q** for which the query ?**q** finitely fails. We shall restrict our attention throughout to the case where **P** is definite and the inference system is SLD.

Once we know what the finite failure set is relative to SLD inference, we shall also be able to say something about the execution by SLDNF of queries containing *fail* calls—subject, of course, to the assumption that the chosen computation rule is *safe*. We shall *not* say anything in this Theme about the more general situation where *fail* calls may occur also in clause bodies, for the position then is significantly more complicated.

Consider, therefore, the execution of queries of the form ?**q** using a definite program **P** under some SLD computation rule **R**. As indicated in Figure 55.1, the Herbrand base **B(P)** can then be partitioned into three species of ground atoms **q**: those for which ?**q** succeeds, those for which ?**q** finitely fails and those for which ?**q** infinitely fails. The first set we can denote by **SS(P, R)**, the second one by **FF(P, R)** and the third one by **IF(P, R)**.

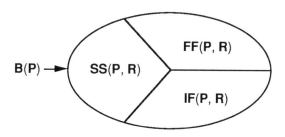

Figure 55.1. Partitioning **B**(**P**) by a computation rule **R**.

An interesting question now arises: in what way does this partitioning depend upon the choice of computation rule **R**? We noted earlier, in Theme 31, that the capacity of a query ?**q** to succeed was *independent* of the computation rule—in other words, that if the query succeeded in one SLD-tree then it succeeded in *all* SLD-trees. Consequently, when it came to denoting the (success) set of all such atoms in Theme 44, we denoted it simply by **SS(P)** in which no qualification according to the choice of **R** was required.

Unfortunately matters are not so tidy in relation to those queries ?**q** which do *not* succeed, because ?**q** may finitely fail under one computation rule yet infinitely fail under another. A simple example is where the program comprises just the clause

$$q \text{ if } r \,\&\, q$$

Under the standard rule (leftmost call) the query ?**q** finitely fails, whereas it infinitely fails under a rule which always selects the rightmost call. Thus the boundary between **FF(P, R)** and **IF(P, R)** depends upon **R**.

There is a simple theoretical way of eliminating this dependence upon **R**—we invoke the idea of a particular sort of computation rule which ensures that any call introduced into a computation is selected after some arbitrary but finite number of execution steps. Such a rule is called a **fair computation rule**. Considering the example again, we might allow a fair computation rule to select 'q' calls any finite number of times, but sooner or later the fairness requirement would demand that an 'r' call be selected, thus immediately forcing finite failure.

With this new concept, we can now state the following facts: ?**q** finitely fails under *some* computation rule if and only if it finitely fails under *all* fair computation rules; equivalently, at least one of its SLD-trees is finitely failed if and only if *all* of its fair SLD-trees are finitely failed. Although fair computation rules are not normally implemented, they certainly tidy up our mathematical account of finite failure. We can denote by **FF(P)**, which carries no qualification as to the choice of **R**, the set of all atoms **q** for which ?**q** has some finitely failed fair SLD-tree, and by **IF(P)** the set of all atoms **q** for which ?**q** has some infinitely failed fair SLD-tree. **FF(P)** is called the (**fair-**) **SLD finite failure set** of **P**. Referring again to the example above, we shall have **FF(P)**={q, r} and **IF(P)**=∅.

The partitioning of **B(P)** for any definite **P** can now be expressed independently of any particular choice of **R**, as shown in Figure 55.2.

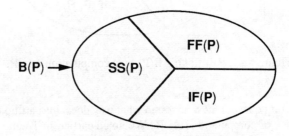

Figure 55.2. Partitioning **B(P)** independently of **R**.

Consider next the extended formalism which generalizes queries so that they may contain *fail* calls besides atomic ones, but with **P** still restricted to be definite. These queries are to be executed using SLDNF under a safe but otherwise arbitrary computation rule (whether fair or otherwise). The following statements then hold true:

$$\text{for all } q \in B(P), \quad q \in FF(P) \quad \text{iff} \quad ?\,fail\,q \quad \text{succeeds under SLDNF}$$
$$q \in SS(P) \quad \text{iff} \quad ?\,q \qquad \text{succeeds under SLDNF}$$

These usefully characterize the outcome of executing queries in any fashion under safe SLDNF in terms of fixed atom-sets associated with **P** alone—equivalently, characterizing the *sound implementation* of finite failure in terms of those atom-sets. In subsequent Themes we shall interpret finite failure in terms of (i) the T_P function and (ii) classical negation ($\neg$). The second of these provides a semantics for *fail* based upon the logical consequences of the completion **Comp(P)**, and hence some soundness and completeness results for SLDNF.

Exercises 55

1.   For this program **P**

> path(X, Z) if arc(X, Z)
> path(X, Z) if arc(X, Y) & path(Y, Z)
> arc(a, b)
> arc(b, c)

identify **SS(P, R)**, **FF(P, R)** and **IF(P, R)** for each of the following kinds of computation rule **R**:

(i)   **R** always selects the leftmost call;
(ii)   **R** always selects the rightmost call;
(iii)   **R** is fair but otherwise arbitrary.

Note—assume **H**={a, b, c}.

(iv)   What difference would it make to these answers if **P** were extended by adding the assertion arc(c, a)?

Theme 56

Mathematical characterization of finite failure

Theme 46 established that, for any definite program P, there exists a particularly simple way of constructing its success set $SS(P)$ using the T_P function: starting with the **bottom element** $\emptyset$ in our lattice of interpretations, repeated application of this function generates a monotonically-increasing chain

$$\emptyset \subseteq T_P(\emptyset) \subseteq T_P^2(\emptyset)$$

whose limit
$$T_P\uparrow\omega = \text{lub}\{T_P^k(\emptyset) \mid k \in N\} = \bigcup_{k \in N} T_P^k(\emptyset)$$

is exactly $SS(P)$ and, moreover, $LFP(T_P)$.

It so happens that there is a somewhat similar method of constructing the finite failure set $FF(P)$. In order to appreciate its rationale it is useful to understand clearly the process by which a ground query $?q$ finitely fails from a definite program P. In particular we need to consider the **depth** within which the failure occurs.

The simplest way for $?q$ to fail finitely is for there to be no clause in P whose heading unifies with q—equivalently, for there to be no clause in $G(P)$ having q as its heading. In this case the failure is said to occur within depth k=1. Relative to the given program P there may be many atoms $q \in B(P)$ for which this is so. The set of all such atoms is denoted by $FF(P, 1)$ and can be characterized very easily using the T_P function. Consider the set of atoms which *do* occur as headings in $G(P)$—this is simply $T_P(B(P))$, as is plain from the definition of T_P:

$$T_P(I) = \{q \mid (q \text{ if body}) \in G(P) \text{ } and \text{ } \mathbf{body} \text{ is } \mathbf{true} \text{ in } I\}$$

since **body** must be **true** when $I=B(P)$. It follows from this that

$$FF(P, 1) = B(P) - T_P(B(P))$$

Consider next the significance of any atom q being in $T_P^2(B(P))$. $G(P)$ must then contain at least one clause whose heading is q and whose body comprises calls each one of which occurs as the heading of at least one clause in $G(P)$. Atoms q which are *not* in $T_P^2(B(P))$ are said to finitely fail within depth k=2. The set of these atoms is denoted by $FF(P, 2)$ and is given by

$$FF(P, 2) = B(P) - T_P^2(B(P))$$

Generalizing this principle, the finite failure set of **P** just contains each atom **q** for which ?**q** finitely fails within *some* depth k∈N:

$$FF(P) = \bigcup_{k \in N} FF(P, k) = B(P) - \bigcap_{k \in N} T_P^k(B(P))$$

Since we assume that **P** has only a finite number of clauses, a query ?**q** can generate from **P** only a finite number of computations. If all of these finitely fail then there must exist some *common* depth k within which they *all* terminate. This is the essential requirement for membership of **q** in **FF(P)**.

Observe that, when we start at the **top element** **B(P)** of our lattice of interpretations, repeated application of the T_P function generates a monotonically-decreasing sequence

$$B(P) \supseteq T_P(B(P)) \supseteq T_P^2(B(P)) \ ...$$

whose limit $\quad$ $glb\{T_P^k(B(P)) \mid k \in N\} = \bigcap_{k \in N} T_P^k(B(P))$

is denoted by $T_P{\downarrow}\omega$ and is pronounced "T_P down omega". Thus we may write

$$FF(P) = B(P) - T_P{\downarrow}\omega$$

This is a *mathematical* characterization of **FF(P)** in terms of T_P and is clearly independent of the execution mechanism. Nevertheless, the atom-set so defined agrees exactly with that described in Theme 55 based upon (fair) SLD.

Example—revisiting our familiar program **P** from Theme 40:

    likes(chris, X) if likes(X, logic)
    likes(bob, logic)

where **B(P)** is {CC, CL, CB, LC, LL, LB, BC, BL, BB} and **G(P)** is

likes(chris, chris) if likes(chris, logic)	CC if CL
likes(chris, bob) if likes(bob, logic)	CB if BL
likes(chris, logic) if likes(logic, logic)	CL if LL
likes(bob, logic)	BL

Then we have

$$
\begin{aligned}
FF(P, 1) &= B(P) - T_P(B(P)) &= \{LC, LL, LB, BC, BB\} \\
FF(P, 2) &= B(P) - T_P^2(B(P)) &= \{LC, LL, LB, BC, BB, CL\} \\
FF(P, 3) &= B(P) - T_P^3(B(P)) &= \{LC, LL, LB, BC, BB, CL, CC\}
\end{aligned}
$$

Since $T_P^k(B(P)) = T_P^3(B(P)) = \{CB, BL\}$ for all k>3 it follows that

$$T_P^3(B(P)) = T_P{\downarrow}\omega$$

and hence that $FF(P) = FF(P, 3) = \{LC, LL, LB, BC, BB, CL, CC\}.$

It is easy to confirm that these are indeed exactly the atoms q for which $?q$ finitely fails under (fair) SLD.

Since $\emptyset \subseteq B(P)$ and T_P is monotonic it is trivial to show that

$$T_P{\uparrow}\omega \subseteq T_P{\downarrow}\omega$$

This fact confers upon the Herbrand Base the structure shown in Figure 56.1.

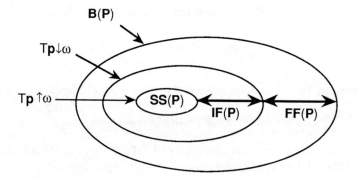

Figure 56.1. Partitioning of $B(P)$ according to the limits of T_P.

Notice that the region between $T_P{\uparrow}\omega$ and $T_P{\downarrow}\omega$ must correspond to $IF(P)$, which we have previously characterized as comprising exactly those atoms which fail infinitely—loosely speaking, those atoms q for which the execution of $?q$ generates a 'loop' and, moreover, generates no successful computations. Interestingly, it turns out that this class of atoms is not homogeneous—more precisely, $IF(P)$ can itself be partitioned into two classes corresponding to two distinct species of infinite failure.

The distinction is best exposed by considering, for any $q{\in}IF(P)$, the fair execution of $?q$ using not P but its ground instantiation $G(P)$. For some programs $G(P)$ this execution will generate an SLD-tree whose infinite depth is owed to the presence of an infinite computation—a genuine 'loop'. But for certain other programs $G(P)$ the SLD-tree will be of infinite depth yet contain no loop. All of its computations will be finitely failed yet there will exist no common depth k within which they all terminate. How is this possible? Consider this rather artificial example, for which $H=\{0, s(0), s(s(0)), ...\}$:

$$\text{num\_exists if num(X)}$$
$$\text{zero(0) if zero(0)}$$
$$\text{num(s(X)) if num(X)}$$

Execution of the query ? num_exists using $\mathbf{G(P)}$ generates the tree shown in Figure 56.2. This tree has infinitely-many computations—moreover, for each $k>1$ there is a computation of length k. Consequently the tree has infinite depth even though each of its individual computations is finitely failed. The atom num_exists neither succeeds nor does there exist any common depth $k \in \mathbf{N}$ within which all of its computations finitely fail—thus it can only belong to $\mathbf{IF(P)}$. The atom zero(0) also belongs to $\mathbf{IF(P)}$ but is not in the same class as num_exists— the tree for the query ? zero(0) comprises just one computation which is infinite. Every other atom in $\mathbf{B(P)}$ belongs to $\mathbf{FF(P)}$. Notice further that the distinction between num_exists and zero(0) might not be immediately apparent from a comparison of their evaluations using $\mathbf{P}$ instead of $\mathbf{G(P)}$—for then, each would generate a tree comprising just one infinite computation.

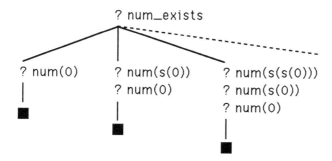

Figure 56.2. An infinitely-deep tree with no infinite computations.

The question now arises of whether we can characterize in mathematical terms this subdivision of $\mathbf{IF(P)}$. In fact it can be shown that the dividing line is the **greatest fixpoint $\mathbf{GFP(T_P)}$**, which always satisfies

$$T_P{\uparrow}\omega \subseteq GFP(T_P) \subseteq T_P{\downarrow}\omega$$

If an atom $\mathbf{q}$ belongs to $(\mathbf{GFP(T_P)} - T_P{\uparrow}\omega)$ then ?$\mathbf{q}$ fails infinitely in the manner of zero(0) in our example; on the other hand, if $\mathbf{q}$ belongs to $(T_P{\downarrow}\omega - \mathbf{GFP(T_P)})$ then ?$\mathbf{q}$ fails infinitely in the manner of num_exists in that example. The latter class of atoms together with $\mathbf{FF(P)}$ constitutes the so-called **ground finite failure set** which is denoted by $\mathbf{GFF(P)}$; this comprises all the atoms $\mathbf{q}$ such that every computation generated from ?$\mathbf{q}$ using $\mathbf{G(P)}$ finitely fails.

Observe, then, that there is an asymmetry in the relationship between the limits and the extremal fixpoints of T_P. Whereas $T_P{\uparrow}\omega$ is always equal to the least fixpoint $\mathbf{LFP(T_P)}$, $T_P{\downarrow}\omega$ does *not* always equal the greatest fixpoint $\mathbf{GFP(T_P)}$. Nevertheless, it is commonly assumed that the latter equality does hold for all 'sensible' programs; at the least, it certainly holds both for non-recursive programs and for programs containing no function symbols. For 'sensible' programs the partitioning of $\mathbf{B(P)}$ is straightforward: atoms either succeed, finitely fail or infinitely fail with respect to *both* $\mathbf{P}$ *and* $\mathbf{G(P)}$. One can take the notion of 'sensible' a stage further by insisting that no atoms should fail infinitely in *any* manner, in which case we would have

$$\mathbf{IF(P)} = \emptyset$$

and hence $\qquad T_P{\uparrow}\omega = T_P{\downarrow}\omega$

and hence $\qquad \mathbf{B(P)} = \mathbf{SS(P)} \cup \mathbf{FF(P)}$

Most logic programs used in practice are, in fact, of this kind: the deliberate incorporation of loops is relatively unusual in conventional logic programming. However, in certain fields such as concurrent logic programming—where one might typically be constructing non-terminating systems software—it is much more common to require this sort of behaviour.

Exercises 56

1. Given the following definite program $\mathbf{P}$:

> A if B
> A if E
> B if C
> D if E
> D

   (i)   determine $\mathbf{FF(P}, k)$ for all $k \in \mathbf{N}$ and hence determine $\mathbf{FF(P)}$;

  (ii) sketch the SLD trees from $?\mathbf{q}$ for each $\mathbf{q} \in \mathbf{B(P)}$ and indicate on the sketches the depths within which any trees are finitely failed.

2. Prove that

$$\cup_{k \in \mathbf{N}}(\mathbf{B(P)} - T_P{}^k(\mathbf{B(P)})) = \mathbf{B(P)} - \cap_{k \in \mathbf{N}}T_P{}^k(\mathbf{B(P)})$$

3. Assuming that $\mathbf{P}$ is definite, prove that

   (i) $T_P{\downarrow}\omega$ is a model for $\mathbf{P}$;

  (ii) $T_P{\uparrow}\omega \subseteq T_P{\downarrow}\omega$.

4. For the program **P** used in the Theme:

$$num\_exists \ \text{if} \ num(X)$$
$$zero(0) \ \text{if} \ zero(0)$$
$$num(s(X)) \ \text{if} \ num(X)$$

determine $T_\mathbf{P}{\uparrow}\omega$, $T_\mathbf{P}{\downarrow}\omega$, **GFP($T_\mathbf{P}$)**, **FF(P)**, **IF(P)** and **GFF(P)**.

5. Prove that, for any definite **P**, **GFF(P)** = **B(P)** − **GFP($T_\mathbf{P}$)**.

Theme 57

The completion semantics for finite failure

The construction of a consequence-oriented semantics for the finite failure extension is more problematic than for pure Horn-clause programs and queries. In the latter case we have a particularly simple connection between logical meaning and operational meaning:

$$\text{for all } q \in B(P), \ P \vDash q \text{ iff } q \in SS(P)$$

As soon as we include *fail* calls in our language no such connection applies— a program containing *fail* is not a construct of classical logic and so is not amenable to the notion of classical logical consequence. Nevertheless, a variety of analogous connections have been suggested. The best-known of these is based upon the so-called **completion semantics**, which relies upon two ideas:

(i) interpreting *fail* as the classical negation connective '¬' (this is why *fail* is commonly referred to as 'negation by failure');

(ii) relating the success or finite failure of calls to logical consequences of **Comp(P)** rather than of **P** alone.

On this basis we can then characterize, in *logical* terms, the execution of ground atomic queries under the (safe-) SLDNF implementation of *fail*:

$$\text{for all } q \in B(P), \quad \text{Comp}(P) \vDash q \quad \text{if } ?\,q \qquad \text{succeeds under SLDNF}$$
$$\text{Comp}(P) \vDash \neg q \quad \text{if } ?\,fail\ q \quad \text{succeeds under SLDNF}$$

Essentially, these are *soundness* results for SLDNF-inference, both of which hold irrespective of whether or not *fail* calls occur also in the clauses of **P**.

Example—consider this program **P**:

$$\begin{array}{l} q \text{ if } \textit{fail } p \\ q \text{ if } r \\ r \end{array}$$

for which **Comp(P)** is

$$\begin{array}{l} q \text{ iff } (\neg p \text{ or } r) \\ r \\ \neg p \end{array}$$

The atomic queries which succeed under SLDNF from this program are ?q and ?r, and it is trivial to verify that both q and r are implied by **Comp(P)**. The only atomic *fail* query which succeeds under SLDNF is ? *fail* p, and it is trivial to verify that ¬p is implied by **Comp(P)**.

The problems come when we seek completeness properties for SLDNF. We would *ideally* like to have the following:

for all $q \in B(P)$, ? q   succeeds under SLDNF if **Comp(P)** ⊨ q

? *fail* q   succeeds under SLDNF if **Comp(P)** ⊨ ¬q

These results do, in fact, hold whenever **P** is definite. Unfortunately, neither of them holds in the more general case where **P** contains *fail* calls.

Note that these idealized requirements are, in any case, inherently weak, for two different reasons. Firstly, it is possible that **Comp(P)** is itself inconsistent, in which case there is no significance in revealing what it implies (since it implies everything). Secondly, to say that a call 'succeeds under SLDNF' is only to say that the call succeeds for *some* safe computation rule—we are not, in the general case, able to specify in advance exactly which such rule will suffice.

You will remember from Theme 55 that in the SLD context we were able to simplify substantially our account of finite failure by referring it to the special class of *fair* computation rules. Unfortunately this device does not transfer satisfactorily into the SLDNF context. To see why this is so, consider the execution of the query

$$Q : \ ? \textit{fail} \ q \ \& \ r$$

using the definite program

$$
\begin{array}{l}
q \ \text{if} \ p \\
q \ \text{if} \ t \\
p \ \text{if} \ p
\end{array}
$$

Observe that Q cannot succeed, but instead must fail either finitely or infinitely. The particular tree which the interpreter constructs will naturally depend upon the policy employed for selecting calls. Figure 57.1 shows one possible tree in a partially-constructed state.

The subtree rooted at ?q is bound to fail infinitely, and so the only way of finitely failing the entire tree is to transfer control out of the subtree—at any stage during its construction—to the latent 'r' call which finitely fails immediately. This is the sort of behaviour we would expect to obtain from a *fair* computation rule. More generally, such a rule would—in order to be truly fair—require the freedom to switch its attention freely back and forth amongst the calls currently in the query.

? **fail** q & r

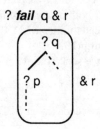

Figure 57.1. A partially-constructed SLDNF-tree.

Now consider the query as depicted in Figure 57.1—what *are* the calls currently in it? We are currently trying both to fail 'p' and to solve 'r', and so it would be tempting to say that our hypothetically-fair computation rule sees the current query as being

$$Q' : \; ? \, \textit{fail} \, p \, \& \, r$$

But this cannot be correct. Whenever any query Q is reduced to some descendant query Q' we understand this to mean that Q can be solved if Q' can be solved. For the example this amounts to saying that

q finitely fails and r succeeds if p finitely fails and r succeeds

which is *unsound*. It is unsound because the correct relationship, according to a straightforward reading of the program, is

q finitely fails and r succeeds if p finitely fails and r succeeds
and t finitely fails

Thus the current state of a partially-constructed SLDNF-tree cannot, in general, be correctly characterized merely as some *homogeneous* set of calls of equal status awaiting selection; rather, it is a *heterogeneous* set of calls and partially-constructed subtrees. Such a structure is incompatible with the standard notion of a sequential computation rule. This is why the definition of a safe computation rule for SLDNF enforces the special restriction that, once a *fail* call has been selected from a query, none of its siblings may be selected until the subtree which it spawns has been *completely* evaluated.

    It is possible, in principle, to envisage some sort of selection policy which dispenses with this restriction and, with sufficiently careful management of the calls and subtrees involved, attempts to be fair to all calls. However, no such policy could overcome the fundamental impediment to truly fair selection—namely that non-ground *fail* calls are not safely selectable. Therefore, since true fairness is unattainable we cannot procure for SLDNF the sort of mathematical tidiness that we could for SLD.

We also mentioned earlier the possibility of **Comp(P)** being inconsistent. In the case where **P** is definite **Comp(P)** must be consistent, but otherwise it may not be. One way of ensuring its consistency is to insist that **P** shall have the property known as **call-consistency**. The simplest way of expressing this property is in terms of the **dependency graph** of **P**, defined as follows:

(i)   the nodes of the graph are the predicate symbols of **P**;

(ii)   for any clause in **P** of the form (**p** if ... & **q** & ...) the graph has a directed edge labelled '+' from the node for **p** to the node for **q**;

(iii) for any clause in **P** of the form (**p** if ... & *fail* **q** & ...) the graph has a directed edge labelled '–' from the node for **p** to the node for **q**.

Then **P** is **call-consistent** if and only if its dependency graph contains no (uniformly-directed) cycle having an odd number of '–' edges. In effect, this property ensures that no predicate symbol **p** is defined in **P**, directly or indirectly, in terms of *fail* **p**, which in turn guarantees that **Comp(P)** is consistent. In practice this restriction is always a reasonable one.

Example— the program in Figure 57.2 is *not* call-consistent, although its completion happens to be consistent.

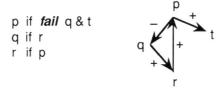

p if *fail* q & t
q if r
r if p

Figure 57.2. A program which is *not* call-consistent.

It is useful also to constrain the class of admissible queries. Specifically, we disallow any query which reduces to the requirement of solving both some call **y**(...) *and* some call *fail* **y**(...). We can formalize the class of admissible queries as follows. Suppose the dependency graph of **P** contains a (uniformly-directed) path from a node **x** to a node **y**; if this path has an even number of '–' edges then we say that **x depends positively** upon **y**, but otherwise we say that **x depends negatively** upon **y**. Now let **Q** be any query: we say that **P** is **strict** with respect to **Q** if and only if

(i)   **Q** does not contain both some call **y**(...) *and* some call *fail* **y**(...);

(ii) when **Q** contains either a call **x**(...) or a call *fail* **x**(...) then, in the dependency graph of **P**, there is no node **y** such that **x** depends upon **y** both positively and negatively.

Example—let **P** be the program in Figure 57.2 and **Q** the query ?r; then **P** is not strict with respect to **Q** since 'r' depends both positively and negatively upon 'q'.

Subject to the assumptions of call-consistency and strictness we can now state some completeness results for SLDNF for programs permitted to contain *fail* calls, provided also that those programs have certain other structural restrictions imposed upon them. For these structurally-restricted programs we have

for all **q**∈**B**(**P**),   ? **q**   succeeds under SLDNF if **Comp**(**P**) ⊨ **q**

?*fail* **q**   succeeds under SLDNF if **Comp**(**P**) ⊨ ¬**q**

The most well-known structural restriction is that the programs shall have the property known as **allowedness**: a program is **allowed** if and only if, for each of its clauses, every variable occurring in the clause occurs in at least one non-*fail* call, in which case floundering is impossible. The above results then hold.

More generally we are interested in compound and possibly non-ground queries of the form ?**calls**. The soundness and completeness properties of SLDNF for such queries can be combined and summarized as follows:

if **P** is allowed, call-consistent and strict with respect to ?**calls**, then

(i)   ? **calls** succeeds with answer substitution θ iff **Comp**(**P**) ⊨ ∀(**calls**θ)

(ii) ? **calls** finitely fails iff **Comp**(**P**) ⊨ ¬∃**calls**

These are just about the simplest correctness results for SLDNF based upon two-valued logic that can be offered at the present time in terms of the classical consequences of **Comp**(**P**) in the case where **P** is call-consistent. They are nevertheless severely restrictive in their presumptions of allowedness and strictness. The latter can be relaxed to some extent for certain subclasses of the call-consistent class, but only at the expense of increased technicality in the mathematical characterization of those subclasses.

Example—consider the following program and query

> **P** :   parent(Y) if *fail* childless(Y)
> childless(Y) if *fail* has_child(Y)
> has_child(Y) if child(X, Y)
> child(brendon, chris)
> child(emlyn, chris)

> **Q** :   ?child(U, V) & *fail* parent(V)

Note that **P** is both call-consistent and strict with respect to **Q**, although it is not allowed (owing to the non-allowedness of each of its first two clauses). Despite this, the grounding effect which the 'child' call in **Q** has upon the *fail* call in **Q** makes it possible to pursue a safe and flounder-free execution under SLDNF, as shown in Figure 57.3. The finite failure of the execution as a whole tells us that no-one can have a child and not be a parent, which is an intuitively correct outcome:

$$\text{Comp(P)} \vDash \neg(\exists U)(\exists V)(\text{child(U, V)} \& \neg\text{parent(V)})$$

By contrast, the query

$$? \text{ child(U, V)} \& \text{parent(V)}$$

succeeds in two ways with answer substitutions

$$\theta 1 = \{U/\text{brendon, V/chris}\}$$
$$\text{and} \quad \theta 2 = \{U/\text{emlyn, V/chris}\}$$

This tells us that

$$\text{Comp(P)} \vDash (\text{child(brendon, chris)} \& \text{parent(chris)})$$
$$\text{and} \quad \text{Comp(P)} \vDash (\text{child(emlyn, chris)} \& \text{parent(chris)})$$

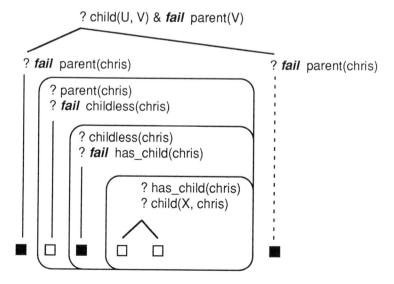

Figure 57.3. SLDNF-execution using the given program and query.

Exercises 57

1. Prove that the completion of the program shown in Figure 57.2 is consistent.

2. For each of the four programs below, sketch its dependency graph and investigate its call-consistency; then construct the program's completion and investigate its consistency.

   (i)   p if *fail* q   (ii)   p if q
          q if *fail* p & r   p if r
          r if *fail* q   q if t
                                             r if *fail* t

   (iii) p if *fail* q   (iv)   p(a) if *fail* q
          q if *fail* t   q   if *fail* t
          t if *fail* p   t   if *fail* p(b)

3. Consider the following indefinite program **P** and assume that the Herbrand domain is {mary, sue, fred, john}:

   > C1 : likes(mary, sue)
   > C2 : likes(fred, sue)
   > C3 : likes(john, mary)
   > C4 : likes(mary, X) if ¬likes(X, mary)

   (i)   Write down all the ground atoms $q \in B(P)$ for which $P \vDash q$.

   (ii)   Suppose the '¬' in clause C4 were changed to *fail*. List all the ground atoms **q** for which ?q succeeds under SLDNF.

   (iii) Show that your answers to (i) and (ii) confirm that SLDNF is incomplete.

   (iv)   Construct **Comp(P)** and show that all your answers to (ii) are sound relative to it, but that not all are sound relative to **P** alone.

   (v)   What aspect of the completion suggests that it improperly formulates the programmer's intentions?

   (vi)   Suppose the programmer had really meant, in place of C4, to say that 'mary' likes anyone who cannot be shown to like 'mary' *using just the unit clauses* of the program. Using just two relations 'likes' and 'LIKES', construct a new program which realizes this intention.

Theme 58

Special applications of SLDNF

The SLDNF inference system has come to be accepted as a staple feature of the logic programming paradigm. It is perhaps in recognition of this that programs and queries containing *fail* calls are now commonly referred to as **normal programs** and **normal queries**—they are what you would *normally* expect to use in practical applications. Up to a point, Prolog employs SLDNF in order to implement its 'not' primitive, which is merely *fail* by another name. Most versions of Prolog do not, however, enforce the safety requirement, leaving this responsibility instead to the programmer.

Given the semantic complications attending SLDNF, could we make do without it and simply stick to SLD? In theory we could do so, since the SLD paradigm is, in principle, capable of computing everything that is computable. But in practice we would pay a heavy price—our programs would be less concise and their executions less efficient. Consider, for example, the problem of showing positively that the element 3 is not a member of the set $\{1, 2\}$. Without the use of *fail* we are obliged to write a program computing a relation 'not_mem' relying, ultimately, upon some built-in inequality primitive $\neq$. Moreover, sets will then have to be represented by structured terms and searched by explicitly-defined recursive procedures:

$$? \text{ not\_mem}(3, 1\cdot2\cdot\text{nil})$$

$$\text{not\_mem}(U, \text{nil})$$
$$\text{not\_mem}(U, V\cdot X) \text{ if } U{\neq}V \text{ \& not\_mem}(U, X)$$

Worse still, a typical application dealing with sets will also require the means of showing that certain elements *are* members of certain sets, in which case we must write a procedure for 'mem' as well as for 'not_mem'. Now compare the formulation above with this one which uses *fail*:

$$?\textit{fail} \text{ mem}(3, \text{set})$$

$$\text{mem}(1, \text{set})$$
$$\text{mem}(2, \text{set})$$

Here, one simple database of ground 'mem' assertions suffices, under SLDNF, for either confirming or disconfirming the membership of particular elements in the given set.

The general hunch amongst many logic programming technologists is that SLDNF, or something very much like it, will play a leading role amongst inference systems serving first-order computational logic. This role is manifested not only in routine programming tasks but also in a wide variety of activities requiring the automated analysis and manipulation of software. In this Theme we briefly illustrate the use of SLDNF for some of these activities.

Simulating classical inference

The relationship between *fail* and '¬' often enables us to achieve, by the use of SLDNF, deductions which would otherwise require the full resources of general resolution applied to general clausal form. Consider the problem of showing subset(a, b) using these definitions (after converting them to clausal form):

$$S1 : \quad subset(X, Y) \text{ iff } (\forall U)(mem(U, Y) \text{ if } mem(U, X))$$
$$S2 : \quad mem(U, a) \text{ iff } U=1$$
$$S3 : \quad mem(U, b) \text{ iff } U=1 \text{ or } U=2$$

We can certainly achieve the task using resolution, although it is then necessary to allow the resolving of derived clauses with their ancestors. Storing the latter in case they are needed later on is an expensive business: this is why SLD and other forms of 'input resolution' are so efficient—they neither retain nor require the ancestors of the current resolvent. Another problem with general resolution applied to biconditional definitions like those shown above is that, without additional controls, it is susceptible to straying into infinite derivations.

We can overcome these difficulties by using SLDNF, provided we first extract and rewrite certain components of the raw material:

$$S1 \vDash \quad subset(X, Y) \text{ if } (\forall U)(mem(U, Y) \text{ if } mem(U, X))$$
$$\vDash \quad subset(X, Y) \text{ if } \neg(\exists U)(mem(U, X) \,\&\, \neg mem(U, Y))$$
$$S2 \vDash \quad mem(1, a)$$
$$S3 \vDash \quad mem(1, b) \text{ and } mem(2, b)$$

With a little reorganization of these implied sentences we can now set up a new program relying upon *fail* instead of '¬':

$$subset(X, Y) \text{ if } \textit{fail } exception(X, Y)$$
$$exception(X, Y) \text{ if } mem(U, X) \,\&\, \textit{fail } mem(U, Y)$$

$$mem(1, a)$$
$$mem(1, b)$$
$$mem(2, b)$$

Then SLDNF solves the problem very efficiently, as evidenced by Figure 58.1.

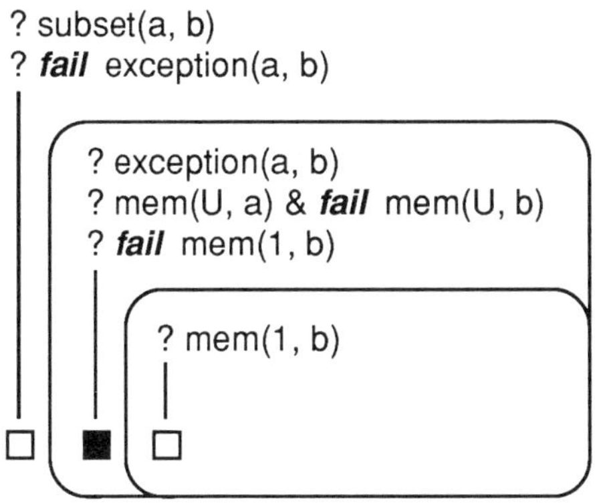

? subset(a, b)
? *fail* exception(a, b)

? exception(a, b)
? mem(U, a) & *fail* mem(U, b)
? *fail* mem(1, b)

? mem(1, b)

Figure 58.1. SLDNF simulating classical inference.

Nevertheless, not all classical inferences can be simulated using SLDNF, as demonstrated by the problem of showing that every set is a subset of itself. The appropriate query in this case is

? subset(α, α)   [skolem constant α]

and is classically refutable by ancestor resolution using just S1 above. However, Figure 58.2 shows that the same query cannot be solved by SLDNF alone (for any safe computation rule) when we reformulate S1 in terms of *fail*—all we get is an inconclusive loop:

subset(X, Y) if *fail* exception(X, Y)
exception(X, Y) if mem(U, X) & *fail* mem(U, Y)
mem(U, Y) if mem(U, X) & subset(X, Y)

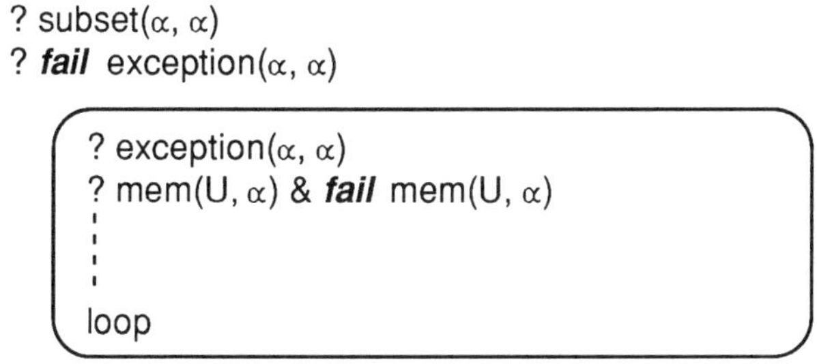

? subset(α, α)
? *fail* exception(α, α)

? exception(α, α)
? mem(U, α) & *fail* mem(U, α)

loop

Figure 58.2. SLDNF failing to simulate classical inference.

The problem here is that SLDNF is not smart enough to perceive metalogically that the derived query

$$? \ mem(U, \alpha) \ \& \ fail \ mem(U, \alpha)$$

contains two calls mem(U, α) and *fail* mem(U, α) which could never be solved conjointly, however 'mem' were defined.

If we could superimpose upon SLDNF an extra rule capable of recognizing and *finitely* failing any query containing conjointly unsolvable calls then the root query in our example would succeed, as desired. Unfortunately such a rule would impose a substantial overhead upon the implementation.

Integrity checking

The adaptation of logic programming to the needs of the database community has contributed substantially to the discipline known as **deductive databases**, which is in turn a sub-discipline of **knowledge assimilation**. The most basic of logical tasks concerned with deductive databases, apart from the elementary business of data retrieval, is that of deciding whether databases remain consistent with respect to their integrity constraints in the course of updating them. An **integrity constraint** is any logical sentence with which the completed database is required always to be consistent. An **update** is any sentence specifying information to be either added to, or deleted from, the database. The simplest formulation of this problem thus comprises a given database **DB**, a set **IC** of integrity constraints and a set **U** of updates, and the aim is to decide the consistency of **Comp(DB)** ∪ **IC** ∪ **U**. A key simplification of this task is to ensure that, prior to the updating, **Comp(DB)** and **IC** are mutually consistent: in that case, any inconsistency arising from the updating must involve **U**, and so the search can be conveniently rooted at **U**.

Let's look at a simple example of how these notions can be implemented through logic programming using SLDNF. In British academic life one's main reward for promotion might be the allocation of an office having more windows than one had previously, thereby increasing one's visibility to outside admirers. A lecturer's office must have two windows, whereas a reader's office must have three. These constraints upon the allocation of offices can be expressed by the clauses

$$windows(X, 2) \ if \ office(Y, X) \ \& \ rank(Y, lecturer)$$
$$windows(X, 3) \ if \ office(Y, X) \ \& \ rank(Y, reader)$$

which, by appropriate use of *transportation of literals*, may be conveniently rewritten in the form of queries:

$$? \ \neg windows(X, 2) \ \& \ office(Y, X) \ \& \ rank(Y, lecturer)$$
$$? \ \neg windows(X, 3) \ \& \ office(Y, X) \ \& \ rank(Y, reader)$$

These may in turn be rewritten using *fail* in place of '¬':

IC1 :   ? *fail* windows(X, 2) & office(Y, X) & rank(Y, lecturer)
IC2 :   ? *fail* windows(X, 3) & office(Y, X) & rank(Y, reader)

IC1 and IC2 jointly constitute the integrity constraint set **IC**. Accompanying these we will have an existing database **DB**:

windows(125, 2)   office(peter, 125)   rank(peter, lecturer)
windows(136, 3)   office(paul, 136)   rank(paul, reader)
windows(218, 2)   :   :
:   :   :
etc.   etc.   etc.

for which **Comp(DB)** is consistent with **IC**.

Suppose a new reader 'james' is now appointed and is allocated office 218 which has 2 windows. The update set **U** is

{ office(james, 218), rank(james, reader)}

This update is inconsistent with **Comp(DB)** ∪ **IC** as attested by the SLDNF graph in Figure 58.3 which begins by reasoning forwards from **U** and subsequently derives □, thereby showing that IC2 has been violated. Note that it is not necessary for this purpose to construct and manipulate **Comp(DB)** explicitly—the completion is exploited implicitly in the way that SLDNF deals with the *fail* calls.

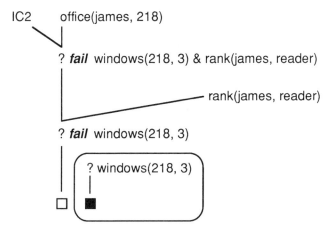

Figure 58.3. Using SLDNF for integrity checking.

Depending upon whether or not inconsistency is detected, the update will be either rejected or accepted. In the present case we must reject it and seek a different office allocation which does not violate the constraints.

The example above exposes only the simplest aspects of database updating under integrity constraints. In particular, it assumes that 'james' is newly appointed rather than promoted from within. Suppose that 'james' had instead been an existing lecturer occupying office 406 having two windows, these facts being already in the database. Then the updating of the database to record the facts of his promotion and new office allocation must also entail the *deletion* of the old facts

$$\text{rank(james, lecturer)}$$
$$\text{office(james, 406)}$$

In the case where **DB** consists only of ground facts (as above) it suffices just to delete explicitly those facts which no longer hold. More generally, however, **DB** may contain rules as well as facts. In this event the data to be deleted may not be explicit in **DB** but implicit in the sense of relying upon the use of rules to derive them. We now have a much harder task: the rules—and possibly some facts as well—must be adjusted in such a way as to eliminate the derivability of the unwanted data yet preserve the derivability of that data which is still required. Moreover, this adjustment must not itself violate the constraints. The problem of achieving all this is called the **view update problem** and is the subject of much interesting and challenging research, to which logic programming is making significant contributions.

Comparison of programs

Given two logic programs, how can we determine whether they compute the same relations? This question assumes importance in the field of **program evolution**: as programs evolve through successive versions, typically in response to changing requirements, we want to be sure that the modifications we make to them do not change those computable relations which we require to be preserved. You might argue that the best way to ensure this is to allow modifications to be made only through the agency of proven transformational tools whose consequence-preservation properties are well-understood. However, it is a fact of computational life that we often need to make modifications which are beyond the scope of the transformational tools available to us: in this event we need methods of analysing change *retrospectively*.

Consider a very simple example in which we alter this program **P1**

$$\text{even(0)}$$
$$\text{even(s(s(X))) \ if \ even(X)}$$

to this new version **P2**:

$$even(0)$$
$$even(s(X)) \text{ if } odd(X)$$
$$odd(s(X)) \text{ if } even(X)$$

The question of whether the modification preserves the denotation of 'even' can be investigated in a variety of ways. One way is as follows. First we rename 'even' as 'even1' in **P1** and as 'even2' in **P2**. Then we require that both the queries

$$? \ even1(X) \ \& \ \textit{fail} \ even2(X)$$
$$? \ even2(X) \ \& \ \textit{fail} \ even1(X)$$

shall fail (whether finitely or infinitely) under SLDNF using **P1** ∪ **P2**. This is tantamount to requiring that $(\exists X)(even1(X) \ \& \ \neg even2(X))$ be consistent with **Comp(P1)** ∪ **Comp(P2)**. Figure 58.4 shows how SLDNF might deal with the first query.

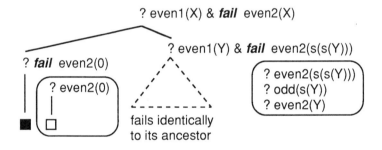

? even1(X) & *fail* even2(X)

? *fail* even2(0)

? even2(0)

? even1(Y) & *fail* even2(s(s(Y)))

? even2(s(s(Y)))
? odd(s(Y))
? even2(Y)

fails identically
to its ancestor

Figure 58.4. Using SLDNF to compare two programs.

There are a number of features to be noted in this tree. First, we have been somewhat liberal in the matter of call selection; in particular, we have not adhered to the safety requirement in selecting *fail* calls. Despite this, the derivations will remain sound for as long as no bindings are made to those call's variables. Secondly, it has suited our purpose to evaluate the *fail* call only partially. Thirdly, we have had to show that the tree is infinite. The conclusion that □ is underivable anywhere in the tree is drawn from the fact that the root query reduces either to finite failure (the leftmost leaf) or to a descendant (the rightmost leaf) whose (infinite) evaluation replicates the same pattern of failure as its ancestor. The overall failure establishes that every tuple in the 'even' relation as computed by **P1** is a tuple of the 'even' relation as computed by **P2**.

Both database updating and program modification under specified constraints are just specific instances of knowledge assimilation, in which consistency-analysis plays a vital role. As we have just seen, the use of SLDNF to investigate consistency requires, in general, additional mechanisms for recognizing those derivations which are bound to fail, since relying merely upon the derivation of finite failure is not a sufficiently powerful strategy—it also needs to recognize mutually unsolvable conjunctions of calls and to recognize loops and/or infinite trees. Loop-detection is a particularly important mechanism in a wide variety of contexts besides that just considered, being contained within the slightly broader topic of **termination analysis**; this is the subject of the next Theme.

Exercises 58

1. Following the approach taken in the Theme for the 'subset' example, use SLDNF to show that every set is a subset of the universal set.

2. Suppose that the database in the Theme is updated by adding the following facts, signifying the appointments of a new lecturer 'ann' and a new reader 'jane', and their decision to share office 112:

> office(ann, 112)   rank(ann, lecturer)
> office(jane, 112)   rank(jane, reader)

Assuming that the database also declares how many windows there are in office 112,

(i)   identify the condition under which the updated database would satisfy both the integrity constraints IC1 and IC2;

(ii)   compose an additional integrity constraint IC3 which would be violated by that circumstance.

3. Use SLDNF and detection of infinitely-failed trees to show that the following programs compute the same 'num' relation:

P1 :   num(0)   **P2** :   num(0)
           num(s(X)) if num(X)   num(s(0))
                                                num(s(s(X))) if num(X)

Theme 59

Termination analysis

Termination analysis focuses on questions about the finiteness or otherwise of computations. There are a number of contexts in which analysis of this kind can be useful. Perhaps the most familiar of these is where a program interpreter is equipped with a loop-detector whose purpose is to recognize and/or bypass loops (infinite computations). We hinted at another use in the previous Theme, where loop-detection was implicit in a demonstration that a tree was infinitely failed and hence that two programs were computationally equivalent.

Despite its obvious importance, termination analysis has for a long time been a relatively neglected subject amongst logic programming researchers, in contrast to the large body of knowledge about termination already developed for other programming formalisms. It is not clear why this is so, although it could be argued that the logic programmers have been preoccupied with supposedly more exciting issues. The last few years have nevertheless seen a considerable increase in interest, leading to a variety of proposed methods of analysis. It would, however, be premature here to attempt a state-of-the-art summary. In particular, the space available in this Theme permits only a brief excursion into the subject.

The use of a program P to execute a query Q can give rise to a loop only if P is *recursive*. However, whether or not a given recursive program *does* give rise to a loop depends, in general, upon both Q and the computation rule R, besides the structural details of P itself. In what follows, our consideration of this question will be restricted to the case where P is definite and the execution mechanism is SLD.

In order to investigate whether a loop can arise we must identify each **potentially-recursive reduction (PRR)** determined by P and R, and then analyse it in the context of Q. Any such reduction consists of reducing the heading of some clause in P, defining some relation q, to some descendent call to q—loosely speaking, we trace out a subcomputation which would be generated under the control of R if that clause were invoked by a most-general call to q, truncating it when it reaches the point of executing some further call to q. For each initial clause so investigated there may be several alternative PRRs, depending upon which other clauses are invoked *en route*.

Pursued exhaustively, this procedure will eventually uncover all the possible PRRs for the relation q under R, whether the clauses involved be individually or mutually recursive, and whether they be singly or multiply recursive. We next describe how any PRR can be usefully represented by a single newly-constructed clause; to assimilate the details of this you may need to refresh your memory concerning unfolding—if necessary, refer back to Theme 49.

The following abstract example gives an idea as to how the method proceeds. Consider the following program fragment

$$
\begin{array}{lll}
\text{C1:} & \text{A(...)} & \text{if } \text{B(...)} \;\&\; \textbf{others-1} \\
\text{C2:} & \text{B(...)} & \text{if } \text{C(...)} \;\&\; \text{D(...)} \;\&\; \textbf{others-2} \\
\text{C3:} & \text{D(...)} & \text{if } \text{E(...)} \;\&\; \text{A(...)} \;\&\; \textbf{others-3}
\end{array}
$$

which is to be used under the standard (left-to-right) computation rule in order to execute a call A which matches the heading of C1. Invocation of clause C1 by this call generates a call to B which we shall assume capable of invoking C2. We shall further assume that this use of C2 generates a call to D capable of invoking C3, which in turn generates a call to A. Thus we have identified a PRR for the relation A. The reason why this reduction is only *potentially* recursive is that the intermediate calls to C and E might not be solvable, in which case the descendent call to A could not be executed. The solvability or otherwise of these calls would eventually have to be investigated in order to decide whether this PRR were a *realizable* recursive step.

The PRR just identified can be represented by a single clause constructed from a sequence of elementary unfolding operations (EUOs). First apply an EUO to C1 upon its B call using C2 (via some m.g.u. $\theta 1$) and then apply another EUO to the result upon its call $D\theta 1$ using C3 (via some m.g.u. $\theta 2$). These operations jointly derive a new clause C*, recursive on A, which represents our PRR:

$$
\text{C*} : \text{A(...)}\theta* \text{ if } \text{C(...)}\theta* \;\&\; \text{E(...)}\theta* \;\&\; \text{A(...)}\theta* \;\&\; \textbf{others}\theta*
$$

where $\theta*$ is the composition of $\theta 1$ with $\theta 2$ and **others** is the conjunction of **others-1**, **others-2** and **others-3**. This clause signifies one way in which a call to A reduces under **R** to another call to A, provided we can solve both of the intermediate calls $\text{C(...)}\theta*$ and $\text{E(...)}\theta*$: note that these calls might fail, either finitely or infinitely. Note also that, for present purposes, we have no interest in the residue **others**$\theta*$.

Once a PRR has been identified it remains to investigate the question of whether its recursive self-invocation would necessarily terminate. We can reformulate this question in terms of well-founded sets. A **well-founded set** is any structure $[\mathbf{W}, «]$ in which $\mathbf{W}$ is a set, '«' is a strict partial order over $\mathbf{W}$ and there exists no infinite path

$$
\ldots « \text{w}'' « \text{w}' « \text{w}
$$

descending from any $w \in \mathbf{W}$. A simple example is $[\mathbf{N}, «]$ in which $\mathbf{N}$ denotes the natural numbers and '«' is the usual 'less than' relation; any descending path must be finite since it cannot proceed beyond the minimal element **0**.

We can exploit such a structure as follows. Our selected PRR will take the general form

$$C^* : \quad q(t) \text{ if } \textbf{intermediates } \& q(t')$$

in which **t** and **t'** are arbitrary argument tuples and **intermediates** denotes those calls, if any, which the given computation rule schedules before the **q** call. We have omitted the **others** component because it plays no role in the analysis. Starting with some initial query

$$\textbf{Q} : \quad ? \, q(s)$$

in which **s** is an arbitrary argument tuple, any computation generated by repeatedly recursing on C* must take the form

$$
\begin{aligned}
&? \, q(s) \\
&? \, \textbf{intermediates}\theta_1 \, \& \, q(t')\theta_1 \\
&? \, q(t')\phi_1 \\
&? \, \textbf{intermediates}\theta_2 \, \& \, q(t')\theta_2 \\
&? \, q(t')\phi_2 \\
&\quad \vdots \\
&\text{etc.}
\end{aligned}
$$

in which θ_1, θ_2, ..., ϕ_1, ϕ_2, ... etc. denote the compositions of various substitutions induced *en route*. The simplest condition for termination is that C* shall be uninvokable by the initial query—that is, θ_1 does not exist. Otherwise, termination might occur because there exists some i for which **intermediates**θ_i finitely fails. Otherwise, termination depends upon the existence of a well-founded set [**W**, «] and a partial function μ mapping atomic queries to members of **W** such that both of the following **termination conditions** hold:

(i) $(\forall i)(\, \mu[?q(t')\phi_i] \in \textbf{W} \quad \text{if} \quad ?q(t')\phi_i \text{ is derivable })$

(ii) $(\forall i)(\, \mu[?q(t')\phi_{i+1}] \ll \mu[?q(t')\phi_i] \quad \text{if} \quad ?q(t')\phi_{i+1} \text{ is derivable from } ?q(t')\phi_i)$

In other words, the sequence of queries $?q(t')\phi_i$ can be mapped to some path in [**W**, «] which cannot descend indefinitely. Otherwise, the computation does not terminate and we have a 'loop'.

Example—**P** is the familiar 'append' program

$$
\begin{aligned}
&\text{A1} : \quad \text{append(nil, W, W)} \\
&\text{A2} : \quad \text{append(U} \cdot \text{X, Y, U} \cdot \text{Z) if append(X, Y, Z)}
\end{aligned}
$$

and **R** is the standard computation rule. We require to investigate termination for the class **Q*** of all atomic queries taking the form

$$\textbf{q} : \quad ? \, \text{append}(\textbf{ground list, ground list, variable})$$

We have just one PRR which is clause A2 as it stands. By considering its heading we see that it must be invokable by any $q \in Q^*$. Since there are no intermediate calls, termination depends upon whether repeated recursion on A2 descends through some well-founded set.

Choose **W** as the set of natural numbers and let '«' be the usual 'less than' relation—thus giving a well-founded set. Define μ as the function which maps **Q*** to **W** such that, for any such $q \in Q^*$, $\mu[q]$ gives the *length* of q's first argument. From consideration of the argument tuples in A2 it is clear that every invocation of A2 by some query $q \in Q^*$ must derive some descendent query $q' \in Q^*$. This ensures that condition (i) above is satisfied. Consideration of the same tuples in A2 shows that the first argument in **q'** must have a length less than that of the first argument in **q**, and so condition (ii) above is also satisfied. Consequently the computation must terminate. It does so when it derives some **q'** which μ maps to some minimal element of **W**, which in the present case can only be **0**: at this point **q'** must have the form

$$? \ append(nil, ..., ...)$$

which clearly cannot reinvoke A2.

This example was particularly easy to analyse and scarcely deserved all the formalization expended upon it. The next example is somewhat more challenging, as it involves one recursion within another.

Example—P is the program

> C1 :   q(X, Z) if X>100 & Z is X–10
> C2 :   q(X, Z) if X≤100 & U is X+11 & q(U, Y) & q(Y, Z)

and **R** is the standard computation rule. We require to investigate termination for the class **Q*** of all atomic queries taking the form

$$q : \ ? \ q(\textbf{integer}, \textbf{integer})$$

This doubly-recursive program has the interesting property that, if a query $q \in Q^*$ of the form ?q(**m**, **n**) is solvable then **n**=91 if **m**≤100 but **n**=**m**–10 otherwise. (It is a famous example in the literature dealing with recursive programs.) We shall make use of this property in analysing the question of termination.

We have two PRRs to investigate, one dealing with the inner recursion and another dealing with the outer one: their single clause representations are respectively

> C3 :   q(X, Z) if X≤100 & U is X+11 & q(U, Y)
> C2 :   q(X, Z) if X≤100 & U is X+11 & q(U, Y) & q(Y, Z)

Both are invokable by any call to 'q' since their headings are most-general.

Taking C3 first, choose **W** as the set of all integers and define '«' such that, for any two integers **m** and **n**,

$$m \ll n \text{ iff } n < m \leqslant 111$$

Then [**W**, «] is well-founded with minimal element 111. Define μ as the mapping from **Q*** to **W** such that for any query in **Q*** of the form ?q(U, Y) we have

$$\mu[?q(U, Y)] = U$$

Suppose such a query **q'** is derivable by invoking C3 with a query $q \in Q^*$ having the form ?q(X, Z). Then U must be an integer and therefore $\mu[q'] \in W$; hence condition (i) is satisfied. The intermediate calls must have been solved and therefore X≤100 and U=X+11, implying X<U≤111; consequently U«X and condition (ii) is also satisfied—the inner recursion therefore terminates.

Taking C2 next, choose **W** again as the set of all integers but now define '«' such that, for any two integers **m** and **n**,

$$m \ll n \text{ iff } n < m \leqslant 101$$

Then [**W**, «] is well-founded with minimal element 101. Define μ as the mapping from **Q*** to **W** such that for any query in **Q*** of the form ?q(Y, Z) we have

$$\mu[?q(Y, Z)] = Y$$

Suppose such a query **q'** is derivable by invoking C2 with a query $q \in Q^*$ having the form ?q(X, Z). Then X must be an integer and therefore $\mu[q'] \in W$; hence condition (i) is satisfied. The intermediate calls must have been solved, and so we know that X≤100, U=X+11 and q(U, Y) is solvable; the latter in turn implies that

$$Y=91 \text{ if } U \leqslant 100 \text{ but } Y=U-10 \text{ otherwise}$$

Trivial manipulation of these consequences establishes that X<Y≤101 and hence that Y«X, so satisfying condition (ii). Therefore the outer recursion also terminates. The summary conclusion is that execution of any query in **Q*** using **P** under the standard computation rule must terminate. The next example shows a case in which we can recognize that termination is impossible.

Example—take **P** to be the program

> E1 :   even(0)
> E2 :   even(s(s(X))) if even(X)

and let **Q*** be the class of queries having the form ? even(**variable**). The only PRR is E2 as it stands.

The argument tuples in E2 are such that, whenever E2 is invoked by some query $q \in Q^*$ of the form ? even(V), we obtain a derived query $q' \in Q^*$ of the form ? even(V'). Since the names of query variables are drawn from an arbitrary and (theoretically) infinite set determined only by the interpreter, there is no basis on which to define a mapping μ from Q^* to the domain W of any well-founded set—in short, there is no well-founded descent that one can associate with the derived queries. Termination is consequently impossible.

More generally, there exists no perfect procedure by which we can decide for all PRRs whether or not they terminate. This is merely a re-statement of the well-known 'Halting Problem'. In practice, however, we usually have a pretty good idea of the well-founded descents underlying our recursive programs, since—in any sensible methodology—the former must have guided the design of the latter. Therefore termination analysis is usually not so much a matter of *searching* for an appropriate well-founded descent as a matter of trying to *confirm* that some known and intended descent is indeed achieved by the given program for the queries of interest; on the whole, this is a more feasible exercise.

The approach described above relies upon *static* (or 'compile-time') analysis of the program and queries, in contrast to *dynamic* (or 'run-time') analysis of evolving computations. A moderate amount of knowledge exists concerning run-time loop-detection and deals mostly with detecting various instance relations between derived calls. For example, if in some computation we find that a call q' is generated from an ancestral call q such that $q = q'\theta$ for some θ then that computation is necessarily a loop; ultimately, any such observation can be reformulated as a comment upon the non-existence of a well-founded descent. Having detected such a situation, the interpreter can then abort this computation and pursue some other one instead. There are all sorts of variations on this theme, but they lie beyond the scope of this course.

Exercises 59

1. Prove that for the interchange-sort program discussed in Exercises 38

        S1 : sort(Y, Y) if ord(Y)
        S2 : sort(X, Y) if append3(X1, U•V•nil, X2, X) & V<U &
                               append3(X1, V•U•nil, X2, Z) &
                               sort(Z, Y)

execution under the standard computation rule must terminate for the class Q^* of all queries having the form

? sort(**ground list, variable**)

You may assume without proof that executions of calls to the auxiliary relations must terminate.

2. The greatest common divisor gcd(X, Y) of any two positive integers X and Y is computable from the program

> G1 : gcd(X, X, X)
> G2 : gcd(X, Y, Z) if X>Y & U is X–Y & gcd(U, Y, Z)
> G3 : gcd(X, Y, Z) if Y>X & V is Y–X & gcd(X, V, Z)

Prove that for this program under the standard computation rule execution must terminate for the class **Q*** of all queries having the form

> ? gcd(**positive integer, positive integer, variable**)

Again, assume that executions of calls to the auxiliary relations must terminate.

3. Show that for the following program

$$\text{shift(a, X, Y, Z) if shift(Y, Z, X, b)}$$

execution must terminate for the class **Q*** of all queries having the form

> ? shift(...)

irrespective of their arguments.

Theme 60

Program verification

We have seen that deduction can be applied to logic programs in order either to compute answers to queries (by total evaluation) or to derive new programs (by partial evaluation). In this Theme we look at the use of deduction for showing that programs are **correct** relative to logic specifications. In this context correctness is taken to be the property whereby, in relation to any query, the answers logically determined by the progam are exactly those logically determined by the specification.

A **logic specification** is a set **S** of logic sentences, asserted independently of the program, which defines all the relations named in that program. In general it is both natural and sufficient for each sentence in **S** defining a relation **R** to take the propositional form

$$\mathbf{R} \text{ iff } \mathbf{F}_1 \text{ or } \mathbf{F}_2 \text{ or ...}$$

where the **R** predicate is most-general and each $\mathbf{F}_i$ is an arbitrary formula. Here are some examples showing how we might specify some familiar relations:

$$\text{parent}(X, Y) \text{ iff } \text{mother}(X, Y) \text{ or father}(X, Y)$$

$$\begin{aligned}
\text{append}(X, Y, Z) \text{ iff } & (X=\text{nil} \ \& \ Y=Z) \text{ or} \\
& (\exists U \exists X' \exists Z')(X=U{\cdot}X' \ \& \ Z=U{\cdot}Z' \ \& \\
& \qquad\qquad \text{append}(X', Y, Z'))
\end{aligned}$$

In general, each such sentence defines the relation **R** in terms of other relations which must be defined in turn by further sentences within **S**.

Occasionally it is useful to regard **S** as comprising both a set **if(S)** consisting of the sentences' if-components

$$\mathbf{R} \text{ if } \mathbf{F}_1 \text{ or } \mathbf{F}_2 \text{ or ...}$$

and a set **only-if(S)** consisting of the sentences' only-if components

$$\mathbf{R} \text{ only-if } \mathbf{F}_1 \text{ or } \mathbf{F}_2 \text{ or ...}$$

Moreover, the requirement that the **R**-predicate shall be most-general typically introduces the '=' relation—hence we shall assume that **S** includes the appropriate equality theory **Eq(H, S)**. Recalling Theme 52, you will now observe that **S** has been put in the form of a completed database.

We shall further demand that **S** is sufficiently informative about the named relations that, for any ground atom **R(t)**, we may determine from **S** whether or not **R(t)** holds: that is, either **S** implies **R(t)** or **S** implies ¬**R(t)**. This property is commonly referred to as **ground-categorical completeness**.

Suppose we develop a program **P** intended for querying a relation **R** defined by **S**. The requirement that **P** and **S** shall agree upon the denotation of **R** (that is, upon the tuples it contains) can be formulated as two conditions:

a) **partial correctness** of **P** w.r.t. **S** for relation **R**:

$$(\forall t \in H)(S \vDash R(t) \quad \text{if} \quad P \vDash R(t))$$

b) **completeness** of **P** w.r.t. **S** for relation **R**:

$$(\forall t \in H)(S \vDash R(t) \quad \text{only-if} \quad P \vDash R(t))$$

Informally, the first part requires that any answer logically computable from (implied by) the program shall be an answer according to the specification, whilst the second part requires that any answer prescribed (implied) by the specification shall be logically computable from the program.

Note that these ideas presume nothing about *execution strategy*. We know that the choice of strategy influences *effective* computability, in that an unfair strategy may be such as to enable a loop to block access to a derivation yielding some logically-computable answer. In order to determine whether or not the logically-computable answers were effectively computable we would need to undertake the separate activity of control-flow analysis, which neither owes anything nor contributes anything to the correctness conditions considered above.

Given a specification **S** and a program **P** there are various ways of investigating whether they satisfy the correctness conditions. The simplest way is to try to show that **S** logically implies (the clauses of) **P**; this is an intuitively sensible relationship which usually—though not invariably—prevails when **P** is correct w.r.t. **S**. If **S** does imply **P** then **P** must be partially correct because of the following:

$$\text{for any } R(t), \text{ if } \quad S \vDash P \text{ and } P \vDash R(t)$$
$$\text{then } S \vDash R(t) \qquad [\text{by the transitivity of } \vDash]$$

The simplest way of showing completeness as well as partial correctness is to deduce **P** from **S** in such a manner as to preserve information about each relation named in whichever sentences of **S** are used. What this requires in practice is that whenever *choices* arise in any deduction step, all those choices are explored. We shall make this notion more concrete in due course.

Meanwhile, observe that the deduction of **P** from **S** can be viewed either as a **verification**, when the program is already given, or as a **synthesis** when the program is not initially given. Thus we have a common, logically-based principle on which to base both of those activities. Any suitable first-order deduction system may be used. One option is to employ resolution—in refutational mode— after converting to clausal-form both **S** and the negations of the clauses in **P** (a task comparable to that explored in Question **7**(iii) of Exercise 53). Alternatively, one might try to derive **P** by unfolding and folding applied to the clausal-form conversion of **S**. Such approaches, however, generally incur a loss of intuitiveness owing to the enigmatical nature of the clauses (often indefinite and skolemised) being manipulated. Usually it is more intuitive and less cumbersome to work directly upon the *unconverted* specification by applying to it various **equivalence transformations**, which are just particular kinds of inference rules applicable to any sentences of first-order logic.

To illustrate this we shall use the familiar 'subset' example. The sentences of the specification are maintained in full if-and-only-if form, rather than being split into their if-parts and only-if parts. Our specification **S** comprises the following sentences:

S1 : subset(X, Y) iff $(\forall U)(U \in Y$ if $U \in X)$
S2 : empty(X) iff $(\forall U) \neg U \in X$
S3 : select(V, X, X') iff $\neg V \in X'$ & $(\forall U)(U \in X$ iff $U \in X'$ or $U = V)$
S4 : **R**(V) iff $(\forall U)(\mathbf{R}(U)$ if $U = V)$

where S4 has been drawn from Axiom **10** of **Eq(H, S)** and applies to each relation **R** named in **S**. The specification anticipates that a program manipulating any set X needs to consider both the case where X is 'empty' and the case where it is not so—in which case it must be possible to 'select' from it a member V leaving a residual set X'.

Given any sentence s containing any subformula **F1**, we may substitute a new formula **F2** for **F1** whenever **S** implies an appropriate **substitution lemma**—that is, whenever we have

either $\mathbf{S} \vDash (\mathbf{F1}$ iff $\mathbf{F2})$ [a 'type-1' lemma]

or $\mathbf{S} \vDash (\mathbf{F1}$ iff $\mathbf{F2})$ if $\mathbf{F3}$ [a 'type-2' lemma]

In the latter case we add to the substituted sentence the formula **F3** as an extra condition. The important point, however, is that in either case we shall have that

if $\mathbf{S} \vDash$ s then $\mathbf{S} \vDash$ s'

Loosely, we say that s has been transformed into s' by virtue of **F2** being (conditionally or unconditionally) 'equivalent' to **F1** according to the given lemma.

Taking our example, we can begin by choosing **F1** as the subformula $U \in X$ in S1 and observing that S3 implies a suitable type-2 lemma

$$(U \in X \text{ iff } U \in X' \text{ or } U = V) \text{ if } select(V, X, X')$$

Applying it gives

$(subset(X, Y) \text{ iff } (\forall U)(U \in Y \text{ if } U \in X' \text{ or } U = V)) \text{ if } select(V, X, X')$
$\vDash \quad subset(X, Y) \text{ if } (\forall U)(U \in Y \text{ if } U \in X' \text{ or } U = V) \text{ \& } select(V, X, X')$
$\equiv \quad subset(X, Y) \text{ if } (\forall U)(U \in Y \text{ if } U \in X') \text{ \& }$
$\qquad\qquad\qquad (\forall U)(U \in Y \text{ if } U = V) \text{ \& } select(V, X, X')$

Next, we can use both S1 and S4 as type-1 lemmas to obtain the target clause

$$subset(X, Y) \text{ if } subset(X', Y) \text{ \& } V \in Y \text{ \& } select(V, X, X')$$

This clause is just a slightly abstract version of the recursion we would customarily employ in a program to solve ? subset(X, Y)—select any element V from X to leave X', check that V occurs also in Y and solve ? subset(X', Y).

This is not the complete story. We started by substituting for $U \in X$ on the condition select(V, X, X'). It is easy to show that

$$\{S2, S3\} \vDash \neg empty(X) \text{ if } select(V, X, X')$$

and thus the derivation above covers the case of $U \in X$ where X is not empty. So we have not yet dealt with the case of $U \in X$ where X *is* empty. To cover this possibility we must *backtrack* to S1 and then substitute again for $U \in X$, this time using a lemma drawn from S2:

$$(\forall U)(U \in X \text{ iff } False) \text{ if } empty(X)$$

We then obtain

$(subset(X, Y) \text{ iff } (\forall U)(U \in Y \text{ if } False)) \text{ if } empty(X)$
$\vDash \quad subset(X, Y) \text{ iff } (\forall U)(U \in Y \text{ if } False) \text{ \& } empty(X)$
$\equiv \quad subset(X, Y) \text{ if } (\forall U)(True) \text{ \& } empty(X)$
$\equiv \quad subset(X, Y) \text{ if } empty(X)$

which is the other target clause. It should be clear from the above that we have lost no information about 'subset' relative to that contained in our starting-point S—owing to this we can be sure that the derived program is complete with respect to the specification.

If we wanted to make the program more concrete we could extend the specification so as to introduce concrete term-based data structures, thus:

$$S5: \quad empty(X) \text{ iff } X=nil$$
$$S6: \quad select(V, X, X') \text{ iff } X=V \bullet X'$$

Using these as lemmas to perform equivalence transformations upon our abstract program yields the more concrete and familiar program

$$subset(nil, Y)$$
$$subset(V \bullet X', Y) \text{ if } V \in Y \ \& \ subset(X', Y)$$

The deduction system just illustrated, although quite intuitive and effective in many practical cases, is not complete. It is possible to devise examples in which a program is implied by a ground-categorical complete specification yet is not deducible from it using just the equivalence transforms proposed above. In such cases the extra necessary ingredients are—not surprisingly—additional inference rules and/or induction schemata.

It is also possible that the program may agree with the specification yet not be implied by it. Various other verification procedures have been devised which are able to deal with this situation, but they are significantly more complicated and are consequently beyond the scope of this Theme.

Exercises 60

1. (i)   Compose a logic specification, comprising one sentence, for the predicate $cp(U, V, L)$ which expresses that in the list L the member V consecutively follows the member U. The only auxiliary relation allowed is '='.

   (ii)   Compose a logic specification, comprising one sentence, for the predicate $ord(L)$ which expresses that the list L is strictly ordered. The only auxiliary relations allowed are '<' and 'cp'.

   (iii)   Using the combined answers to (i) and (ii) and the appropriate equality theory, prove the partial correctness of the program

$$ord(nil)$$
$$ord(U \bullet nil)$$
$$ord(U \bullet V \bullet T) \text{ if } U < V \ \& \ ord(V \bullet T)$$

2. (i)   Compose a logic specification, comprising one sentence, for the predicate $length(L, N)$ which expresses that the list L has length N.

Use the auxiliary relations '≤' and 'item', where item(U, K, L) expresses that the member U occupies position K in L.

(ii)   Compose a logic specification, comprising one sentence, for the predicate non-empty(L) which expresses that the list L has at least one member. The only auxiliary relation allowed is 'item'.

(iii)   Using the combined answers to (i) and (ii), derive the clause

non-empty(L) if 1≤K & K≤N & length(L, N)

(iv)   Suggest an additional sentence specifying '≤' which would be sufficient in order to simplify the derived clause in (iii) to

non-empty(L) if 1≤N & length(L, N)

3. From suitable logic specifications of the 'subset' and 'singleton' relations, derive the clause

subset(X, Y) if V∈Y & singleton(X, V)

where singleton(X, V) expresses that X is a set comprising just a single member V.

Answers to exercises

Answers 1–4

You must find your own answers to all of these.

Answers 5

1. Clearly you are just an instance of Anyone. Since you are sensible (by the third clause) you must buy this_book (by the second clause) and hence chris must like you (by the first clause).

2. No—each clause (A if B) offers some conclusion A which can be inferred if we have already inferred B. Conclusions drawn from the program can only be instances of the clauses' conclusions, none of which are negated propositions.

3. The following three conclusions only may be inferred:

    sensible(you)
    buys(you, this_book)
    likes(chris, you)

4. nephew(You, Neph) if brother(You, Bro) & son(Neph, Bro)
   nephew(You, Neph) if sister(You, Sis) & son(Neph, Sis)

Answers 6

Again, you must find your own answer to this one.

Answers 7

Appropriate points to consider might include these:

(a) what is meant by the 'direct' expression of knowledge, and can that notion be supported in, for example, (i) a functional programming language, (ii) an object-oriented language or (iii) a conventional procedural language?

(b) whether there is any reason for believing that the mathematical analysis of software is necessarily facilitated by writing that software in logic;

(c) whether the separation of knowledge from use is (i) realistic and (ii) likely to be beneficial;

(d) whether the uniformity entailed in using one formalism for multiple activities is compatible with the natural human liking for diversity and free choice.

Answers 9

1. (i) $(\forall X)((\exists Y)parent(X, Y)$ if $father(X)$ or $mother(X))$
    (ii) $(\forall X)((\exists Y)mother(X, Y)$ if $parent(X)$ & $female(X))$
    (iii) $(\forall X)((\exists Y)(\exists Z)parent(Y, Z)$ if $father(X)$ or $mother(X))$
    (iv) $(\exists Y)child(Y)$ if $(\forall X)parent(X)$

2. (i) $(\forall X)(\forall Y)\neg likes(X, Y)$
    (ii) $(\forall X)(\forall Y)\neg likes(X, Y)$ [*same answer as* (i)]
    (iii) $(\forall X)likes(X, X)$
    (iv) $(\forall X)(\forall Y)(likes(X, Y)$ if $\neg X=Y)$
    (v) $(\exists Y)(\forall X)(likes(X, Y)$ & $(\forall Z)(Z=Y$ if $likes(X, Z)))$
    (vi) $(\forall X)(\forall Y)(likes(X, Y)$ iff $(X=chris$ & $Y=chris))$
    (vii) $(\forall X)(\neg likes(X, X)$ or $(\exists Y)\neg likes(Y, X))$

Answers 10

1. (i)   First label the quantifiers distinctly as follows:

    $(\forall_1 X)(((\forall_2 X)p(X)$ & $(\forall_3 Y)p(Y)$ & $q(X))$ if $(p(X)$ & $q(Y)))$

    The scope of $(\forall_1 X)$ is the subformula

    $(((\forall_2 X)p(X)$ & $(\forall_3 Y)p(Y)$ & $q(X))$ if $(p(X)$ & $q(Y)))$

    The scope of $(\forall_2 X)$ is the left-most subformula $p(X)$.
    The scope of $(\forall_3 Y)$ is the subformula $p(Y)$.

    (ii) X in the left-most $p(X)$ is quantified by $(\forall_2 X)$.
    Y in $p(Y)$ is quantified by $(\forall_3 Y)$.
    X in $q(X)$ is quantified by $(\forall_1 X)$.
    X in the right-most $p(X)$ is quantified by $(\forall_1 X)$.

    (iii) Only Y in $q(Y)$ is not quantified by any quantifier.

2. The instance is $tree(t(Y, U))$ $\{Y/t(U, X), U/X\}$.

Note—the occurrence of U in the term t(Y, U) is not affected by the replacement U/X; when we construct an instance we apply all the replacements simultaneously and independently.

3.   has_niece(brother(Y)) if (∃X)daughter(X, Y) &
                                        sibling(brother(Y), Y)

Note—the X in daughter(X, Y) is unaffected, since it is bound.

Answers 11

1. The sentence is **true** if we assign, for example,

        false to A , **true** to B and anything to C

The sentence is **false** if we assign, for example,

        true to A , **false** to C and anything to B

2.   (A if B) if C is **false**   iff   (A if B) is **false** and C is **true**
                                            iff   A is **false**, B is **true** and C is **true**
            A if (B & C) is **false**   iff   A is **false** and (B & C) is **true**
                                            iff   A is **false**, B is **true** and C is **true**

Thus the two sentences always have identical truth-values.

3. There are 4 ways of associating the constants with the domain and there are
   $4 \times 4 = 16$ ways of associating 'likes' with relations on the domain. Therefore
   there are $4 \times 16 = 64$ distinct interpretations.

4. Choose the domain as {chris} in each case. Then

   (i)   interpret 'likes' as {<chris, chris>};
   (ii)   same as for (i);
   (iii)   interpret 'likes' as ∅.

5. Choose the domain {**0, 1**} in each case. Then

   (i)   interpret 'even' as {**0**} and 'odd' as {**0**};
   (ii)   same as for (i);
   (iii)   interpret 0 as **0**, interpret 's' as the function which maps every
            element in the domain to **0** and interpret '=' as identity;
   (iv)   interpret 's' as in (iii), interpret 'odd' as {**0**} and 'even' as {**1**};
   (v)   **false** in *all* interpretations—e.g. interpret 'even' as {**0**}.

Answers 12

1. Let the atomic formula be p(t) where p is n-ary and t is some ground n-tuple. Choose *any* domain **D**. We may freely associate each constant in t with *any* d∈**D** and freely associate each function symbol in t with *any* function from D^n to **D**. Whichever way we make these associations, their net effect is to associate t with *any* $d^*∈D^n$ of our choosing. Finally we may freely associate p with *any* relation R⊆D^n.

   (i)   Then, p(t) can always be satisfied by arranging that $d^*∈R$.

   (ii)   However, p(t) cannot be valid since this would require $d^*∈R$ to hold *necessarily*, which it clearly does not.

2. {A, B} ⊨ C means that, for every interpretation **I**,

$$\textbf{I} \text{ satisfies C if } \textbf{I} \text{ satisfies } \{A, B\}$$
$$\text{if } \textbf{I} \text{ satisfies A and } \textbf{I} \text{ satisfies B}$$

{A} ⊨ (C if B) means that, for every interpretation **I**,

$$\textbf{I} \text{ satisfies (C if B) if } \textbf{I} \text{ satisfies A}$$

   i.e.   (**I** satisfies C if **I** satisfies B) if **I** satisfies A

   i.e.   **I** satisfies C if (**I** satisfies B and **I** satisfies A)

These accounts are clearly equivalent.

3. (i)   Let the domain be **D**={d} where d is arbitrary. Then there are just two possible interpretations—we may associate P either with ∅ or with {d}. In the first interpretation the sentence evaluates to

        ¬(¬**false** or **false**) which is **false**

     and in the second interpretation it evaluates to

        ¬(**false** or **true**) which is also **false**

     Therefore the sentence is not satisfiable on this domain.

  (ii)   Let the domain be **D**={d1, d2} where both d1 and d2 are arbitrary. The sentence can then be viewed as

     ¬ ((¬P(d1) or P(d1))
       & (¬P(d1) or P(d2))
       & (¬P(d2) or P(d2))
       & (¬P(d2) or P(d1)))

This evaluates to **true** if (and only if) we associate the predicate symbol 'P' with {d1, d2}, and therefore the sentence is satisfiable.

4. A suitable interpretation is the following:

>   choose the domain **N**={**0, 1, 2, 3**, ...}
>   associate 0 with **0**
>   associate 's' with the successor function on **N**
>   associate 'even' with {**0, 2, 4**, ...}
>   associate 'odd' with {**0, 1, 3, 5**, ...}

Answers 13

1. (i)   ¬(B iff C)   ≡   ¬((B if C) & (C if B))

  ≡   ¬(B if C) or ¬(C if B)

  ≡   ¬(B or ¬C) or ¬(C or ¬B)

  ≡   (¬B & ¬¬C) or (¬C & ¬¬B)

  ≡   (¬B & C) or (¬C & B)

  ≡   (¬B or ¬C) & (¬B or B) & (C or ¬C) & (C or B)

  ≡   ¬(B & C) & *True* & *True* & (B or C)

  ≡   (B or C) & ¬(B & C)

(ii)   (A if B) iff (B if A)   ≡   ((A if B) & (B if A)) or
  (¬(A if B) & ¬(B if A))

  ≡   (A iff B) or ¬((A if B) or (B if A))

  ≡   (A iff B) or ¬(A or ¬B or B or ¬A)

  ≡   (A iff B) or ¬*True*

  ≡   (A iff B) or *False* ≡ (A iff B)

(iii)   (A or B) iff ¬A   ≡   ((A or B) & ¬A)) or (¬(A or B) & ¬¬A)

  ≡   ((A & ¬A) or (B & ¬A)) or (¬A & ¬B & A)

  ≡   (*False* or (B & ¬A)) or (*False* & ¬B)

  ≡   (B & ¬A) or *False*

  ≡   (¬A & B)

(iv)   (∀X)(A if B(X))   ≡   (∀X)(A or ¬B(X))

  ≡   A or (∀X)¬B(X)

  ≡   A or ¬(∃X)B(X)

  ≡   A if (∃X)B(X)

(v)   (∀Y)((∃X)A(X) if A(Y))   ≡   (∃X)A(X) if (∃Y)A(Y) [using (iv)]

  ≡   (∃X)A(X) if (∃X)A(X)
  [renaming bound variables]

  ≡   (∃X)A(X) or ¬(∃X)A(X)

  ≡   *True*

(vi)   ($\exists$X)(A(X) if B(X)) $\equiv$ ($\exists$X)(A(X) or $\neg$A(X))
                                    $\equiv$ ($\exists$X)A(X) or ($\exists$X)$\neg$B(X)
                                    $\equiv$ ($\exists$X)A(X) or $\neg$($\forall$X)B(X)
                                    $\equiv$ ($\exists$X)A(X) if ($\forall$X)B(X)
                                    $\equiv$ ($\exists$X)A(X) if ($\forall$Y)B(Y)

2. (i)   A & B $\vDash$ (A & B) or $\neg$B
                  $\vDash$ (A or $\neg$B) & (B or $\neg$B)
                  $\vDash$ (A if B) & *True*
                  $\vDash$ (A if B)

   (ii)   (A or B) & ($\neg$A or C) $\vDash$ (A or $\neg\neg$B) & (C or $\neg$A)
                                      $\vDash$ (A if $\neg$B) & (C if A)
                                      $\vDash$ (C if $\neg$B)
                                      $\vDash$ (C or B)
                                      $\vDash$ (B or C)

   (iii) (A iff B) if C $\vDash$ ((A if B) & (B if A)) if C
                           $\vDash$ ((B if A) & (A if B)) if C
                           $\vDash$ ((B if A) if C) & ((A if B) if C)
                           $\vDash$ (B if A) if C
                           $\vDash$ B if (A & C)
                           $\vDash$ B if (C & A)

Answers 14

1. (i) $\neg$likes(X, Y)
   (ii) $\neg$likes(X, Y) [*same as* (i)]
   (iii)   likes(X, X)
   (iv)   likes(X, Y) if $\neg$X=Y
   (v)   {likes(chris, chris), ($\neg$likes(X, Y) or $\neg$X=chris or $\neg$Y=chris)}

2.   blessed(X) if pure_in_heart(X)
           shall_see(X, god) if blessed(X)

To ensure that only the pure in heart shall see God, use either these clauses

           blessed(X) if shall_see(X, god)
           pure_in_heart(X) if blessed(X)

or this single clause

           pure_in_heart(X) if shall_see(X, god)

depending upon how you interpret the requirement.

3.   friends(X, Y) or enemies(X, Y)
            friends(X, Y) if likes(X, Y) & likes(Y, X)
            likes(X, Y) if friends(X, Y)
            likes(Y, X) if friends(X, Y)
            enemies(X, Y) or likes(X, Y) or likes(Y, X)
            ¬likes(X, Y) or ¬enemies(X, Y)
            ¬likes(Y, X) or ¬enemies(X, Y)

4. (i)   {glitters(something) , ¬gold(something)}
   (ii)   well(X) if ends_well(X)
   (iii)   ¬island(X) if man(X)
   (iv)   justifies(Y, X) if end(X) & means(X, Y)

Answers 15

1. (i)   indefinite
   (ii)   negative
   (iii)   indefinite
   (iv)   negative
   (v)   definite

2. (i)   non-Horn
   (ii)   Horn
   (iii)   non-Horn
   (iv)   Horn
   (v)   Horn

3. (i)   rule
   (ii)   query
   (iii)   rule
   (iv)   query
   (v)   rule

4. The two clauses p(X) and (p(X) or p(X)) are logically equivalent.

5. (i)   Horn(X) or non-Horn(X) or ¬clause(X)
   (ii)   Horn_or_non-Horn(X) if clause(X)

Answers 16

1. (i)   insect(X) if six_legs(X)
   (ii)   evergreen(X) or deciduous(X) if tree(X)
   (iii)   vertebrate(X) if ¬invertebrate
   (iv)   omniscient(god) if *True*
   (v)   *False* if *True*

2 . (i)   ¬weed(X) or plant(X)

    (ii)   ¬lunch(X) or ¬free(X)

    (iii)   I've_seen(X) or ¬I've_seen(Y) or ¬elephant(Y) or ¬flies(Y)

    (iv)   will_be_saved(X) or ¬repents(X)

Answers 17

1 . (i)   parent(X, f(X)) if father(X)   [skolem function f]

          parent(X, g(X)) if mother(X)   [skolem function g]

    (ii)   mother(X, f(X)) if parent(X) & female(X)   [skolem function f]

    (iii)   parent(f(X), g(X)) if father(X)   [skolem functions f, g]

          parent(h(X), k(X)) if mother(X)   [skolem constants h, k]

    (iv)   child(α) if parent(β)   [skolem constants α, β]

2 . (i)   LHS   ≡ A or ¬(A or ¬B) ≡ A or (¬A & ¬¬B)

                 ≡ A or (¬A & B)

                 ≡ (A or ¬A) & (A or B)

                 ≡ *True* & (A or B) ≡ A or B ≡ RHS

    (ii)   LHS   ≡ (A if B) if C

                 ≡ (A or ¬B) or ¬C

                 ≡ A or ¬B or ¬C

          RHS   ≡ A if (B & C)

                 ≡ A or ¬(B & C)

                 ≡ A or ¬B or ¬C ≡ LHS

    (iii)   LHS   ≡ (∀X)(A or ¬B(X))

          RHS   ≡ A if (∃X)B(X)

                 ≡ A or ¬(∃X)B(X)

                 ≡ A or (∀X)¬B(X)

                 ≡ (∀X)(A or ¬B(X))

                 ≡ LHS

Answers 18

1 . (i)   likes(chris, Y)

    (ii)   likes(chris, skolem)

    (iii)   likes(X, Y)

    (iv)   likes(X, skolem(X))

    (v)   likes(skolem, Y)

    (vi)   likes(skolem1, skolem2)

    (vii)   ¬likes(skolem(X), chris)

    (viii)   likes(X, skolem(X))   [same as (iv)]

    (ix)   ¬likes(X, Y)

    (x)   ¬likes(X, skolem(X))

Worked solution for (x):

$$\neg(\exists X)(\forall Y)\text{likes}(X, Y) \;\Rightarrow\; (\forall X)\neg(\forall Y)\text{likes}(X, Y)$$

$$\Rightarrow\; (\forall X)(\exists Y)\neg\text{likes}(X, Y)$$

Y potentially depends upon X, and so must be
replaced by a skolem function of X to give

$$\Rightarrow\; (\forall X)\neg\text{likes}(X, \text{skolem}(X))$$

$$\Rightarrow\; \neg\text{likes}(X, \text{skolem}(X))$$

2. (i)   likes(chris, chris)
           ¬likes(chris, X) if ¬X=chris

   (ii)   likes(X, X)
           X=Y if likes(X, Y)

   (iii)   likes(X, Y) if ¬X=Y
           ¬X=Y if likes(X, Y)

3.   A if B & C & D
           A if B & ¬C & ¬D
           B if A
           C if D & A
           D if C & A

4. (i)   path(X, Y) if go(Y)
           path(X, Y) if ¬go(X)
           go(Y) if path(X, Y) & go(X)

   (ii)   empty(X) if ¬f(X)∈X
           ¬U∈X if empty(X)

   (iii)   function(F) if g(F)=h(F)
           function(F) if ¬maps(F, f(F), g(F))
           function(F) if ¬maps(F, f(F), h(F))
           Y=Z if function(F) & maps(F, X, Y) & maps(F, X, Z)

Answers 19

1. (i)   < a, aba, ababa, aca, acaba, acababa, acabababa, acabaca >
   (ii)   {a} ∪ {(aX)^{n}a | X∈{b, c}, n∈{1, 2, 3, ...}}

2. (i)   < E, D, C, B, A >
   (ii)   {A, B, C, D, E}

3. $< D, C, A >$ is a proof of A, and
          $< D, C, B, \neg A >$ is a proof of $\neg A$.

Answers 20

1. $p(0)$
          $p(s(X))$ if $p(X)$

Explanation—the program has only symbols to work with. How we interpret those symbols is up to us. The relation 'p' computable from the program is

$$p = \{0, s(0), s(s(0)), ...\}$$

and, again, how we interpret this relation is up to us. If we interpret the program over the domain $N = \{0, 1, 2, ...\}$ then 'p' denotes the set of natural numbers provided we interpret

   '0' as **0**
   's' as the function on **N** which maps **x** to **x+1**.

Alternatively, 'p' denotes the set of even numbers provided we interpret

   '0' as **0**
   's' as the function on **N** which maps **x** to **x+2**.

Alternatively, 'p' denotes the set of prime numbers provided we interpret

   '0' as **2**
   's' as the function on **N** which maps **x** to the smallest prime number which is greater than **x**.

2. The simplest condition is that I_1 and I_2 shall be **isomorphic**, that is, have the same structure:

          let the respective domains be D_1 and D_2
          and make a 1:1 mapping between D_1 and D_2;

          then for every n-ary predicate symbol **p** in the language,
          let **p** denote in I_1 the relation $R_1 \subseteq D_1^n$,
          let **p** denote in I_2 the relation $R_2 \subseteq D_2^n$,
          and make a 1:1 mapping between R_1 and R_2.

3. Add the assumptions

harriet=harry
christine=chris

Another, less convincing, possibility is to add the assumptions

harriet=Anyone
christine=Anyone

Answers 21

1. (i)   This is sound since the implication

$$\{A, B\} \vDash A \text{ if } B$$

does hold—if A and B are both **true** then (A if B) is **true**.

(ii)   This is unsound since the following implication does not hold:

$$\{(A \text{ if } C), (B \text{ if } C)\} \vDash A \text{ if } B$$

as seen from the case where A and C are both **false** and B is **true**.

(iii)   This is sound since the following implication does hold:

$$\{(A \text{ or } B), (\neg A \text{ or } C)\} \vDash B \text{ or } C$$

as seen by rewriting the assumption-set as the equivalent conjunction

$$(A \text{ or } B) \mathbin{\&} (\neg A \text{ or } C)$$

which is in turn equivalent to

$$(A \text{ if } \neg B) \mathbin{\&} (C \text{ if } A)$$

which, by the transitivity of 'if' (see Theme 13) must imply

$$(C \text{ if } \neg B) \text{ which is equivalent to } (B \text{ or } C)$$

2. The rule *modus mistakens* is unsound since the implication

$$\{A, A \text{ if } B\} \vDash B$$

does not hold—as seen from the case where **A** is **true** and **B** is **false**.

3. The following example indicates the general principle:

given clauses		in rewritten form
A if B ≡ ¬B if ¬⊢.		B* if A*
B if C ≡ ¬C if ¬B		C* if B*
C ≡ ¬¬C		¬C*

Here, A* renames ¬A, B* renames ¬B and C* renames ¬C. In order to show A, for instance, it is sufficient to apply *modus ponens* to the given clauses. Alternatively we can provisionally deny A, by asserting (A* if *True*), add this to the rewritten form of the clauses and then apply *modus tollens*:

$$\{¬C^*, (C^* \text{ if } B^*)\} \quad \vdash \quad ¬B^*$$
$$\{¬B^*, (B^* \text{ if } A^*)\} \quad \vdash \quad ¬A^*$$
$$\{¬A^*, (A^* \text{ if } True)\} \quad \vdash \quad ¬True \equiv False$$

By proving *False* we have shown that the new assumptions are unsatisfiable and hence that we must retract our denial of A—thus concluding that A must hold.

Answers 22

1. We require to prove that

$$\text{if } S \vDash s \text{ then } S{-}\{s_i\} \vDash (s \text{ if } s_i) \qquad [\text{for any i}]$$

First, assume that $S \vDash s$, so that every model for S is a model for s. Secondly, assume that there exists some interpretation I which is a model for $S{-}\{s_i\}$ but is not a model for (s if s_i). Since I is not a model for (s if s_i) it must be a model for s_i but not for s. Therefore I is a model both for $S{-}\{s_i\}$ and for $\{s_i\}$, and hence for their union, which is S. Therefore I is a model for S but not for s, contradicting the first assumption. In order to maintain the first assumption the second one must be retracted, hence establishing the proof.

2.

((A if B) if C) if D ≡	(A if B) if (C & D)	[exportation law]
≡	A if (B & (C & D))	[again]
≡	A if (B & C & D)	

3. If a sentence-set **S** is satisfied by an interpretation **I** then **I** must satisfy every subset of **S**, including ∅. Thus if ∅ has any dissatisfying interpretation **I*** then so does **S**. This would hold for any **S**—hence every **S** would have a dissatisfying interpretation (**I***).

Note—since there clearly *are* sentence-sets which are satisfied by all interpretations, it follows from the above that ∅ must also be satisfied by all interpretations. You could alternatively reach the same conclusion by using the Compactness Theorem.

Answers 23

1. (i)   **H** = { a, f(a), g(a), f(f(a)), f(g(a)), g(f(a)), g(g(a)), ...,
                    b, f(b), g(b), f(f(b)), f(g(b)), g(f(b)), g(g(b)), ...}

   (ii)   **H** = {a, t(a, a), t(t(a, a), a), t(a, t(a, a)), t(t(a, a), t(a, a)), ...}

   (iii)   **H** = {a, f(a), f(f(a)), f(f(f(a))), ...}

   Note—by convention, this case is dealt with by extending the language by introducing an arbitrary constant 'a'.

2. The program's second clause for 'int' can be viewed as shorthand for the set of all its ground instances, the simplest two of which are these:

   G1 :   int(s(0)) if int(0)   [choosing X as 0]
   G2 :   int(s(s(0))) if int(s(0))   [choosing X as s(0)]

   Then the proof requires just two steps of *modus ponens* involving only the terms 0, s(0) and s(s(0)):

   G1 ∪ {int(0)}   ⊢ int(s(0))
   G2 ∪ {int(s(0))} ⊢ int(s(s(0)))

3. Let **D** denote the domain of all strings whose members all belong to the set {**a, b**}. One possible interpretation over **D** is then as follows:

   associate '0' with the string **a**;

   associate 's' with the function from **D** to **D** which maps any element *string* to the element **a***string*;

   associate 'p' with the function from **D** to **D** which maps any element *string* to the element **b***string*;

   associate 'int' with **D**.

Note—under this interpretation, the given program determines just this subset of the meaning of 'int':

$$\{a, aa, aaa, ...\}$$

Strictly, there is no obligation upon us to provide an association for 'p' since it does not appear in the program under consideration. However, in later Themes we also need to consider queries posed to programs and to discuss their interpretations as well. Clearly, a query may well contain some function symbol such as 'p' which occurs in the language yet not in the program, and so it does no harm here to provide a meaning for it.

Answers 24

1. last(f(a, nil), a)
   last(f(nil, nil), nil)
   last(f(f(a, a), nil), f(a, a))
   last(f(f(a, nil), nil), f(a, nil))
   last(f(f(nil, a), nil), f(nil, a))
   last(f(f(nil, nil), nil), f(nil, nil))
   :
   etc.

   last(f(a, a), a) if last(a, a)
   last(f(a, a), nil) if last(a, nil)
   last(f(a, nil), a) if last(nil, a)
   last(f(a, nil), nil) if last(nil, nil)
   last(f(nil, a), a) if last(a, a)
   last(f(nil, a), nil) if last(a, nil)
   :
   etc.

2. One step of *modus ponens* suffices:

   { last(f(a, nil), a),

   last(f(a, f(a, nil)), a) if last(f(a, nil), a)} ⊢ last(f(a, f(a, nil)), a)

3. First, note that we can add the atomic sentence *True* to any set of assumptions with altering its logical properties. Likewise we can rewrite any atomic sentence **A** as the sentence (**A** if *True*). Then the reflexivity property can be viewed as this step of *modus ponens*:

   {*True*, (**A** if *True*)} ⊢ **A**

Answers 25

1. (i)   There are 39 ground clauses in $\mathbf{G}(\mathbf{P} \cup \neg\mathbf{C})$ which may be enumerated systematically as follows:

$$g_1 \ : \ \neg\textbf{path(a, c)}$$
$$g_2 \ : \ \textbf{arc(a, b)}$$
$$g_3 \ : \ \textbf{arc(b, c)}$$
$$g_4 \ : \ \text{path(a, a) if arc(a, a)}$$
$$g_5 \ : \ \text{path(a, b) if arc(a, b)}$$
$$g_6 \ : \ \text{path(a, c) if arc(a, c)}$$
$$g_7 \ : \ \text{path(b, a) if arc(b, a)}$$
$$g_8 \ : \ \text{path(b, b) if arc(b, b)}$$
$$g_9 \ : \ \textbf{path(b, c) if arc(b, c)}$$
$$\vdots$$
$$g_{13} \ : \ \text{path(a, a) if arc(a, a) \& path(a, a)}$$
$$\vdots$$
$$g_{20} \ : \ \textbf{path(a, c) if arc(a, b) \& path(b, c)}$$
$$\vdots$$
$$g_{39} \ : \ \text{path(c, c) if arc(c, c) \& path(c, c)}$$

(ii)   For $k = 1, 2, \ldots$ we test whether $\{g_1, \ldots, g_k\}$ is unsatisfiable. The test will not succeed until k reaches 20, whereupon unsatisfiability becomes detectable amongst the five clauses shown in bold face.

Answers 26

1. Suppose that the first parent has m positive literals and that the second has n positive literals. Then the resolvent must have $(m+n-1)$ positive literals, since one positive literal is eliminated in the complementary pair. If both parents are Horn clauses then we must have $m \leqslant 1$ and $n \leqslant 1$, in which case $(m+n-1) \leqslant 1$; so the resolvent must be a Horn clause.

2. Showing that ((A if B) if A) is valid is equivalent to showing that its negation is unsatisfiable, which is in turn equivalent to showing that $\square$ is resolution-derivable from the clausal form of the negation. The negation in clausal form is $\{A, \neg A, B\}$ from which $\square$ is resolution-derivable in one step: thus the original sentence must be valid.

3. If the inference were sound then, by definition, we should have

$$\{A, A \text{ if } B\} \vDash B$$

and hence that {A, A if B, ¬B} were unsatisfiable and hence that □ were resolution-derivable. But no resolvent is derivable (since no two clauses resolve) and so the inference must be unsound.

4. If it were affirmation-complete then (A if B) would be derivable as a resolvent (whether directly or indirectly) from {A, B}. But those two clauses have no resolvent and therefore resolution cannot be affirmation-complete.

Answers 27

1. (i)   likes(mum(Y), dad(chris))
   (ii)   likes(mum(chris), dad(chris))
   (iii)   tree(t(t(U, U), t(U, U)))
   (iv) $(\exists X)$wife(X, Y) if man(Y) & married(Y, elizabeth)

   Note—the X in wife(X, Y) is not replaced since it is bound.

2. (i)   not strictly legal, as it is not idempotent.
   (ii)   legal, by convention, and called an **identity substitution**.
   (iii)   legal, and called the **null substitution**.
   (iv)   illegal due to not being functional.
   (v)   technically illegal, despite being effectively functional.
   (vi)   not strictly legal, as it is not idempotent.
   (vii)   same answer as (v).
   (viii)   illegal—only variables may be replaced.

3. $\sigma^1 = \{X/f(a, Y), Y/f(b, Z), Z/c\}$ is not idempotent
          $\sigma^2 = \{X/f(a, f(b, Z)), Y/f(b, c), Z/c\}$ is not idempotent
          $\sigma^3 = \{X/f(a, f(b, c)), Y/f(b, c), Z/c\}$ is idempotent
          so the answer is n=3.

4. $\sigma^* = \{X/f(a, b), W/f(U, Z), Y/b, V/c\}$

        p(V, X, Y, W)σ*   = p(c, f(a, b), b, f(U, Z))
        p(V, X, Y, W)σ1   = p(V, f(a, Y), Y, f(U, Z))
        (p(V, X, Y, W)σ1)σ2 = p(c, f(a, b), b, f(U, Z))

Answers 28

1. The initial clauses are

        C1 : likes(chris, Y) or likes(Y, chris)
        C2 : ¬likes(X, chris)

   Note—rename X in C1 as Y to distinguish it from X in C2.

Now derive the following resolvents:

   C3 : likes(chris, chris) [parents C1 and C2]
   C4 : □   [parents C2 and C3]

2. The initial clauses are

   C1 : likes(chris, Y) or likes(Y, chris)
   C2 : ¬likes(X, chris) or ¬likes(chris, X)

Note—these *are* unsatisfiable; to see this, just take the instances C1{Y/chris} and C2{X/chris}, and do a propositional truth-analysis.

Let [+ +] denote the class of all clauses having two positive literals, let [− −] denote the class having two negative literals and let [+ −] denote the class having one positive literal and one negative literal. Now observe the following:

  (a) if two clauses from any of these classes resolve with one another then every resolvent directly or indirectly derivable from them is also in one of those classes;
  (b) C1 is in [+ +] and C2 is in [− −];
  (c) □ is not in any of the three classes.

Hence no refutation is derivable.

Note—the point is that one of the initial clauses (C1) is *indefinite*; in order to obtain refutations from unsatisfiable, indefinite clause-sets, one must sometimes supplement resolution with another inference rule called **factoring**—see Theme 39.

3. The initial clauses are

   C1 : helps(X, Y) or helps(Y, Y)
   C2 : ¬helps(α, α)   [skolem constant α]

Now derive the following resolvents:

   C3 : helps(α, α)   [parents C1 and C2]
   C4 : □   [parents C2 and C3]

4. The initial clauses are

   C1 : path(X, Y) if go(Y)
   C2 : path(X, Y) if ¬go(X)
   C3 : go(Y) if path(X, Y) & go(X)

(i)   First deny **reflexivity** by adding the clause

      C4 : ¬path(α, α)   [skolem constant α]

and then derive the following resolvents:

      C5 : ¬go(α)   [parents C1 and C4]
      C6 : go(α)   [parents C2 and C4]
      C7 : □   [parents C5 and C6]

(ii)   First deny **transitivity** by adding the clauses

      C4 : ¬path(α, γ)   [skolem constants α, β, γ]
      C5 : path(α, β)
      C6 : path(β, γ)

and then derive the following resolvents:

      C7 : ¬go(γ)   [parents C1 and C4]
      C8 : ¬path(X, γ) or ¬go(X)   [parents C3 and C7]
      C9 : ¬go(β)   [parents C6 and C8]
      C10 : ¬path(W, β) or ¬go(W)   [parents C3 and C9]
      C11 : ¬go(α)   [parents C5 and C10]
      C12 : path(α, Y)   [parents C2 and C11]
      C13 : □   [parents C4 and C12]

5. The initial clauses are

      C1 : path(X, Y) if go(Y)
      C2 : path(X, Y) if ¬go(X)
      C3 : go(Y) if path(X, Y) & go(X)
      C4 : go(c) if go(b)
      C5 : go(b) if go(a)
      C6 : ¬path(a, c)

Now derive the following resolvents:

      C7 : ¬go(c)   [parents C1 and C6]
      C8 : ¬go(b)   [parents C4 and C7]
      C9 : ¬go(a)   [parents C5 and C8]
      C10 : path(a, Y)   [parents C2 and C9]
      C11 : □   [parents C6 and C10]

6. The initial clauses are

> C1 : subset(X, Y) if f(X, Y)∈Y   [skolem function f]
> C2 : subset(X, Y) if ¬f(X, Y)∈X
> C3 : U∈Y if subset(X, Y) & U∈X
> C4 : U∈a if U=1
> C5 : U∈b if U=1
> C6 : U∈b if U=2
> C7 : U=1 if U∈a
> C8 : U=1 or U=2 if U∈b
> C9 : ¬subset(a, b)

Now derive the following resolvents:

> C10 : f(a, b)∈a   [parents C2 and C9]
> C11 : f(a, b)=1   [parents C7 and C10]
> C12 : f(a, b)∈b   [parents C5 and C11]
> C13 : subset(a, b)   [parents C1 and C12]
> C14 : □   [parents C9 and C13]

7. The initial clauses are

> C1 : X=Y if R(X, Y) & R(Y, X)   [antisymmetry of R]
> C2 : X=Y if Y=X   [symmetry of =]
> C3 : S(X, Y) if R(X, Y)
> C4 : S(X, Y) if X=Y
> C5 : R(X, Y) or X=Y if S(X, Y)
> C6 : S(α, β)   [skolem constants α, β]
> C7 : S(β, α)
> C8 : ¬α=β

Now derive the following resolvents:

> C9 : ¬R(α, β) or ¬R(β, α)   [parents C1 and C8]
> C10 : α=β or ¬S(α, β) or ¬R(β, α)   [parents C5 and C9]
> C11 : ¬S(α, β) or ¬R(β, α)   [parents C8 and C10]
> C12 : ¬R(β, α)   [parents C6 and C11]
> C13 : β=α or ¬S(β, α)   [parents C5 and C12]
> C14 : α=β or ¬S(β, α)   [parents C2 and C13]
> C15 : ¬S(β, α)   [parents C8 and C14]
> C16 : □   [parents C7 and C15]

Answers 29

1. (i) $(\forall X)(\forall Y)(\forall Z)\neg$append(a•X•nil, Y•nil, Z)

(ii)

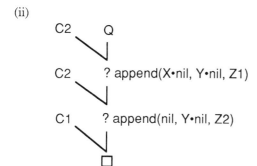

```
C2    Q
       \
C2     ? append(X•nil, Y•nil, Z1)
        \
C1     ? append(nil, Y•nil, Z2)
        \
         □
```

(iii) $(\exists X)(\exists Y)$append(a•X•nil, Y•nil, a•X•Y•nil)

2. (i)

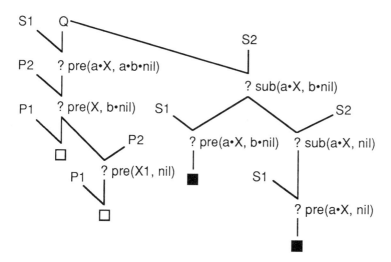

(ii)   sub(a•nil, a•b•nil)
        sub(a•b•nil, a•b•nil)

(iii)   sub(X, Y) if append(Y1, X, Y2) & append(Y2, Y3, Y)

Answers 30

1. (i)   finite and successful
   (ii)   infinite and successful
   (iii) finitely failed
   (iv)   infinite and successful
   (v)   finitely failed

   Note—this query cannot be resolved with the second 'append' clause, as that
   would require a disallowed substitution $\{U/U \cdot X\}$ which makes U an infinite
   term outside the language.

   (vi)   infinite and successful
   (vii) infinitely failed

2. (i)

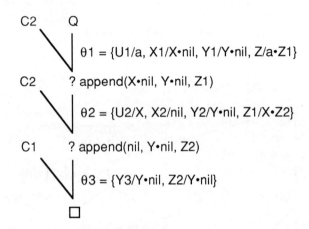

   (ii) $\theta1 \circ \theta2 = \{$ U1/a, X1/X·nil, Y1/Y·nil, Z/a·X·Z2,
            U2/X, X2/nil, Y2/Y·nil, Z1/X·Z2$\}$

   $\theta1 \circ \theta2 \circ \theta3 = \{$ U1/a, X1/X·nil, Y1/Y·nil, Z/a·X·Y·nil,
            U2/X, X2/nil, Y2/Y·nil, Z1/X·Y·nil,
            Y3/Y·nil, Z2/Y·nil$\}$

   $\Phi = \{Z/a \cdot X \cdot Y \cdot nil\}$ [the bindings significant to Q]

   computed answer $= (\exists X)(\exists Y)$append(a·X·nil, Y·nil, a·X·Y·nil)
   universal closure $= (\forall X)(\forall Y)$append(a·X·nil, Y·nil, a·X·Y·nil)

3. We know that **P** solves ?R(Y) without requiring Y to take any particular
   value, since the answer substitution $\Phi = \{Y/X\}$ leaves X unbound (and hence

Y effectively unbound). This means that **P** would also solve any *instance* of ?R(Y) and, in particular, any instance ?R(α) where α is a Skolem constant. Thus **P** $\cup$ {¬R(α)} must be unsatisfiable. However, the latter is the clausal form version of **P** $\cup$ {¬($\forall$X)R(X)}, which must therefore also be unsatisfiable. It follows immediately that **P** ⊨ ($\forall$X)R(X).

Answers 31

1. The clause-set **C** obtained by converting ¬**s** to clausal form is

$$\{odd(\alpha), \neg even(s(\alpha))\} \qquad \text{[skolem constant } \alpha \text{]}$$

SLD resolution must begin with the negative clause; however, this clause resolves with no clause—thus, since no refutation is obtainable from **P** $\cup$ **C** it follows that **P** does not imply **s**.

Note—it should be clear from the above that **P** cannot, in fact, imply *any* sentence of the form ($\forall$X)(even(s(X)) if ...).

2. (i)   The SLD tree consists here of just one computation:

        ? one-and-zero(1•0•1•0•nil)
        ? ones(1•0•1•0•nil) & zeros(1•0•1•0•nil)
        ? ones(1•0•nil)   & zeros(1•0•1•0•nil)
        ? ones(nil)   & zeros(1•0•1•0•nil)
        ? zeros(1•0•1•0•nil)
        ? zeros(1•0•nil)
        ? zeros(nil)
        □

      No efficiency gain would be achieved by using a rightmost computation rule for this query.

(ii)   for the query ? one-and-zero(1•2•1•0•nil) it would be more efficient to use the right most rule, because it would have the effect of inspecting first those positions in the list where 0s were expected; thus execution would terminate (as soon as the 2 were found) without wasting time in checking the 1s.

(iii)   a computation rule which selected whichever call had the longest argument would solve both queries efficiently by giving equitable attention to the positions of both 0s and 1s.

Answers 32

1. (i)   The four relevant clauses identified in the Theme are

G1 : ¬gr(am, br)
G2 : gr(am, br) if p(am, ch) & p(ch, br)
G3 : p(am, ch)
G4 : p(ch, br)

Let **mp** abbreviate *modus ponens*, **mp** abbreviate *modus tollens* and **tol** abbreviate *transportation of literals*. Then we can infer the following clauses:

G5 : gr(am, br) or ¬p(am, ch) if p(ch, br)   [**tol** on G2]
G6 : gr(am, br) or ¬p(am, ch)   [**mp** on G4, G5]
G7 : gr(am, br) if p(am, ch)   [**tol** on G6]
G8 : gr(am, br)   [**mp** on G3, G7]
G9 : □   [**mt** on G1, G8]

There are lots of other ways of deriving □. Here is one way using propositional resolution:

G7 is the resolvent of G2 and G4
G8 is the resolvent of G3 and G7
G9 is the resolvent of G1 and G8

(ii)   One counter-model is that which assigns **true** to just the three atoms gr(am, br), p(am, ch) and p(ch, br); this satisfies G2, G3 and G4, but not G1.

Alternatively, assign **true** to just the atoms p(am, ch) and p(ch, br); this satisfies G1, G3 and G4, but not G2.

Note—these are the two simplest counter-models.

2. In order to get the desired effect we need only further eliminate those subsets which comprise just two or more negative clauses, of which there are merely 11. Thus the number of potentially relevant subsets becomes reduced to $2^{71}-2^{67}-15$ (which is scarcely a significant improvement upon the original total).

Answers 33

1. The stack **S** initially contains only a finite number of term-pairs. Thereafter, each step removes one of those term-pairs and may must be syntactically smaller than the one removed since it is a proper subcomponent of it. Since any term-pair can be reduced only to a finite number of proper subcomponents, the stack clearly cannot grow indefinitely; thus it must eventually either become completely emptied, hence terminating the algorithm

with 'success', or else yield up an irreconcilable term-pair and thereby terminate the algorithm with 'failure'.

Note—the result can be proved formally, but with no significant difficulty, by using structural induction.

2. **Note**—let l.g.u. denote any less-general unifier.

(i)   m.g.u. = {Y/a, X/b}; no l.g.u.
(ii)   m.g.u. = {X/Y, Z/Y}; l.g.u. = {X/a, Y/a, Z/a}
(iii)   m.g.u. = {X/Y1, Y/X1}; l.g.u. = {X/a, Y/b, X1/b, Y1/a}

Note—variables have been renamed in (iii) so that no two atoms have a variable in common.

(iv)   m.g.u. = {X/a, Z/t(a, b)}; no l.g.u.
(v)   no m.g.u.
(vi)   m.g.u. = {X/f(Y1), X1/f(Y)}; l.g.u. = {X/f(a), X1/f(b), Y1/a, Y/b}

Note—variables have been renamed in (vi) so that no two atoms have a variable in common.

(vii)   no m.g.u.

Answers 34

1. Depending upon the manner in which we deal with any term-pair comprising two variables, the algorithm will yield

$$\text{either} \quad \{X/W, W/f(W)\}$$
$$\text{or} \quad \{W/X, X/f(X)\}$$

These replacement sets are not fundamentally distinct—each one is just a **variant** (uniformly-renamed version) of the other.

Note—the desire to avoid this complication is what motivated the choice of the slightly more elaborate example in the Theme.

2. An apparently suitable assertion is

$$A : \quad \text{put\_on\_end}(U, \text{diff}(L, U \bullet \text{nil}), L)$$

Resolving A with Q1 solves Q1 and yields the m.g.u.

$$\{U/c, X/L, L/c \bullet \text{nil}, Y/c \bullet \text{nil}\}$$

The value c•nil assigned to Y is intuitively correct provided we interpret diff(X, X) as the empty list.

The outcome using Q2 is rather more subtle. Since Q1 succeeds, you might expect Q2 also to succeed; however, it does not—the occur check precludes resolving A with Q2. If the occur-check were suppressed then Q2 would be 'solved' and Y would be assigned the value X where X was itself assigned to X•nil—in effect, assigning Y an infinite value. That answer would certainly be wrong, so we can be grateful to the occur-check for blocking it. Does Q2 have an intuitively correct answer? It can be read as seeking to add the arbitrary element X to the empty list, so the result Y should be the unit list X•nil. Yet we cannot compute this answer because the occur check forces Q2 to fail. The problem arises fundamentally from not having proper regard for *types*. The use of diff(X, X) to represent the empty list entails that X is itself a list, since 'diff' refers to the difference of two lists. But the appearance of X also as the first argument in Q2 treats X as a potential member of the latter class of lists. If we want to maintain the latter role for X then we shall have to represent the empty list in Q2 in a less risky way. Using diff(V•nil, V•nil) solves the problem.

Moral—when using difference lists, take care not to violate implicit assumptions about types.

3. (i)   We seek to derive □ from the clausal form of {A1, ¬A2}, which comprises the two clauses:

append(f(U), U, U)   [skolem function f]
¬append(V, g(V), g(V))   [skolem function g]

Occur-check failure prevents these from resolving and so A1 does not imply A2. If the occur-check were suppressed then the clauses would resolve and we would conclude, incorrectly, that the implication did hold.

Note—in the usual interpretation, which associates 'append' with concatenation over the domain of lists, both A1 and A2 are **true** and you might have expected that the implication would hold. To see that it does not, consider an interpretation over the domain {1, 2} which associates 'append' with the 3-ary relation {<1, 1, 1>, <2, 2, 2>}. Then this is a model for A1 but a counter-model for A2.

(ii)   We now seek to derive □ from the clausal form of {A2, ¬A1}, which comprises the two clauses:

append(α, U, U)   [skolem constant α]
¬ append(V, β, β)   [skolem constant β]

These resolve (with or without the occur-check) to give □ as the resolvent, correctly confirming that A2 implies A1.

Answers 35

1. (i) (a) **select**(Query, Call, Others) if append(Call•nil, Others, Query)

   combine(New_calls, Others, New_query)
   if append(New_calls, Others, New_query)

   (b) **select**(Query, Call, Others) if append(Others, Call•nil, Query)

   combine(New_calls, Others, New_query)
   if append(Others, New_calls, New_query)

(ii)

```
                              ? solve(one-and-zero(1•0•1•0•nil)•nil)
        _____
? empty(...)              :
  |                       :
  ■                          ? solve(ones(1•0•1•0•nil)•zeros(1•0•1•0•nil)•nil)
   _____
? empty(...)              :
  |                       :
  ■                          ? solve(ones(1•0•nil)•zeros(1•0•1•0•nil)•nil)
   _____
? empty(...)              :
  |                       :
  ■                          ? solve(ones(nil)•zeros(1•0•1•0•nil)•nil)
   _____
? empty(...)              :
  |                       :
  ■                          ? solve(zeros(1•0•1•0•nil)•nil)
   _____
? empty(...)              :
  |                       :
  ■                          ? solve(nil)
   _____
? empty(nil)              ? select(nil, Call, Others) & ...
  |                         |
  □                         ■
```

Note—The initial query is coded as the *list of calls* one-and-zero(nil)•nil. The simulated execution by **M** then proceeds as shown above, where intermediate steps dealing with calls to '**select**', '**reduce**', etc. have been omitted for brevity.

2. 1.   Each node in the tree is

either the empty query □
or a non-empty query having no immediate descendants
or a query having one or more immediate descendants.

Nodes of the first two kinds are called **leaf nodes** and nodes of the third kind are called **non-leaf nodes**.

2.   The search begins by **generating** the tree's **root node**, which constitutes the tree's first **layer**.

3.   A **search step** from a non-leaf node generates any one of that node's so-far-ungenerated immediate descendants.

4.   A **layer step** comprises all possible search steps from non-leaf nodes in the current layer; the nodes thereby generated jointly constitute the next layer.

5.   If the current layer contains no non-leaf nodes then the entire tree has been generated, otherwise another layer step is performed.

Answers 36

1. (i)   Leftmost selection, otherwise the tree will be infinite.
(ii)   Rightmost selection, otherwise the tree will be infinite.
(iii)   There is not much difference—both cases yield a single computation having 10 steps. However, with rightmost selection the derived queries are generally shorter than those obtained using leftmost selection, so in the former case there may be some advantage in memory utilization.

2. The SLD-tree looks like this:

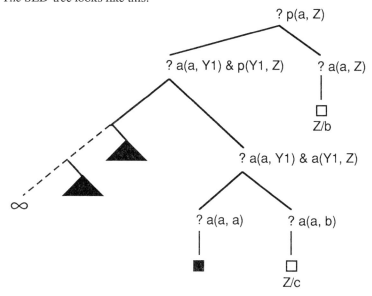

Answers 37

1. (i) θ_{in} = {U/a, X/T•nil, Y/b•V} and θ_{out} = {W/a•Z}.

Note—you might argue that the data 'a' passed to W in θ_{out} has come not from the procedure but from the query's own call. However, such a view is an over-simplification. What actually happens here is that 'a' is first passed from the call as *input* to the procedure via the variable U, from which it is subsequently passed back again to the call as *output* to W. You can regard U as a *channel* in the procedure through which data can be routed from the query, as indicated below:

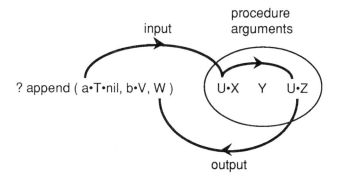

(ii) θ_{in} = {Z/a•b•nil}

         θ_{out} = {W/nil, X/b•nil, V/a}

Similar channelling behaviour occurs here, too. It is easiest to perceive it in distinct stages: first, the query's data 'a' is routed through the procedure variable Z to the query variable V; then b•nil is routed through Z to the query variable X; finally, b•nil is passed back again from X as further input to Z.

Answers 38

1. The program as first given is highly inefficient. The standard interchange-sort algorithm is just a deterministic iteration, in each cycle of which it suffices to identify and invert any *one* disordered pair V<U in the current state of the list. This program is inefficient because, having selected any one such pair it subsequently backtracks (on the first 'append3' call) to seek alternative disordered pairs in that same state of the list. The consequent redundancy can be seen in this simplified view of the execution of the suggested query, where selected pairs have been underlined:

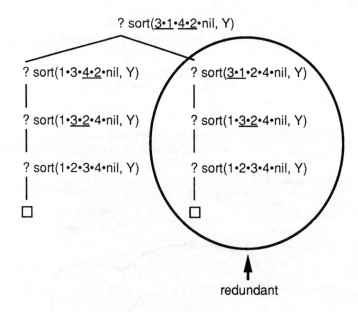

(i)   This modification would be disastrously wrong: if in some cycle the program failed to detect disorderedness in the first pair of the list, then the cut would prevent backtracking to the first 'append3' call for the purpose of seeking other pairs—thus execution might incorrectly fail.

(ii) This version would work correctly and the effect of the cut would be to eliminate the redundant subtree shown above. So it is more efficient than the original version.

(iii) This version is very risky because S3 is not **true** in the intended interpretation. However, it *does* work correctly for all **standard queries** in which the input list contains only distinct numbers; also, it is more efficient than version (ii) because it omits the final test ord(Y). An example of a **standard query** which incorrectly succeeds using version (iii) is

$$? \text{ sort}(1 \bullet 1 \bullet \text{nil}, Y)$$

Clearly, sort(1•1•nil, 1•1•nil) is not **true** in the intended interpretation because 1•1•nil is not in strictly ascending order.

Note—version (iii) will also incorrectly succeed with non-standard queries such as ? sort(silly, Y).

2. (i) It is motivated by recognizing that if the call greater_or_equal(X, Y) succeeds then

(a) whichever way it succeeds (for instance, by X>Y), there is no purpose in trying to solve it another way (for instance, by X=Y), and

(b) only the first clause for 'least' should be used to solve the query.

(ii) Both queries are correctly solved as follows:

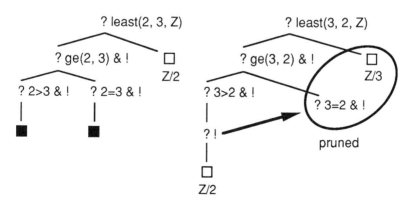

(iii)   No—for example, it incorrectly succeeds for the query

? least(3, 2, 3)

due to using this clause which is **false** in the intended interpretation:

least(X, Y, X)

3. Consider the result of executing the query ? one-way(P, q) using the supposed algorithm **A** with program **P** as the available data. If the query succeeds, this means that the call one-way(P, q) in **P** must succeed, in which case ?q succeeds from **P** in two ways—hence **A** has produced the wrong answer. Otherwise, if the query fails, this means that the call one-way(P, q) in **P** must fail, in which case ?q succeeds from **P** in one way—hence **A** has again produced the wrong answer. The conclusion is that algorithm **A** cannot exist.

Note—in this exercise we have glossed over the metalogical question of whether the notion of a program **P** referring to itself is fully formalizable in first-order logic.

Answers 39

1. (i)   The initial clauses from which we seek to derive $\square$ are

C1 : A(X) or A(Y)
C2 : ¬A(W) or ¬A(Z)

However, $\square$ is underivable for exactly the same reasons as given in the answer to Question **2** of Exercises 28.

(ii)   Factoring C1 gives A(X) and factoring C2 gives ¬A(W); resolving these factored clauses gives $\square$ immediately.

Note—factored clauses are always logically *implied* by the original clauses; in this example they happen also to be *equivalent* to them.

Answers 40

1.   Each interpretation is some subset of **H**, and the number of such subsets is 2^n.

2.   **B(P)** is always an **H**-model.

3.   **P** must contain no assertions (positive unit clauses).

4. **P** must be such that, for every relevant atom in **P**, **P** implies **q**.

Note—equivalently, every ground atom in **G**(**P**) must be ultimately reducible, using the clauses in **G**(**P**), to some conjunction of ground assertions in **G**(**P**). This restricts the choice of relevant models to those which make the body of each clause (and hence also its heading) **true**; there can be only one such model, which consists of just the relevant atoms in **P**.

Consider this counter-example in which **H**={god, chris}:

"... *and without him was not anything made that was made.*"

In clausal form this becomes the program **P**

made_by(X, god) if was_made(X)

whose ground instantiation **G**(**P**) is

made_by(god, god)   if was_made(god)
made_by(chris, god) if was_made(chris)

Here, **P** has 9 distinct relevant **H**-models. Observe that, in **G**(**P**) as it stands, no atom **q** is such that **q** is implied by **P**. The simplest way of remedying this is to add to **P** the assertion

was_made(X)

The resulting program then has exactly one relevant **H**-model:

{ made_by(god, god), was_made(god)
made_by(chris, god),was_made(chris)}

Note that this way of forcing a unique meaning upon the new program also yields, as a logical consequence, the fact

made_by(X, god)

Thus we have conceded St. John's preceding claim:

"*All things were made by him;*"

5. Here, every clause in **P** has to be valid (tautological). For this to be so, the consequent atom **q** in every ground clause **g** in **G**(**P**) must also be an antecedent atom in **g**. Thus, whatever interpretation **I**⊆**B**(**P**) we take, **g** must be **true** irrespective of whether or not **q** belongs to **I**.

6. The **H**-models here are just {A, C}, {B, C} and {A, B, C}.

7. The smallest **H**-model is this set of ground atoms:

$$\{list(t) \mid t \in \{nil, a \cdot nil, a \cdot a \cdot nil, a \cdot a \cdot a \cdot nil, ...\}\}$$

8. The interpretations are $\emptyset$, {p(1)}, {p(2)} and {p(1), p(2)}. Only the last of these is an **H**-model for the clause.

Answers 41

1. (i)

R(X, X)	**reflexivity**
X=Y if R(X, Y) & R(Y, X)	**antisymmetry**
R(X, Z) if R(X, Y) & R(Y, Z)	**transitivity**

   (ii)

C1 :	¬R(Y, X) if R(X, Y)	**asymmetry**
C2 :	R(X, Z) if R(X, Y) & R(Y, Z)	**transitivity**
	¬R(X, X)	**irreflexivity**
C3 :	R(α, α)	**denial of irreflexivity**
		[skolem constant α]

   Resolving C1 and C3 gives

   C4 : ¬R(α, α)

   Resolving C4 and C3 gives $\square$.

2. (i) Both **S** and **s** have no lower bound but have one upper bound **a**.
   (ii) **S** has no least element but has a greatest element **a**.
         s has neither a least nor a greatest element.
   (iii) **S** has one maximal element **a** and three minimal elements **c**, **d** and **g**.
         s has two maximal elements **b** and **e**, and three minimal elements **c**, **d** and **e**.

3. Since **S** is itself a subset of **S** it follows that **S** has a greatest lower bound which, being a member of **S**, must be the (unique) least element of **S**.

   Since the empty set $\emptyset$ is a subset of **S** it follows that $\emptyset$ has a greatest lower bound and, because all the lower bounds of $\emptyset$ are exactly all the members of **S**, the greatest of them must be the (unique) greatest element of **S**.

   The existence of both a least and a greatest element establishes the complete lattice property.

Note—this proof is directly analogous to that given in the Theme.

Answers 42

1. (i) minimal symmetric model = {BL, LB, CB, BC}
maximal symmetric model = **B(P)**

   (ii) {BL, LB, CB, BC, LL, CL, LC, CC}

2. (i) Since every model includes **MM(P)** we must have at least the atoms BL and CB ; then reflexivity requires that we must also have BB, LL and CC. In fact {BL, CB, BB, LL, CC} is the minimal reflexive model for this program.

   (ii) There are several irreflexive models, the minimal one being **MM(P)**. Another example is {BL, CB, LB, LC}.

   (iii) There are several transitive models, the minimal one being {BL, CB, CL, CC} and the maximal one being **B(P)**. An intermediate one is {BL, CB, CL, CC, LL, BB}.

3. **B(P)** is certainly not a counter-model. Try removing any one atom from **B(P)**—then we find that the following are counter-models:

$$B(P)-\{CC\}$$
$$B(P)-\{CB\}$$
$$B(P)-\{CL\}$$
$$B(P)-\{BL\}$$

These are the only maximal ones. Note that in each case we have removed from **B(P)** an atom in the heading of some clause in **G(P)** whose body remains **true**, thereby making the clause **false**.

4. The simplest counter-example is the case where **P1**={B} and **P2** is {A if B}. Then **MM(P1)**={B} and **MM(P2)**=∅, so that their union is {B}; however, **MM(P1 ∪ P2)**={A, B}.

Answers 43

1. **Assumption A1:**   **I** is the intersection of several models
                             M_1, ... and M_n for **P**, where **P** is definite.

   Assumption A2:   **I** is not a model for **P**.

   If **A2** holds   then   some clause (**q** if **body**) of **G(P)** is **false** in **I**
                      then   **q**∉**I** and **body** is **true** in **I**
                      then   **q**∉M_i and **body** is **true** in M_i for some i

then $\mathbf{M_i}$ is not a model for (**q** if **body**)

then $\mathbf{M_i}$ is not a model for **P**

which contradicts **A1**. Thus to maintain **A1** we have to deny **A2**, which gives the result.

Note— first, **I** need not be the intersection of *all* models of **P**;

secondly, the result does not generally hold if **P** is indefinite.

Answers 44

1. The part of **MM(P)** computed by the given query is

$$\{ \text{ append(nil, nil, nil)}$$
$$\text{append(nil, a•nil, a•nil)}$$
$$\text{append(nil, a•a•nil, a•a•nil)}$$
$$\vdots$$
$$\text{etc.}\}$$

2. The output determines that the part of **SS('arc')** computed by the query is {arc(a, b), arc(a, c)} and that the part of **SS('path')** computed is {path(b, d), path(c, d)}; the part of **MM(P)** computed altogether is the union of these sets.

3. Since the query interrogates *every* relation (here, just 'p') in **P** and does so in the most-general way, it must compute the whole of **MM(P)**. The computed output tells us that **MM(P)** must be

$$\{ \text{p(0, 0),} \qquad \text{p(0, s(0)),}$$
$$\text{p(0, s(0)),} \qquad \text{p(s(0), s(s(0))),}$$
$$\text{p(0, s(s(0))),} \quad \text{p(s(s(0)), s(s(s(0)))),}$$
$$\vdots \qquad\qquad \vdots$$
$$\text{etc.} \qquad\qquad \text{etc.}\}$$

4. Construct the minimal model for the first program as follows:

even(0) must be **true** to make the first clause **true**;

for the case X=0, the second clause says that

$$\text{even(s(s(0)))} \text{ if } \text{even(0)}$$

which is **true** only if even(s(s(0))) is **true**, as even(0) is **true**;

odd(s(0)) must be **true** to make the third clause **true**;

for the case X=s(0), the fourth clause says that

$$\text{odd(s(0))} \text{ if } \text{even(s(s(0)))}$$

which is **true** since both of its atoms are **true**.

Continuing this sort of reasoning in order to make *all* instances of the clauses **true** soon makes it clear that the set of atoms which have to be **true** (i.e. the minimal model) is

$$\{even(0), even(s(s(0))), even(s(s(s(s(0))))), ...\}$$
$$\cup \ \{odd(s(0)), odd(s(s(s(0)))), ...\}$$

Similar analysis of the second program yields the same minimal model. Hence the programs have identical success sets and so must answer all queries identically.

Answers 45

Note— abbreviate atoms as in the Theme;
abbreviate 0 by **0**, s(0) by **1**, s(s(0)) by **2**, ... etc.;
abbreviate 'even' by 'e' and 'odd' by 'o';
abbreviate {e(**0**), e(**2**), e(**4**), ...} by **EV**;
an atom-set followed by ↺ is a fixpoint.

1. (i)   **B(P)** → {CC, CL, CB, BL} → {CC, CB, BL} → {CB, BL} ↺
   (ii)   {LL, BB} → {CL, BL} → {CC, CB, BL} → {CB, BL} ↺
   (iii)   Ø → {BL} → {CB, BL} ↺

2. (i)   Ø → Ø ↺
   (ii)   Ø → {e(**0**)} ↺
   (iii)   Ø → {e(**0**), o(**1**)} → {e(**0**), o(**1**), e(**2**)} ↺
   (iv)   Ø → {e(**0**)} → {e(**0**), e(**2**)} → ... → **EV** ↺

3. (i)   **B(P)** → **B(P)**–{e(**0**), e(**1**)}
                       → **B(P)**–{e(**0**), e(**1**), e(**2**), e(**3**)} → ... → Ø ↺
   (ii)   **B(P)** → {e(**0**), e(**2**), e(**3**), e(**4**), ...} → {e(**0**)} ↺
   (iii)   **B(P)** → {e(**0**), o(**1**), e(**2**), e(**3**), ...} → {e(**0**), o(**1**), e(**2**)} ↺
   (iv)   **B(P)** → **B(P)**–{e(**1**)} → **B(P)**–{e(**1**), e(**3**)} → ... → **EV** ↺

4. C could be any one of the following clauses:

         p(a)
         p(a) if p(a)
         p(a) if p(a) & p(a)
         p(a) if p(a) & p(a) & p(a)
         :
         etc.

Suppose we begin the construction with {p(a)}. For the program **P**={**C**}, where **C** is any of the above clauses other than the first, the method converges at {p(a)}, yet the minimal model is Ø.

5. The step {p(a)} → {p(b)} determines that the program must contain either or both of the clauses

$$p(b) \qquad p(b) \text{ if } p(a)$$

However, the second step {p(b)} → {p(b), p(c)} retains p(b), suggesting that the program does contain the clause p(b). (Recall that each step re-introduces the program's unit clauses.) Alternatively the program might contain such a clause as

$$p(b) \text{ if } p(b)$$

which also has the effect of retaining p(b)—however, we can reject this possibility because it is not the *simplest* one. The second step further suggests that the program contains the clause

$$p(c) \text{ if } p(b)$$

Note that including the unit clause p(c) instead would not be correct, since p(c) is not introduced by the first step. Thus the simplest program satisfying the conditions is

$$p(b)$$
$$p(c) \text{ if } p(b)$$

Answers 46

1. Note—an atom-set followed by ↺ is a fixpoint.

   (i)   Ø → Ø ↺
           hence the minimal model is Ø.

   (ii)   Ø → {p(0)} → {p(0), p(s(0))} → ... → {p(t) | t∈**H**} ↺
           hence the minimal model is {p(t) | t∈**H**}.

   (iii)   Ø → {p(t) | t∈**H**} ↺
           hence the minimal model is {p(t) | t∈**H**}.

   Note—in (i) and (iii) we *reach* the fixpoint in a finite number of steps, but in (ii) we have to *infer* the fixpoint by determining the limit (least upper bound) of an infinite set of atom-sets.

2. **Note**— abbreviate 'permute' by 'p';
   abbreviate $\{a<b, b<c, a<c\}$ by **L**.

$$\emptyset \rightarrow \mathbf{L}$$
$$\rightarrow \mathbf{L} \cup \{ p(a, b, c)\}$$
$$\rightarrow \mathbf{L} \cup \{ p(a, b, c), p(b, a, c), p(a, c, b)\}$$
$$\rightarrow \mathbf{L} \cup \{ p(a, b, c), p(b, a, c), p(a, c, b),$$
$$p(b, c, a), p(c, a, b)\}$$
$$\rightarrow \mathbf{L} \cup \{ p(a, b, c), p(b, a, c), p(a, c, b),$$
$$p(b, c, a), p(c, a, b), p(c, b, a)\} \; \circlearrowleft$$

3. Assuming that **P** is definite, $T_\mathbf{P}$ constructs a complete lattice—inwhich case every subset of it has a least upper bound (lub). In particular, any such subset $\{x, y\}$ has a lub and itself constitutes a complete lattice, in which case $T_\mathbf{P}$ must be continuous over it. Without loss of generality suppose we have $x \subseteq y$, so that $y = \text{lub}\{x, y\}$. Then continuity implies

$$T_\mathbf{P}(\text{lub}\{x, y\}) = T_\mathbf{P}(y) = \text{lub}\{T_\mathbf{P}(x), T_\mathbf{P}(y)\}$$

which implies $T_\mathbf{P}(x) \subseteq T_\mathbf{P}(y)$ and hence monotonicity.

4. (i) If **I** is a model then $T_\mathbf{P}(\mathbf{I}) \subseteq \mathbf{I}$. So by monotonicity we must have $T_\mathbf{P}(T_\mathbf{P}(\mathbf{I})) \subseteq T_\mathbf{P}(\mathbf{I})$. But whenever $T_\mathbf{P}(\mathbf{J}) \subseteq \mathbf{J}$, **J** is a model; so taking **J** as $T_\mathbf{P}(\mathbf{I})$ it follows that $T_\mathbf{P}(\mathbf{I})$ is a model.

   (ii) Assume that **I** is a model but that $T_\mathbf{P}(\mathbf{I})$ is not; then there must be some clause (**q** if **body**) in **G(P)** such that **body** is **true** in $T_\mathbf{P}(\mathbf{I})$ and $q \notin T_\mathbf{P}(\mathbf{I})$. Since **I** is a model, $T_\mathbf{P}(\mathbf{I}) \subseteq \mathbf{I}$ and therefore **body** must also be **true** in **I**. But then the definition of $T_\mathbf{P}(\mathbf{I})$ demands that $q \in T_\mathbf{P}(\mathbf{I})$, which contradicts the earlier conclusion. The initial assumption must be false and so the desired result must hold.

Answers 47

1. (i) A single hyper-resolution step clearly yields the same resolvent as obtained by the following sequence of resolution steps:

   resolve B_1 with   **q** if b_1 & b_2 & ... & b_m
   resolve B_2 with   (**q** if b_2 & ... & b_m)θ
   :
   resolve B_m with   (**q** if b_m)θ

   yielding the resolvent $q\theta$

   from which we may conclude that $\vdash_{\text{HYP}}$ is *sound*.

Moreover, $\vdash_{HYP}$ must also be *complete* since resolution is affirmation-complete with respect to atomic conclusions. Hence we have, for all $q \in B(P)$,

$$P \vdash_{HYP} q \quad \text{iff} \quad P \vDash q \quad \text{iff} \quad q \in SS(P)$$

from which the desired result then follows directly.

(ii)   It is easy to see that hyper-resolution applied to $G(P)$ directly implements the construction of the least fixpoint using T_P, since each step corresponds to a single application of T_P. Hence we have

$$P \vdash_{HYP} q \quad \text{iff} \quad q \in LFP(T_P)$$

Answers 48

1. The evaluation here is deterministic:

> ? append(U•nil, Y, Z)
> ? append(nil, Y, Z1)   [binding Z/U•Z1]
> □   [binding Z1/Y]

yielding the clause append(U•nil, Y, U•Y).

2. Here the evaluation is more interesting:

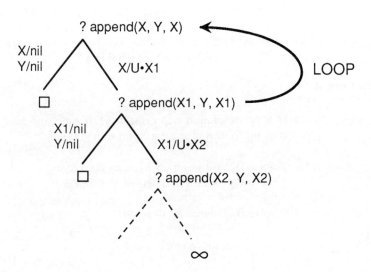

As usual, we can truncate the computations wherever we wish. The simplest case is where we truncate them immediately below the second layer of the tree—doing this yields the program

> append(nil, nil, nil)
> append(U•X1, Y, U•X1) if append(X1, Y, X1)

However, the tree contains an infinite computation from which all other computations branch off to force Y/nil—so we know that 'nil' is the only possible value for Y. Moreover, each branch forces X to be some list in {nil, U•nil, U•U1•nil, ...} where U, U1, ... etc. are arbitrary—which clearly covers the class of all lists. Thus, provided that X is a list we conclude that the original program can be replaced by just the single clause

> append(X, nil, X)

Note—a rigorous proof of this requires the use of structural induction over the class of all lists.

3. The relevant computation here is:

> ? even(Y)
> ? num(X) & twice(X, Y)
> ? num(s(U)) & twice(U, Z)   [X/s(U), Y/s(s(Z))]
> ? num(U) & twice(U, Z)

which we truncate at this point to yield the clause

> even(s(s(Z))) if num(U) & twice(U, Z)

Answers 49

1. (i)   A complete one-step unfolding of

> even(s(X)) if odd(X)

yields two clauses which can safely replace it, namely

> even(s(s(0)))
> even(s(s(X))) if even(X)

whilst a complete one-step unfolding of

> odd(s(X)) if even(X)

also yields two clauses which can safely replace it, namely

odd(s(0))
odd(s(s(X))) if odd(X)

(ii)   A partial evaluation of ? even(X) is shown below:

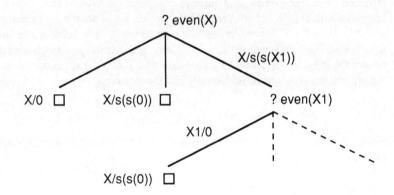

The solution X/s(s(0)) in the second layer is obtained by using the
clause even(s(s(0))). However, it is repeated in the next layer by using
the clause even(0) instead. This pattern is repeated throughout the
tree—hence no solutions would be lost by deleting the clause
even(s(s(0))).

2. (i)   A complete one-step unfolding of the clause

one-and-zero(X) if ones(X) & zeros(X)

upon its first call yields two clauses which can replace it:

one-and-zero(nil) if zeros(nil)
one-and-zero(1•V•Y) if ones(Y) & zeros(1•V•Y)

Complete one-step unfoldings of these upon their 'zeros' calls yield
two more clauses which can replace them:

one-and-zero(nil)
C :   one-and-zero(1•0•Y) if ones(Y) & zeros(Y)

(ii)   The only way to solve one-and-zero(Y), according to the original
program, is to solve both ones(Y) and zeros(Y). We can express this
knowledge by writing the sentence

one-and-zero(Y) iff ones(Y) & zeros(Y)

A similar argument applied to clause C tells us that

one-and-zero(1•0•Y) iff ones(Y) & zeros(Y)

These two 'iff' sentences imply a third one

one-and-zero(1•0•Y) iff one-and-zero(Y)

which both implies the new clause

one-and-zero(1•0•Y) if one-and-zero(Y)

and ensures (by the 'only-if' component) that its substitution for C in the derived program preserves all the computable answers.

3. The SLD tree would look like this:

? cp(3, 4, 1•2•3•4•5•nil)

? cp(3, 4, 4•5•nil)

and the program which generates it is

cp(U, V, U•V•X)
cp(U, V, W•U•V•X)
cp(U, V, W•W1•U•V•X)
cp(U, V, W•W1•W2•Y) if cp(U, V, Y)

Answers 50

1. **Note**—use CD, DC, ... etc. to abbreviate the atoms.

(i)	**P** ∪ {¬CD, ¬CC, ¬DC, ¬DD}	consistent
(ii)	**P** ∪ {¬CD, ¬DC, ¬DD}	inconsistent
(iii)	**P** ∪ {¬CD, ¬CC, ¬DC, ¬DD}	inconsistent
(iv)	**P** ∪ {¬CD}	consistent
(v)	**P** ∪ {¬DC}	inconsistent

2. (i)   Since **CWA(P)** contains neither of the literals ¬likes(dov, chris) and ¬likes(dov, dov), we know that **P** must imply both likes(dov, chris) and likes(dov, dov). Thus it is sufficient to make **P** consist of just those two assertions.

   (ii)   Alternatively, **P** may consist of just the assertion likes(dov, X), whose ground instantiation is identical to the answer given in (i).

3. When **P** is definite, **CWA(P)** = **P** ∪ {¬q | q∈B(P), q∉MM(P)}.

Let **M** be any (**H**-)model of **CWA(P)**. Then **M** must be a model for both **P** and {¬q | q∈B(P), q∉MM(P)}. The latter requirement implies that, for any q∈B(P),

$$
\begin{array}{lll}
 & \text{M satisfies } \neg q & \text{if } q\notin MM(P) \\
\text{so} & q\in MM(P) & \text{if M satisfies } q \\
\text{so} & q\in MM(P) & \text{if } q\in M \\
\text{so} & M\subseteq MM(P) &
\end{array}
$$

Therefore **M** is some model for **P** included within **MM(P)**. The only such model is **MM(P)** itself, which is thus the unique model for **CWA(P)**.

4. If **MM(P)=B(P)**   then   {¬q | q∈B(P), q∉MM(P)} = ∅

   then   **CWA(P)** = **P** ∪ ∅ = **P**.

Answers 51

1. (i)   A iff (B or ¬C)
            ¬C
            B

   (ii)   A iff (¬B & C)
            B iff C
            C

   (iii)   A iff ((A & C) or B)
            C iff ¬B
            ¬B

2. (i)   A if ¬B

   Here **Comp(P)** has just one model {A}.

(ii)   A if ¬B
        B if B

Here **Comp(P)** has just two models {A} and {B}.

3. By the definition of T_P,

> for all $q \in B(P)$ and $I \subseteq B(P)$,
> $q \in T_P(I)$ iff   for some clause (**q** if **body**-i) in **P**,
>   **body**-i is **true** in **I**

When $I = MM(P)$, $T_P(I) = MM(P)$ since **I** is then a fixpoint. So the above implies

> S1 :   for all $q \in B(P)$,
> $q \in MM(P)$ iff for some clause (**q** if **body**-i) in **P**,
>   **body**-i is **true** in **MM(P)**

Each sentence in **Comp1(P)** has the form

> S2 :   **q** iff (**body**-1 or ... or **body**-n)

where (**q** if **body**-i) occurs in **P** for each i. So S1 and S2 imply

> for all $q \in B(P)$,
> $q \in MM(P)$ iff (**body**-1 or ... or **body**-n) is **true** in **MM(P)**

which in turn implies that **MM(P)** is a model for S2 and hence for **Comp1(P)**.
Each sentence in **Comp2(P)** has the form

> S3 :   ¬**r**

where no clause in **P** has **r** as its heading. In this case S1 immediately implies that $r \notin MM(P)$. So **MM(P)** is a model for S3 and hence for **Comp2(P)**. Thus **MM(P)** is a model for both parts of **Comp(P)**.

Note—not every definite program **P** is such that **Comp(P)** has a unique model. The simplest counter-example is {**q** if **q**} whose completion {**q** iff **q**} has two models ∅ and {**q**}.

Answers 52

1. (i)   is(Y, Z) if Y=love_of_money & Z=source_of(X) & evil(X)

(ii)   relies_upon(X, Y) if Y=X & self_sufficient(X)
(iii)   append(L1, Y, L2) if L1=U•X & L2=U•Z & append(X, Y, Z)

2. (i)   num(Y) iff Y=0 or (∃X)(Y=s(X) & num(X))
(ii)   dup(Y) iff (∃U)(∃X)(Y=U•X & U∈X) or
                          (∃V)(∃X)(Y=V•X & dup(X))

Note—this could be written more compactly as

dup(Y) iff (∃U)(∃X)(Y=U•X & (U∈X or dup(X)))

(iii)   knows(W, Y) iff (W=frank & (∃X)(computer(X)
                                         & aspect_of(X, Y))) or
                         (W=chris & tells(frank, Y, chris))

Informally, frank knows everything about computers, chris knows
everything that frank tells him, neither of them knows anything else
and no-one else knows anything at all.

3. First generalize the clauses so as to make their 'p' literals both most- general
and identical:

r(X) if p(A, F) & A=a & F=f(X)
p(A, F) if F=f(b) & q(A)

Use *modus ponens* and *transportation of literals* to infer

r(X) if A=a & F=f(X) & F=f(b) & q(A)

By suitably instantiating certain axioms of the equality theory (refer back to
Theme 52 if necessary) we obtain the following consequences:

q(A) if q(a) & A=a   [from Axiom **10**]
F=f(X) if F=f(b) & f(X)=f(b)   [from Axiom **10**]
f(X)=f(b) if X=b   [from Axiom **9**]

Using the above inference rules and merging identical literals yields

r(X) if A=a & F=f(b) & X=b & q(a)

Since, in the presence of the equality theory, generalization is reversible with
no loss of consequence, the desired result follows immediately:

r(b) if q(a)

Note—the last step (de-generalization) is analogous to the application of a substitution:

$$r(X) \quad \text{if} \quad A=a \ \& \ F=f(b) \ \& \ X=b \ \& \ q(a)$$
$$\equiv \quad (r(X) \ \text{if} \ q(a)) \ \text{if} \ (A=a \ \& \ F=f(b) \ \& \ X=b)$$
$$\equiv \quad (r(X) \ \text{if} \ q(a)) \ \{A/a, \ F/f(b), \ X/b\}$$
$$\equiv \quad (r(b) \ \text{if} \ q(a))$$

and this in turn corresponds to the final stage of a resolution step where we apply the m.g.u. to the resolvent's literals.

Answers 53

1. The program **P** contains the clauses

$$\text{CL}: \quad \text{A} \quad \text{if} \ ... \ \& \ \textbf{calls} \ \& \ ...$$
$$\text{C} \quad \text{if} \ \textbf{calls}$$

from which folding yields the clause

$$\text{F(CL)}: \quad \text{A} \quad \text{if} \ ... \ \& \ \text{C} \ \& \ ...$$

So the new program is $\textbf{P} \cup \{\text{F(CL)}\} - \{\text{CL}\}$. As explained in the Theme, the process of deriving this program can be viewed as performing a complete-unfolding-and-replacement on **Comp(P)**, and we know that this process preserves the atomic consequences. Thus for all $q \in \textbf{B(P)}$ we shall have the following:

$$\textbf{Comp(P)} \vDash q \quad \text{iff} \quad \textbf{Comp(P)} \cup \{\text{F(CL)}\} - \{\text{CL}\} \vDash q$$
so
$$\textbf{P} \vDash q \quad \text{iff} \quad \textbf{P} \cup \{\text{F(CL)}\} - \{\text{CL}\} \vDash q$$

since the **only-if** component of **Comp(P)** cannot contribute towards the determination of atomic consequences when **P** is definite.

2. Our program **P** is

$$A(Y) \quad \text{if} \quad B(X, X, Y)$$
$$C \quad \text{if} \quad B(U, 2, 3)$$
$$B(1, 2, 3)$$

and so it follows that $\textbf{Comp(P)} \vDash A(Y)$ iff $(\exists X)B(X, X, Y)$
$$\vDash A(3) \quad \text{iff} \quad (\exists X)B(X, X, 3)$$

Moreover,   **Comp(P)** ⊨ B(U, V, W) iff U=1 & V=2 & W=3

⊨ B(X, X, 3) iff X=1 & X=2 & 3=3

iff **false** (by equality axioms)

So in all models of **Comp(P)**, (∃X)B(X, X, 3) must be **false** and therefore A(3) must be **false**. But **Comp(P)** must have some models, such as **B(P)**, in which C is **true**. Since these cannot be models for (A(3) if C), the latter cannot be implied by **Comp(P)**.

3. Unfold (A if B & C)   with (C if D1) to give (A if B & D1).
   Unfold (A if B & D1) with D1   to give (A if B)

   Unfold (A if B & C)   with (C if D2)   to give (A if B & D2).
   Fold   (A if B & D2) with (E if B & D2) to give (A if E)

Note—the question asks you only to *derive* these clauses, not to say whether they may correctly *replace* existing clauses.

4. We are initially given this clause C for 'last':

   C : last(L, U) if append(W, U•nil, L)

   Unfold C with clause A1 to obtain last(U•nil, U) as required.
   Unfold C with clause A2 to obtain

   last(V•Z, U) if append(X, U•nil, Z)

   Fold this using C to obtain the other required clause

   last(V•Z, U) if last(Z, U)

5. We are initially given this clause C for 'sub':

   C : sub(X, Y) if append(Y1, X, Y2) & append(Y2, Y3, Y)

   Unfold C on its first call using A1 to give

   sub(X, Y) if append(X, Y3, Y)

   Fold this using the given 'pre' clause D to obtain the required clause

   sub(X, Y) if pre(X, Y)

   Unfold C on its first call using A2 to obtain

sub(X, Y) if append(L1, X, L3) & append(U•L3, Y3, Y)

Unfold this on its second call using A2 to obtain

sub(X, U•Y') if append(L1, X, L3) & append(L3, Y3, Y')

Fold this using C to obtain the other required clause for 'sub'.

Unfold D using A1 to obtain the required clause pre(nil, Y).
Unfold D using A2 to obtain

pre(V•X', V•Z) if append(X', Y, Z)

Fold this using D to obtain the other required clause for 'pre'.

6. Trivially, the clause N1 in each program is directly derivable from the other program.

Unfold clause N4 using N3 to obtain clause N2 in **P1**.
Unfold clause N2 using itself to obtain clause N3 in **P2**.
Clause N4 in **P2** is underivable from **P1**.

7. (i) Trivially, the clause E1 in each program is directly derivable from the other program.

Unfold O2 in **P1** using E2 to obtain O3 in **P2**.
E3 in **P2** is underivable from **P1**.
Unfold E3 in **P2** using O3 to obtain E2 in **P1**.
Unfold O3 in **P2** using E1 to obtain O1 in **P1**.
O2 in **P1** is underivable from **P2**.

(ii) $T_{\mathbf{P1}}(\emptyset)$ = {even(0)} $\cup$ {odd(s(0))}
$T_{\mathbf{P1}}^{2}(\emptyset)$ = {even(0), even(s(s(0)))}
$\cup$ {odd(s(0)), odd(s(s(s(0))))}

continuing *ad infinitum* establishes that

MM(P1) = {even(x) | x $\in$ {0, s(s(0)), ...}}
$\cup$ {odd(x) | x $\in$ {s(0), s(s(s(0))) ...}}

$T_{\mathbf{P2}}(\emptyset)$ = {even(0)}
$T_{\mathbf{P2}}^{2}(\emptyset)$ = {even(0)} $\cup$ {odd(s(0))}
$T_{\mathbf{P2}}^{3}(\emptyset)$ = {even(0), even(s(s(0)))} $\cup$ {odd(s(0))}

continuing *ad infinitum* establishes that

$$\mathbf{MM(P2)} = \{\text{even}(x) \mid x \in \{0, s(s(0)), ...\}\}$$
$$\cup \{\text{odd}(x) \mid x \in \{s(0), s(s(s(0))) ...\}\} = \mathbf{MM(P1)}$$

(iii)

(a)   One counter-model is $\mathbf{MM(P1)} \cup \{\text{even}(s(0))\}$.

Note—this does not falsify any clause in $\mathbf{G(P2)}$, but does falsify this clause in $\mathbf{G(P1)}$:

        odd(0) if even(s(0))

(b)   The clauses in our assumption set are those of **P2**:

        E1 :   even(0)
        E3 :   even(s(X)) if odd(X)
        O3 :   odd(s(X)) if even(X)

together with those from the conversion of ¬C:

        Q :   ? odd(c)   [skolem constant c]
        E4 :   even(s(c))

Any refutation must involve the negative clause Q, since all the other clauses are definite and therefore jointly consistent. But since Q resolves with no clause of **P2** there can be no refutation.

(iv)   Convert $\mathbf{Comp(P2)} \cup \{\neg C\}$ to the clause-set

        even(Y) if Y=0
        even(s(X)) if odd(X)
        Y=0 or Y=s(f(Y)) if even(Y)   [skolem function f]
        Y=0 or odd(f(Y)) if even(Y)

        ? odd(c)   [skolem constant c]
        even(s(c))

together with the appropriate equality theory.

The following resolution graph shows that a refutation is obtainable, and hence that $\mathbf{Comp(P2)}$ does imply C.

Note—to reduce clutter, the graph omits the side clauses, but you should have no difficulty in identifying these.

? odd(c)
|
? odd(f(Y)) & c=f(Y) (using equality theory)
|
Y=0 if even(Y) & c=f(Y)
|
s(c)=0 if c=f(s(c))
|
? c=f(s(c)) (using equality theory)

  even(s(c))
  |
  s(c)=0 or s(c)=s(f(s(c)))
  |
  s(c)=s(f(s(c))) (using equality theory)
  |
  c=f(s(c)) (using equality theory)

☐

Answers 54

1. (i)

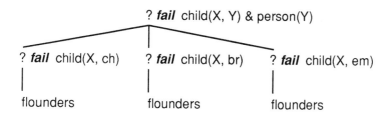

? **fail** child(X, Y) & person(Y)

? **fail** child(X, ch)   ? **fail** child(X, br)   ? **fail** child(X, em)
| | |
flounders   flounders   flounders

Note—here we have interpreted 'safe left-to-right computation rule' to mean that the rule considers only the safely-selectable calls and then selects the left-most of these; hence, in the first step, the rule skips over the *fail* call and selects the 'person' call instead. A stricter interpretation would be that the left-most of *all* the calls must be selected, subject to safety—in this event, the computation would flounder immediately.

(ii)

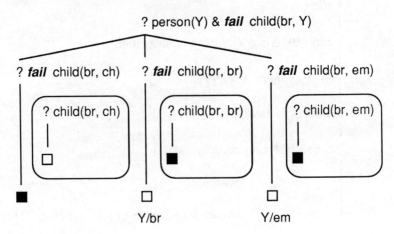

(iii)

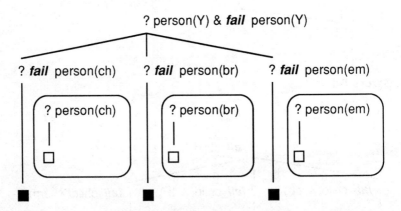

(iv)

? *fail* child(X, X)

flounders

2. (i)   p if *fail* r & **others**   [introducing some new atom 'r' which must
              r if q(X)   be ground when the *fail* call is activated]

    (ii)   **Note**—the transform for the particular example is

childless(Y) if ***fail*** r(Y)   [note that the (ground) value of Y has
r(Y) if child(X, Y)   to be conveyed through the ***fail*** call]

(a)

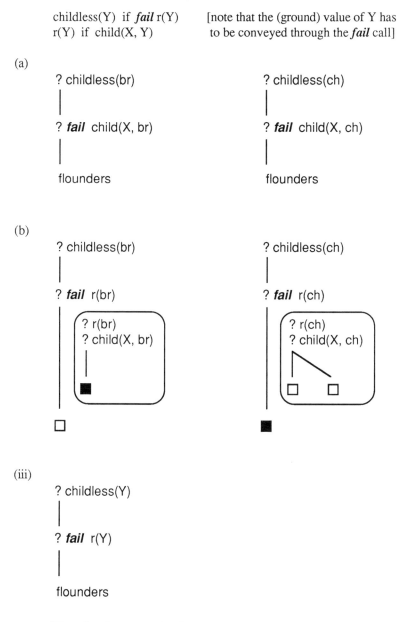

? childless(br)

|

? ***fail*** child(X, br)

|

flounders

? childless(ch)

|

? ***fail*** child(X, ch)

|

flounders

(b)

? childless(br)

|

? ***fail*** r(br)

    ? r(br)
    ? child(X, br)

□

? childless(ch)

|

? ***fail*** r(ch)

    ? r(ch)
    ? child(X, ch)

□ □

■

(iii)

? childless(Y)

|

? ***fail*** r(Y)

|

flounders

The simplest remedy *for this particular example* is to modify
the first clause of the transform to

childless(Y) if person(Y) & ***fail*** r(Y)

Answers 55

1. (i)   **SS(P, R)** = { arc(a, b), path(a, b),
                      arc(b, c), path(b, c),
                                  path(a, c) }

     FF(P, R) = { arc(a, a), path(a, a),
                      arc(a, c),
                      arc(b, a), path(b, a),
                      arc(b, b), path(b, b),
                      arc(c, a), path(c, a),
                      arc(c, b), path(c, b),
                      arc(c, c), path(c, c) }

     IF(P, R) = ∅

   (ii)   **SS(P, R)** = as in (i) but with path(a, c) omitted.

     FF(P, R) = { arc(a, a),   **IF(P, R)** = { path(a, a),
                      arc(a, c),
                      arc(b, a),   path(b, a),
                      arc(b, b),   path(b, b),
                      arc(c, a),   path(c, a),
                      arc(c, b),   path(c, b),
                      arc(c, c) }   path(c, c) }

   (iii)   answers all as in (i).

2. (i)   **SS(P, R)** = { arc(a, b), path(a, a),
                      arc(b, c), path(a, b),
                      arc(c, a), path(a, c),
                                  path(b, a),
                                  path(b, b),
                                  path(b, c),
                                  path(c, a),
                                  path(c, b),
                                  path(c, c) }

     FF(P, R) = { arc(a, a),
                      arc(a, c),
                      arc(b, a),
                      arc(b, b),
                      arc(c, b),
                      arc(c, c) }

$$\mathbf{IF(P, R)} = \emptyset$$

(ii) answers all as in (i).
(iii) answers all as in (i).

Answers 56

1. Note—$\mathbf{B(P)} = \{A, B, C, D, E\}$.

(i) $T_\mathbf{P}(\mathbf{B(P)})$ $= \{A, B, D\}$, therefore $\mathbf{FF(P, 1)} = \{C, E\}$
  $T_\mathbf{P}^2(\mathbf{B(P)})$ $= \{A, D\}$,   therefore $\mathbf{FF(P, 2)} = \{B, C, E\}$
  $T_\mathbf{P}^3(\mathbf{B(P)})$ $= \{D\}$,   therefore $\mathbf{FF(P, 3)} = \{A, B, C, E\}$
  $T_\mathbf{P}^k(\mathbf{B(P)})$ $= \{D\}$ for all $k > 3$

Thus $\mathbf{FF(P)} = \{C, E\} \cup \{B, C, E\} \cup \{A, B, C, E\}$
    $= \mathbf{B(P)} - (\{A, B, D\} \cap \{A, D\} \cap \{D\})$
    $= \{A, B, C, E\}$

(ii) **Note**—take the root node to be at a depth of 1. Then to say that an atom **q** finitely fails within depth k is to say that, in the fair SLD tree for ?**q**, every computation terminates unsuccessfully at a leaf node whose depth does not exceed k.

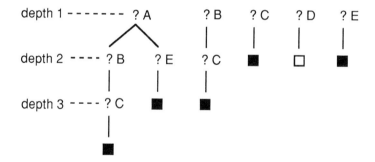

2. This relationship is owed only to elementary properties of set union, complement and intersection, and directly follows from

$$(B-T1) \cup (B-T2) = B-(T1 \cap T2)$$

3. (i) We know that, when **P** is definite, **I** is a model if and only if $T_\mathbf{P}(\mathbf{I}) \subseteq \mathbf{I}$. Thus, since $\mathbf{B(P)}$ is a model, so is $T_\mathbf{P}(\mathbf{B(P)})$. By the monotonicity of $T_\mathbf{P}$ it follows that $T_\mathbf{P}^k(\mathbf{B(P)})$ must be a model for all $k \in \mathbf{N}$. Finally, the intersection

$$\bigcap_{k \in \mathbf{N}} T_P{}^k(B(P))$$

must be a model due to the model intersection property of definite programs.

(ii)   We know that $\emptyset \subseteq B(P)$. Since T_P is monotonic it follows that

$$T_P(\emptyset) \subseteq T_P(B(P))$$
$$T_P{}^2(\emptyset) \subseteq T_P{}^2(B(P))$$
$$\vdots \qquad \qquad \vdots$$
$$\text{etc.} \qquad \text{etc.}$$

and hence that $T_P{\uparrow}\omega \subseteq T_P{\downarrow}\omega$

4. $T_P{\uparrow}\omega \quad = \emptyset$
   $T_P{\downarrow}\omega \quad = \{\text{zero}(0), \text{num\_exists}\}$
   $\mathbf{GFP}(T_P) = \{\text{zero}(0)\}$
   $\mathbf{FF}(P) \quad = \{\text{num}(X) \mid X \in H\}$
   $\mathbf{IF}(P) \quad = \{\text{zero}(0), \text{num\_exists}\}$
   $\mathbf{GFF}(P) \quad = \{\text{num}(X) \mid X \in H\} \cup \{\text{num\_exists}\}$

5. $\mathbf{GFF}(P) \quad = \mathbf{FF}(P) \cup (T_P{\downarrow}\omega - \mathbf{GFP}(T_P))$
   $\qquad\qquad = (B(P) - T_P{\downarrow}\omega)) \cup (T_P{\downarrow}\omega - \mathbf{GFP}(T_P))$
   $\qquad\qquad = B(P) - \mathbf{GFP}(T_P)$

Answers 57

1. **Note**—a set of sentences is consistent if and only if it has a model. Here, the completion is consistent owing to the model $\emptyset$:

$$p \text{ iff } \neg q \ \& \ t$$
$$q \text{ iff } r$$
$$r \text{ iff } p$$
$$\neg t$$

2. (i)   This program is not call-consistent since there is a cycle $(q{\rightarrow}r{\rightarrow}q)$ having one '$-$' edge:

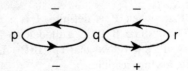

The completion is consistent owing to the model {p, r}:

$$p \text{ iff } \neg q$$
$$q \text{ iff } \neg p \& r$$
$$r \text{ iff } \neg q$$

(ii) This program is call-consistent since there are no cycles in its graph:

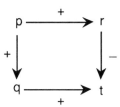

The completion is consistent owing to the model {p, q, t}:

$$p \text{ iff } (q \text{ or } r)$$
$$q \text{ iff } t$$
$$r \text{ iff } \neg t$$

(iii) This program is not call-consistent since there is a cycle (p→q→t→p) having three '−' edges:

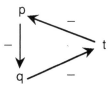

The completion is inconsistent as it implies (p iff ¬p) which is **false**—hence it has no model:

$$p \text{ iff } \neg q$$
$$q \text{ iff } \neg t$$
$$t \text{ iff } \neg p$$

(iv) This program is not call-consistent since the graph is identical to that in (iii). However, the completion has the model {p(a), t, a=a, b=b}:

$$p(X) \text{ iff } X=a \& \neg q$$
$$q \text{ iff } \neg t$$
$$t \text{ iff } \neg p(b)$$

together with **Eq(H, P)** where **H**={a, b}.

Note—the call-consistency criterion for completion-consistency is stronger than necessary when it is based only upon the program's predicate symbols: as the example above shows, programs may have consistent completions even when they are not call-consistent. There is, however, a more discriminating criterion. Construct a dependency graph whose nodes are the ground atoms of **G(P)** and base the determination of its labelled edges upon the entire atoms rather than upon their predicate symbols alone. We define **P** as being **locally-call consistent** if and only if this graph contains no cycle having an odd number of '–' edges. Then we have this criterion: if **P** is locally call-consistent then **Comp(P)** is consistent.

In the example above, **P** is locally call-consistent and therefore we know that it must be completion-consistent.

3. **Note**—use simple propositional abbreviations for the ground atoms, such as MS for likes(mary, sue), FJ for likes(fred, john) and so on.

(i)   Clauses C1—C3 of **P** trivially determine that **P** implies MS, FS and JM. The ground instantiation of C4 written in classical format is

$$
\begin{array}{ll}
\text{MM} & \text{or} \quad \text{MM} \\
\text{MS} & \text{or} \quad \text{SM} \\
\text{MF} & \text{or} \quad \text{FM} \\
\text{MJ} & \text{or} \quad \text{JM}
\end{array}
$$

Only the first of these ground clauses implies an atomic consequence, namely MM. Thus the atoms **q** for which **P** implies **q** are just MS, FS, JM and MM.

(ii)   Under SLDNF the queries ?MS, ?FS and ?JM all succeed trivially using C1—C3. The only other queries that need to be investigated are those capable of invoking C4, these being ?MM, ?MF, ?MS and ?MJ. ?MM infinitely fails due to generating only a loop. ?MF succeeds since ?*fail* FM finitely fails. ?MS succeeds in two ways, once using C1 and once using C4 (since ?*fail* SM succeeds). ?MJ finitely fails. Thus the atoms **q** for which ?**q** succeeds are just MS, FS, JM and MF.

(iii)   The incompleteness of SLDNF is attested by the fact that MM is implied by **P** but is not computable from it under SLDNF.

(iv)   The completion **Comp(P)** is

likes(Y, X) iff (Y=mary & X=sue)   or
                 (Y=fred & X=sue)   or
                 (Y=john & X=mary) or
                 (Y=mary & ¬likes(X, mary))

together with **Eq(H, P)**.

Since **Comp(P)** ⊨ **P**, **Comp(P)** trivially implies MS, FS and JM. It remains only to investigate whether **Comp(P)** implies MF. Using **Eq(H, P)** to replace ground '=' atoms by either *True* or *False*, we can show that **Comp(P)** implies the instance

likes(mary, fred) iff (*True & False*)   or
                       (*False & False*)   or
                       (*False & False*)   or
                       (*True & ¬likes(fred, mary)*)

⊨   likes(mary, fred) iff ¬likes(fred, mary)

Moreover, **Comp(P)** also implies the instance

likes(fred, mary) iff (*False & False*)   or
                       (*True & False*)   or
                       (*False & True*)   or
                       (*False & ¬likes(mary, mary)*)

⊨   likes(fred, mary) iff *False*

Combining this with the former result then gives

likes(mary, fred) iff ¬*False*
≡   likes(mary, fred)

Thus **Comp(P)** implies MF. This establishes that all the four atoms computable under SLDNF are implied by **Comp(P)**, and so are sound relative to it; however, MF is not sound relative to **P** since it is not implied by **P**.

(v)   The completion is suspect in that it implies

likes(mary, mary) iff ¬likes(mary, mary)

which is **false**; thus **Comp(P)** is inconsistent. This is not surprising, since **P** is not locally call-consistent.

(vi)   Change 'likes' to 'LIKES' in C1-C3 and change C4 to

likes(mary, X) if ¬LIKES(X, mary)

Then add a new clause

likes(Y, X) if LIKES(Y, X)

Answers 58

1. Let u denote the universal set and define it by the clause

mem(U, u)

The appropriate query is ?subset(α, u) where 'α' is a skolem constant, and the only other clauses needed are those given in the Theme:

subset(X, Y) if ***fail*** exception(X, Y)
exception(X, Y) if mem(U, X) & ***fail*** mem(U, Y)
mem(U, Y) if mem(U, X) & subset(X, Y)

The query is then solvable using SLDNF as follows:

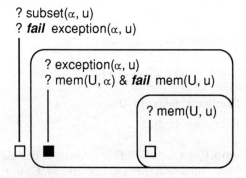

Here we have used a computation rule which always selects the right- most call. The selection of the call ***fail*** mem(U, u) is technically unsafe but, because the evaluation of mem(U, u) does not bind U, the computation is nevertheless sound.

2. (i) The database would have to declare both that office 112 had 2 windows *and* that it had 3 windows.

(ii) The new constraint IC3 sufficient to eliminate this possibility is

? *fail* (windows(X, 2) & windows(X, 3))

which could be rewritten in our standard syntax as a pair of clauses

? *fail* has-both(X)
has-both(X) if windows(X, 2) & windows(X, 3)

3. Firstly, rename 'num' as 'num1' in program **P1** and as 'num2' in program **P2**. Then the proof that the programs compute 'num' identically lies in the fact that no refutation can be obtained from either of the two following evaluations:

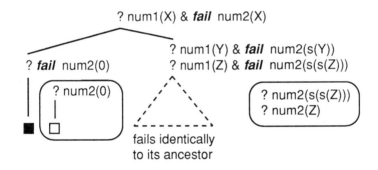

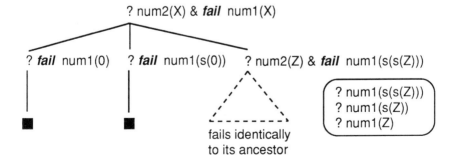

Answers 59

1. The interchange-sort algorithm works by repeatedly searching for any disordered pair of adjacent members in the current state of the list and then correcting it by interchanging its elements. It is tempting at first to seek a well-founded descent based upon the current number of such disordered pairs, but this turns out not to work—correcting any one of them does not necessarily reduce the total number in the list. For example, the list 4•1•3•2•nil has two such pairs; correcting the first of them gives the new list 1•4•3•2•nil which still has two. Suppose we count instead the number of 'general inversions' in the current state of the list—each of these is a pair of members **e1** and **e2** such that **e1** precedes **e2** in the list and satisfies **e2<e1**. It is then easy to prove that the total number of such pairs strictly decreases whenever an adjacent disordered pair is corrected. In the example above, this number reduces from 4 to 3. Thus, for our single PRR

$$\text{sort}(X, Y) \quad \text{if} \quad \text{append3}(X1, U \cdot V \cdot \text{nil}, X2, X) \ \& \ V < U \ \&$$
$$\text{append3}(X1, V \cdot U \cdot \text{nil}, X2, Z) \ \&$$
$$\text{sort}(Z, Y)$$

we choose the well-founded set $[N, <]$ on the natural numbers and define μ from Q^* to N such that $\mu[?\text{sort}(X, Y)]$ gives the number of general inversions in X when X is ground. Then condition (i) is satisfied because every derived query $?\text{sort}(X, Y)$ is such that X is ground and so must contain some number $n \in N$ of general inversions. Condition (ii) is satisfied because whenever the intermediate calls

$$\text{append3}(X1, U \cdot V \cdot \text{nil}, X2, X) \ \& \ V < U \ \&$$
$$\text{append3}(X1, V \cdot U \cdot \text{nil}, X2, Z)$$

succeed they implement the correction of a disordered adjacent pair and so achieve a descent through $[N, <]$. Finally, no other PRRs need be considered because the exercise stipulates that all derived calls to all auxiliary relations must terminate.

2. For the 'gcd' program there are three PRRs to consider:

$$\begin{aligned} \text{G2:} \quad & \text{gcd}(X, Y, Z) \quad \text{if} \quad X > Y \ \& \ U \text{ is } X-Y \ \& \ \text{gcd}(U, Y, Z) \\ \text{G3:} \quad & \text{gcd}(X, Y, Z) \quad \text{if} \quad Y > X \ \& \ V \text{ is } Y-X \ \& \ \text{gcd}(X, V, Z) \\ \text{G4:} \quad & \text{gcd}(X, Y, Z) \quad \text{if} \quad X > Y \ \& \ U \text{ is } X-Y \ \& \\ & \qquad\qquad\qquad\qquad Y > U \ \& \ V \text{ is } Y-U \ \& \\ & \qquad\qquad\qquad\qquad \text{gcd}(U, V, Z) \end{aligned}$$

Taking G2 first, choose the well-founded set $[N, <]$ and define μ from Q^* to N such that $\mu[?\text{gcd}(X, Y, Z)]$ gives $\max(X, Y)$—the maximum of X and Y.

Then condition (i) is satisfied because for any such query in Q^* the value of $\max(X, Y)$ is in N. Condition (ii) must also be satisfied because, for any query ?gcd(U, Y, Z) derived using G2 from a query ?gcd(X, Y, Z) in Q^*, Y is positive, in which case $\max(U, Y) < \max(X, Y)$ since $X > Y$ and U is $X{-}Y$; thus each recursive step achieves a descent through $[N, <]$. An exactly similar argument applies to the use of G3. In the case of G4, recursion is not possible because the intermediate calls cannot be solved conjointly—in effect they require both that $X > Y$ and that $2Y > X$, which is impossible. Thus termination is assured whichever PRR is considered.

3. Choose the well-founded set $[N, <]$ and define μ from Q^* to N such that $\mu[?\text{shift}(...)] = (4{-}n)$ where n is the number of query arguments identical to 'b'. Then condition (i) is satisfied because $(4{-}n)$ must be in N. The only PRR to consider is the given recursive clause. Suppose that ?shift($a2$, $a3$, $a1$, b) is derivable using this clause from ?shift(a, $a1$, $a2$, $a3$) and that k members of $\{a1, a2, a3\}$ are identical to 'b'. Then $\mu[?\text{shift}(a, a1, a2, a3)] = (4{-}k)$ and $\mu[?\text{shift}(a2, a3, a1, b)] = (3{-}k)$, showing that the recursive step achieves a descent through $[N, <]$. Thus termination is assured.

Answers 60

1. (i) cp(U, V, L) iff $(\exists W)(\exists S)($ L=W•S &
$((W{=}U \ \& \ (\exists T)S{=}V{\bullet}T) \text{ or cp(U, V, S)})))$

(ii) ord(L) iff $(\forall U)(\forall V)(U{<}V$ if cp(U, V, L))

(iii) Substitute L/nil in (i) and simplify as follows:

cp(U, V, nil) iff $(\exists W)(\exists S)($nil=W•S & ...)
$\Rightarrow$ cp(U, V, nil) iff $(\exists W)(\exists S)($**false** & ...)   [using equality]
$\Rightarrow$ cp(U, V, nil) iff **false**

Now use this result as a lemma for making an equivalence substitution in (ii), again substituting L/nil:

ord(nil) iff $(\forall U)(\forall V)(U{<}V$ if cp(U, V, nil))
$\Rightarrow$ ord(nil) iff $(\forall U)(\forall V)(U{<}V$ if **false**)   [using lemma]
$\Rightarrow$ ord(nil) iff $(\forall U)(\forall V)($**true**)
$\Rightarrow$ ord(nil) iff **true**
$\Rightarrow$ ord(nil)

The second clause of the target program is similarly obtained by making the substitution L/U'•nil in both (i) and (ii).

To obtain the third clause we substitute L/U'•V'•T' in (i) and so obtain:

cp(U, V, U'•V'•T') iff (∃W)(∃S)(U'•V'•T'=W•S &
                                ((W=U & (∃T)S=V•T) or
                                cp(U, V, S)))

which serves as a lemma for making an equivalence substitution in
(ii) for the instance L/U'•V'•T':

    ord(U'•V'•T') iff (∀U)(∀V)(U<V if cp(U, V, U'•V'•T'))
⇒ ord(U'•V'•T') iff (∀U)(∀V)(U<V if (∃W)(∃S)(U'•V'•T'=W•S
                                & ((W=U & (∃T)S=V•T)
                                or cp(U, V, S))))
⇒ ord(U'•V'•T') iff (∀U)(∀V)(∀W)(∀S)(U<V if U'•V'•T'=W•S
                                & ((W=U & (∃T)S=V•T)
                                or cp(U, V, S)))
⇒ ord(U'•V'•T') iff (∀U)(∀V)(∀W)(∀S)(∀T)
                                (U<V if U'•V'•T'=W•S & W=U & S=V•T) &
                                (∀U)(∀V)(∀W)(∀S)
                                (U<V if U'•V'•T'=W•S & cp(U, V, S))
⇒ ord(U'•V'•T') iff U'<V' &
                                (∀U)(∀V)(U<V if cp(U, V, V'•T'))

Note—the last simplification entails several minor manipulations
using the equality theory and, in particular, the following lemmas
about '=':

    (∀X)(q(X) if X=t & p) iff (q(t) if p)
    where t is any term and **X** does not occur in **p**

    (∀X)(q if X=t & p) iff (q if p)
    where t is any term and **X** does not occur in either **p** or **q**.

Continuing:

⇒ ord(U'•V'•T') iff U'<V' & ord(V'•T') [using (ii) as a lemma]

whose 'if' part is (a variant of) the target clause.

Thus each of the three clauses has been shown to be implied by the
specification.

2. (i)   length(L, N) iff (∀K)((∃U)item(U, K, L) iff 1⩽K & K⩽N)

    (ii)   non-empty(L) iff (∃K)(∃U)item(U, K, L)

    (iii)   The following lemma is implied by (i):

$$((\exists U)\mathrm{item}(U, K, L) \quad \mathrm{iff} \quad 1{\leqslant}K \ \& \ K{\leqslant}N) \quad \mathrm{if} \ \mathrm{length}(L, N)$$

We can use this to make a conditional equivalence substitution in (ii), giving

$$(\mathrm{non\text{-}empty}(L) \quad \mathrm{iff} \quad (\exists K)(1{\leqslant}K \ \& \ K{\leqslant}N)) \ \mathrm{if} \ \mathrm{length}(L, N)$$
$\vDash$ $\mathrm{non\text{-}empty}(L) \quad \mathrm{if} \quad (\exists K)(1{\leqslant}K \ \& \ K{\leqslant}N) \ \& \ \mathrm{length}(L, N)$
$\vDash$ $\mathrm{non\text{-}empty}(L) \quad \mathrm{if} \quad 1{\leqslant}K \ \& \ K{\leqslant}N \ \& \ \mathrm{length}(L, N)$

(iv)   The final simplification can be obtained using the following lemma about '$\leqslant$':

$$1{\leqslant}N \quad \mathrm{iff} \quad (\exists K)(1{\leqslant}K \ \& \ K{\leqslant}N)$$

Applying it to the derived sentence above

$$\mathrm{non\text{-}empty}(L) \quad \mathrm{if} \quad (\exists K)(1{\leqslant}K \ \& \ K{\leqslant}N) \ \& \ \mathrm{length}(L, N)$$

gives the desired result

$$\mathrm{non\text{-}empty}(L) \quad \mathrm{if} \quad 1{\leqslant}N \ \& \ \mathrm{length}(L, N)$$

3. The specifications of 'subset' and 'singleton' are as follows:

$$\mathrm{subset}(X, Y) \quad \mathrm{iff} \quad (\forall U)(U{\in}Y \ \mathrm{if} \ U{\in}X)$$

$$\mathrm{singleton}(X, V) \quad \mathrm{iff} \quad (\forall U)(U{\in}X \ \mathrm{iff} \ U{=}V)$$

The second of these implies the lemma

$$(U{\in}X \ \mathrm{iff} \ U{=}V) \ \mathrm{if} \ \mathrm{singleton}(X, V)$$

which can be used to apply an equivalence substitution to the first specification, giving

$$(\mathrm{subset}(X, Y) \quad \mathrm{iff} \quad (\forall U)(U{\in}Y \ \mathrm{if} \ U{=}V)) \ \mathrm{if} \ \mathrm{singleton}(X, V)$$
$\vDash$ $\mathrm{subset}(X, Y) \quad \mathrm{if} \quad (\forall U)(U{\in}Y \ \mathrm{if} \ U{=}V) \ \& \ \mathrm{singleton}(X, V)$
$\vDash$ $\mathrm{subset}(X, Y) \quad \mathrm{if} \quad V{\in}Y \ \& \ \mathrm{singleton}(X, V)$

where the last step employs this lemma about '$=$'

$(\forall X)(\mathbf{q}(X) \ \mathrm{if} \ X{=}\mathbf{t} \ \& \ \mathbf{p}) \ \mathrm{iff} \ (\mathbf{q}(\mathbf{t}) \ \mathrm{if} \ \mathbf{p})$
where $\mathbf{t}$ is any term and X does not occur in $\mathbf{p}$

INDEX